FANCLUB

Sue Stafford

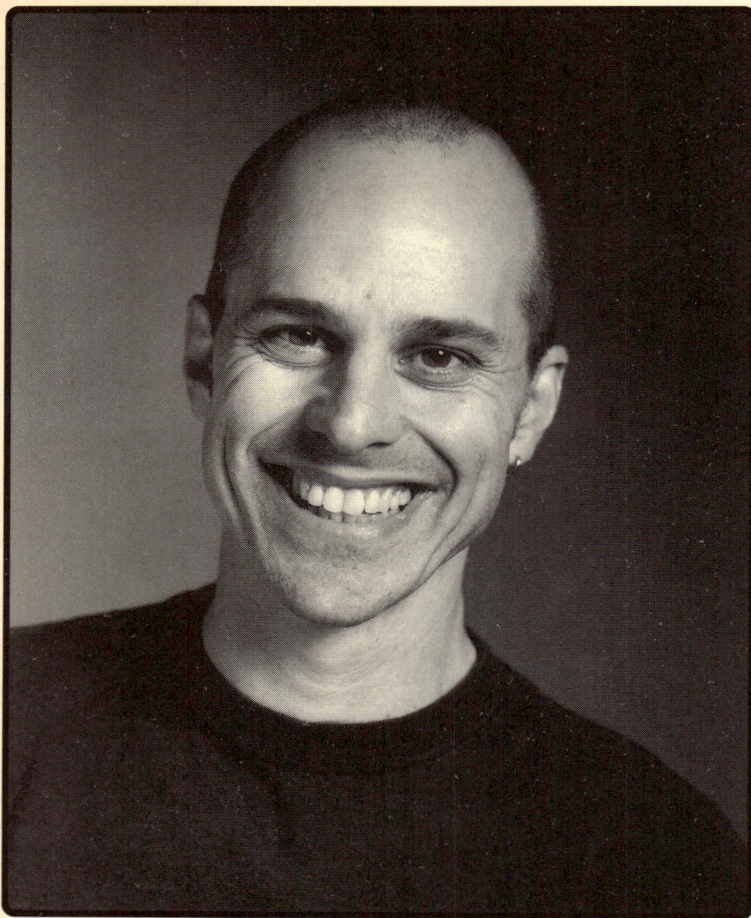

Barry Divola lives in Sydney, and for the past nine years he has somehow managed to convince people to pay him money to write full-time about music, movies, television and pop culture. You may have read his weekly album review column in *Who Weekly* and, if so, perhaps you've sent him hate mail, especially if your're a Celine Dion fan. His stuff also appears in *Cleo*, *Max* and *Rolling Stone*. He's a big fan of yours, especially if you buy this book.

FANCLUB

**IT'S A FAN'S WORLD
POP STARS JUST LIVE IN IT**

BARRY DIVOLA

ALLEN & UNWIN

First published in 1998 by
Allen & Unwin
9 Atchison Street
St Leonards NSW 1590
Australia
Phone: (61 2) 8425 0100
Fax: (61 2) 9906 2218
E-mail: frontdesk@allen-unwin.com.au
Web: http://www.allen-unwin.com.au

National Library of Australia
Cataloguing-in-Publication entry:

Divola, Barry.
  Fanclub: it's a fan's world—pop stars just live in it.

  ISBN 1 86448 770 4.

  1. Rock music fans—Australia. 2. Rock music—Australia.
  I. Title.

781.660994

Design by Paul McNeil
Back cover photographs: Philip Morris, Mirror Australian Telegraph Publications and Sue Stafford
Typeset in 10/12 pt Glypha by Bookhouse, Sydney
Printed by Australian Print Group, Maryborough, Victoria

10 9 8 7 6 5 4 3 2 1

'Get obsessed and stay obsessed.'

—John Irving,
The Hotel New Hampshire

'It's tough having heroes. It's the hardest thing
in the world. It's harder than being a hero.'

—Lester Bangs

'You don't have to be a star, baby,
to be in my show.'

—Marilyn McCoo and Billy Davis Jr.

CONTENTS

FANTALES

COME TOGETHER

BANDS AS FANS

FANBREAKS

Acknowledgements

Hey, couldn't have done it without …

Kathy Graham—for her proofing skills, constant encouragement, and even more constant friendship.

Jessica Adams—for co-steering *Fanclub* from the original idea to getting signed up. Buy her next book.

Sue Stafford—quality photography at bargain prices.

Brett Oaten—legal eagle.

John Barker—Mr Mojo risin', and fact-checker extraordinaire.

Cory Messenger—my guide through cyberspace.

Eric Fleming—pop psychologist.

Brad Robinson—coffee breaks and movie career opportunities.

Poli Papapetrou—for the use of her fine Elvis fan photos.

Tony and Janette Dean, Liz Stevenson, Clinton Meredith, Simon Thomson and Annette Walsh—for entrusting me with their band memorabilia.

Sophie Cunningham, Christa Munns and Sandy Webster—for being *Fanclub* fans and kicking my butt at the correct times.

Paul McNeil—props to design dude numero uno.

Sue O'Connor—complicated lady.

Uma—more complicated lady.

My family—see? I do have a real job.

Thanks to the following people for giving me contacts, info, tip-offs and set-ups: Catherine Swan, Carolyn Berry, Lyndie Blake, Mardi Caught, Katie Snarskis, Sue McAullay, Leonie Messer, Angela Vogt, Viv Fantin, John Watson, Kate Stewart, Chris Cooke, Andrew Humphreys, Eddie Greenaway.

Thanks to all the artists who spoke to me especially for the book, and also the ones who simply let me ask them all about their fans when they were probably thinking, Can I talk about my new album now? Special thanks to Tim Rogers, Daniel Johns and Darren Hayes, who contributed to the Bands As Fans sections.

Thanks to the magazines who have given me work during the writing of this thing—particularly *Who Weekly* (cheers, Jeff Collerton), *Cleo*, *Juice*, the *Sydney Morning Herald Metro*, *Max* and *Rolling Stone*. Thanks to Kevin Naughton and Dan Driscoll on 2BL radio. And bless you, Margaret Cott, for

ACKNOWLEDGEMENTS

accepting a Squeeze album review and a *Cocoon* movie review all those years ago.

The Manly gang said I have to thank them, even though they didn't do anything apart from being my buddies and asking, 'Have you finished yet?' at regular intervals. Does writing this book mean I don't have to lie about kissing three girls next Orb Day?

And most importantly, thank you to the many, many fans at concerts, conventions, hotels, airports and instore appearances who shared their stories with me and my tape recorder. There are dozens of you, but I want to mention those who underwent longer interrogations and photo shoots—Loretta Tolnay, Sam Pickard, Clinton Meredith, Peter Green, Annette Walsh, Claire Isaac, John McKechnie, Brett Price, Julie Ledger and Tony Hamlyn. Without all of you folks there would be no *Fanclub*.

Thank you. Thank you very much. I have now left the building.

YOU ARE HERE

INTRODUCTORY NOTE FROM A NERD

'Oh, I just don't know where to begin ...'

—Elvis Costello and The Attractions,
'Accidents Will Happen'

1

I'm driving across the Sydney Harbour Bridge in Wilma. It's 1982. Wilma is my first car, a blue two-door 1969 model Torana. I bought it off a guy who also owned a Charger called Fred. It's a Tuesday night. It's pissing with rain. Fifteen minutes earlier I'd been listening to the radio and heard that Elvis Costello was about to be interviewed live at the station. On an impulse, without even thinking, I'd walked over to my record collection, grabbed my copy of *Get Happy!!* and strolled out the front door. I was going to meet my idol, and he was going to sign my favourite album.

I admit it. I am a fan. I have been obsessive, fanatical and downright sad in my time. In this introduction I could write in detail about any number of instances. I travelled to Athens, Georgia for no other reason than the fact that R.E.M. came from there, and I wanted to see all the landmarks of their existence and take in the atmosphere that helped create their music (I ended up having a beer with Peter Buck at the 40 Watt Club; I also saw Michael Stipe on two separate occasions, but was too nervous to approach him). I went to Boston and searched for the Fenway and the Museum of Fine Arts, solely because they were mentioned in songs by Jonathan Richman. A few years later, I planned another trip so my arrival in Memphis would coincide with the anniversary of Elvis Presley's death, allowing me to take part in the annual candlelight vigil at Graceland.

I consider R.E.M.'s albums *Murmur*, *Fables Of The Reconstruction* and *Lifes Rich Pageant* close to religious experiences, the first album Jonathan Richman did with the Modern Lovers would be my companion on a desert island any day, and I have a vial of dirt from Graceland sitting on a shelf at home. But my conversion to the church of Costello was so unexpected and total that I compare it to Paul's conversion on the road to Damascus.

I was a swot at school. I was skinny and I had braces on my teeth and bad skin. With credentials like that, there was no way I could escape becoming totally engrossed with pop music.

I had a little Panasonic transistor radio that was my constant companion from the age of ten. Every Sunday night I would listen to the Top 40 countdown. I would already know the order, as I religiously cut out the Top 40 listing from the Sunday paper in the morning ('Dad! Have you finished with the paper yet?') and charted the progress of songs, especially noting new entries and the ones that had dropped from the chart. I remember the days when Abba had taken up permanent residence in the charts, with 'Fernando' claiming the top spot week after week after week. I still get a thrill out of the so-called disposable music from that era, and when a recent spate of compilations featuring everything from The Partridge Family to Pilot and Pussyfoot came out, I spun them relentlessly. One-hit wonders had a special resonance—'S-S-S-Single Bed', 'Kung Fu Fighting', 'We Do It', and the hapless Rupert Holmes with 'Escape (The Pina Colada Song)' were all the more memorable for their flash-in-the-pan status.

By the time my braces came off, I was seriously into the music thing. I must have been, because I would spend hours in our rumpus room (this was the 1970s, understand), sitting in a brown velour beanbag (see, it really was the 1970s) wearing a pair of giant white headphones (do you need any more evidence?) and listening to *Bat Out Of Hell, Machine Head, Hotel California* and *Rumours.* Every Saturday night, my friends and I would go to the disco at a local golf club, testing out the moves that my sister had taught us to The Ritchie Family's 'The Best Disco In Town'. The final song was always The Commodores' 'Three Times A Lady', which was our cue to go to the toilets, as we were far too self-conscious to be stuck out on the floor during a slow dance, awkwardly holding a girl. We went to see our first big concerts—ELO, The Beach Boys, Fleetwood Mac. And we eventually ventured into pubs to see The Angels, Flowers and Australian Crawl. Just to prove to you that I wasn't a total dag (oh, what the hell, I'm not convincing anyone), I also used to regularly play a reel-to-reel tape of Beatles songs that my older next-door neighbour (he was in his twenties!) had made for me. Before this, my cousin had been to Japan and brought back copies of *Let It Be* and *Abbey Road,* along with various Monkees albums, and we would sing along and laugh at the strange translations of the lyrics on the back cover. And, hey, I had a copy of *Kiss Alive!*, so I couldn't have been that wussy, could I?

Still, my prospects were looking grim. I had developed a worrying fondness for those twin evils of the music industry—Supertramp and Rick Wakeman.

I can laugh about it now.

Well, no, I can't really.

In fact, without even doing any research, I can quote verbatim a section of overblown narration from Wakeman's *Journey To The Centre Of The Earth*—'cumulus clouds formed heavily in the south like huge wool packs piled up in picturesque disorder'. Sigh.

So, somehow I ended up at university, attempting a degree in science. I use the word attempting loosely. 'Floundering', 'belly-flopping' and 'desperately looking for a way out of this ridiculously ill-conceived decision' are phrases that come more readily to mind. Still, I had fallen in with a small group of folks who became fast friends. Among them was an English girl who had cropped hair and attitude. We bonded over The Beatles and Roxy Music, but her true allegiances lay elsewhere. She kept going on and on about this guy called Elvis Costello. I'd vaguely read about him in a *RAM* magazine I had bought, probably because it had a picture of Supertramp on the cover.

Being a guy, being a nerd, and wanting to be noticed, I immediately began to put Costello down and teased her for liking him. I'd never heard anything that he'd done. This continued throughout the week, until on Friday afternoon my friend arrived at lectures with a plastic bag and thrust it into my arms.

'Listen and learn,' she said.

Inside were copies of *My Aim Is True* and *This Year's Model*.

By Monday I was a disciple. Within six months I was insufferably cool, expounding the merits of The Clash, The Jam, XTC, Squeeze, The Pretenders and The Police (hey, Sting was cool back then!) to anyone who would, or more often wouldn't, listen.

Some wise man once said that music journalists like Elvis Costello because they all look like him. Back then I had no idea you could actually become a music journalist. I just knew that this myopic, knock-kneed English guy was a genius with a snarly voice, and had a knack for taking a chainsaw to a dictionary and coming up with pearls of wisdom. I took to wearing skinny ties and old suit coats. I would carry a tape of *This Year's Model* to daggy parties and casually slip it into the cassette player to replace Bread or James Taylor.

The author unsuccessfully attempts to impress a girl with his rendition of Costello's 'Alison', circa 1979.

INTRODUCTORY NOTE

Eventually I found an ally in a guy called Dave. He could play piano, and as I had recently given up my position as bass player in the largely unlamented and brilliantly named Vaguely Autistic, we started playing together. He, too, thought that Elvis was God. We were into him too late to see his first tour in 1978, the one where the fans ripped up the seats in the Regent Theatre because they felt he hadn't played for long enough. When he finally returned, we went two nights in a row and danced our legs down to bloody stumps, singing along to every word. Of course, we knew every word.

I remember when *Imperial Bedroom* came out. I bought it on the day of release, and rushed home to put it on. It was one of those epiphanies you can only have when you're young and besotted, with way too much time on your hands and no girlfriend. As each song progressed, I felt like I knew where each word, each chord change and each melody progression was going. I felt as if Elvis Costello and I were somehow connected on some invisible wavelength and that he'd written these songs with me in mind.

Eventually I did become a music journalist—I don't wear glasses, but I am a skinny geek. And eventually the intensity of my love waned. After all, he did make *Goodbye Cruel World*. By the time I got to interview him, it was thirteen years after my first flush of love. He had interviews backed up. I got thirteen minutes of phone time. I pointed out to him that this worked out to one minute for every year since I first became a fan. He laughed a little and said he was sorry. He probably thought I was a complete idiot.

I've spoken to him twice since then, and even though they've been pleasant exchanges and he always has interesting things to say, the earth didn't move. I still follow his career with some interest, but now every time a new album comes out, it's more like reading about an old girlfriend's announcement of a second child. 'That's nice, I hope they're happy.' It's not like locking eyes with someone you've never met and getting a jolt of electricity through your spine.

But where were we? On the Harbour Bridge. In Wilma. Rain pissing down. I got to the radio station. Was confronted by a guard who said I couldn't go up there. I explained my mission. I pleaded with him. He said I could leave the record and he'd see what he could do. I drove home. The next day I returned and picked up the record.

I'm looking at it now as I write this. There in the bottom left-hand corner of the front cover it says 'To Barry, Get Happy, Regards Elvis'.

5

It reminds me of being a fan. Being a fan is not about being reasonable. It's about obsession and blind devotion. Each person I talked to for this book spoke with an emotion and enthusiasm that I could relate to. Yes, even those bright-eyed fourteen-year-old girls who earnestly claimed they would love Boyzone until the day they died.

The idea for *Fanclub* started one night when I was sitting with a bunch of friends at a backyard barbecue. Most of us had been unhealthily fascinated by pop music for most of our lives, and on this particular evening we were having one of our regular games of music trivia, where one person has compiled a cassette full of song snippets, and teams have to beat each other in guessing the artist and the title. Yes, this is what pop-culture obsessed thirtysomethings get up to these days.

In our preamble to the contest, apart from drinking too much, we somehow got talking about Skyhooks and Sherbert. A few of the women in our group were big Sherbert fans in the 1970s (a couple of the guys still are), and wondered aloud about all those other girls who filled concert halls and screamed, 'Garth's a spunk!' What happens to these people? Do they still listen to the old records, or did they move on to other things after the lads' fortunes took a slide and they dilly-dallied with unwise name changes like Highway and The Sherbs? Do the fans still follow Daryl Braithwaite's career? Do they still have their scrapbooks? Have they finally given up on marrying Garth Porter? And more importantly, if you put them in a room with a bunch of old Skyhooks fans, would they rip each other limb from limb?

It got me thinking. What if I could find these people? And not just fans of Skyhooks and Sherbert, but Kiss and Abba and Duran Duran and Take That. What makes them tick? Would they be able to put their love into words? It could make a good magazine story. After a week of cursory research and vague note-jotting, it became obvious that a couple of thousand words were not going to cover it. Full-on fans are not only out there (passionate, vocal, obsessed), they're also out there (not very hard to find).

In fact, some of them knew each other, even though the artists they followed had little in common. My Bon Jovi fan put me in touch with a good friend of hers, who became my Michael Jackson fan. When my Sherbert fan met my Skyhooks fan, she was sure she recognised him from big concerts twenty years ago—sadly, for those of us who may have wanted to see blood on the floor, they got on very well, and even admitted to not minding the music of the 'other' side. This happened whenever fans from different camps would meet—there was a common bond in their obsessiveness.

INTRODUCTORY NOTE

The object of their obsession wasn't as important as the fact that they were obsessed. It was as if the subgroups of fans were different branches of some larger secret society. They spoke the same language. They understood each other. In the end, all fans belong to the same club.

FANSTORY

'In the beginning, back in 1955, man didn't know about
a rock 'n' roll show and all that jive'

—AC/DC, 'Let There Be Rock'

Jesus was the first person to have fans. In fact, he was probably the very first pop star. Consider the evidence.

He bided his time before stardom in a normal every day job (a carpenter). Then he became really famous quite quickly, and the fame lasted around three years—the average pop lifespan for someone under the intense scrutiny of the public eye. He had a bunch of guys follow him around on tour throughout the Middle East. Many of them left their jobs as fishermen just to hang out in his entourage and bask in his reflected glory. A few of them decided to start their own fanzine—they called it *The New Testament*. Matthew, Mark, Luke and John gave varying personal accounts of what went on (miracles, wise words, encounters with the general public) and put it in their own language. The main man couldn't turn water into wine or bring a dead guy back to life without these four scribbling it down. One female fan was so enamoured of JC that she washed his feet and used her hair to dry them.

Of course, like any pop phenomenon, there was a backlash. And like a true pop star, he died young and tragically, at the age of 33, and became more popular in death than in life. His fans went on to commemorate his birthday and the day of his death every year. They built shrines in his memory, and created a following of almost (well, literally) religious proportions over the years. Relics and merchandise—crosses, little models of his birth scene, statuettes of his mother—still change hands today. And everything he ever said is quoted, requoted, and dissected for meaning.

The final pop star trademark? His true fans don't believe that he's really dead, and they're eagerly waiting for his comeback.

The fact that you can insert the names Kurt Cobain, Jim Morrison, Elvis Presley or Jeff Buckley in the above paragraphs and, without juggling the facts around too much, see some spooky parallels tells you something about the nature of fame. It follows a pattern. And one element of the star process is essential to the whole thing. The fans. They are the oxygen of pop. Without them, pop would die. Sure, the fans are always looking for someone new to worship and obsess over, especially now, in the high-turnover, celebrity-fixated, channel-surfing, information-overloaded days of the late 1990s. But without fans the star is nothing.

In space, no-one can hear you scream. Or preach. Or play guitar. Or say zigazig-ah.

'Oh, a little bit of everything, I guess.'

Is there any more boring response to the question, 'So, what kind of music are you into?' Someone who will talk your ear off for the better part of an hour about their undying love of, say, Men Without Hats at least has something with which to fill up 60 minutes, even if you don't totally agree with their less-than-persuasive argument that 'The Safety Dance' is the perfect distillation of all that is great in the past 30 years of pop music.

Put simply, obsessives are interesting. They have opinions. They have beliefs. They may be slightly mad. They have an unwavering support for that which they hold dear. And they're willing to fight for it. Sure, they can be exhausting. Even if you're into what they're talking about. Recently I discovered that a work acquaintance was a rabid Elvis Costello fan. An hour and a half after this discovery I was still backing away from his office door, politely nodding along to his assertions about the modal harmonies and classical music influences inherent in Elvis's last couple of albums.

When you venture into the world of fandom, you start to realise that these people have created their own little universes around their idols. They know everything there is to know about them. They talk about them as if they live next door and pop in to visit a couple of times a week to watch 'Friends' or borrow a hairdrier. They might pick the band up on something they said in an interview and knowingly laugh at them for forgetting important facts or dates in their career. The bands don't really care about this stuff—the fans do. Put a pop star up against one of his or her fans in a trivia contest about that star, and the fan will win every time. They're keepers of the flame. They're historians. They're collectors. They're secretaries. They are the Moneypenny to the star's James Bond, fussing over them, putting up with their tardiness, their infidelities, their scrapes, but still loving them madly from a safe distance. Just as Bond and Moneypenny will never have sex, yet maintain a flirtatious coexistence, the fan and the star realise that their relationship is mutually beneficial, even if it's never consummated.

Most of us listen to music, whether we actively seek it out or not. The radio is a backdrop. It's there in taxis, in shops, in workplaces. But for some that's not enough. These are people who would never, ever have to go into a record store and say, 'I'm looking for this song I heard a couple of weeks ago, and I think a girl sings it and it says something about love in the chorus and it's sort of dancey but sort of slow, too.' These are people who care passionately about an artist. Following a band gives their world order. It gives their life meaning. They feel that these musicians are their friends, their strength, their solace, their saviours. Once again, there are religious overtones here.

Sure, the chances of meeting the star in a one-to-one situation are incredibly small (although in the case of Michael Jackson fan Loretta Tolnay, you will find that following one's dream can pay off if you have enough faith and determination). A true fan realises the star is there for them. Through magazine stories, over the airwaves, via their videos, on the Internet, and at the hotels, airports and concert stages the stars frequent on tour, there's a communion between the idol and the faithful. As Golden Earring would say, it's like radar love. You don't necessarily have to see someone in the flesh in order to worship them.

'I'm quite happy with the fact that my audience is predominantly female,' Sir Cliff Richard once said. 'I am predominantly male, after all.'

Putting aside all those persistent rumours about Cliff's celibacy/sexuality for a moment, this is a telling comment. Pop was, and largely still is, a fairly sexist medium. Despite the fact that there are so many female performers now involved in music that those 'women in rock' stories are completely redundant, the fan phenomenon that's characterised by screaming hysteria is still largely the domain of the teenage girl.

If you want to go back through the history books, it's Frank Sinatra and Johnny Ray who were the first real objects of mass desire. Sinatra made his impression in the 1940s as a skinny bloke with a conversational, knowing edge to his balladeering. Girls swooned and screamed in his presence, and even scored themselves a name in the process—bobbysoxers. This sort of thing hadn't happened before, and it marked the new power of the teen market.

Johnny Ray was a perfect teen product. His schtick was to work himself into a teary lather, sobbing his way through the appropriately titled 'Cry' and 'The Little White Cloud That Cried'. For some reason, this didn't scare people and make them run away in droves, but triggered off hysterical reactions, and girls would literally try to rip him apart at his concerts.

'No pop format is any good unless it can be expressed in one sentence,' wrote Nik Cohn in *Awopbopaloobop Alopbamboom*. And he was right.

Look at these three words—Elvis the pelvis.

You couldn't get any simpler than that. Here was a guy who Ed Sullivan couldn't film below the waist because his movements were considered too lewd for the American public. You can imagine the outraged 1950s parents tuning in and scoffing at the no-talent hillbilly. You can also imagine their kids gazing at his sensual mouth and greased-back hair, marvelling at his drawled singing style, and imagining what was going on in that area below the bottom of their TV screens. And you can also imagine the dollar signs flashing on and off in the eyes of Colonel Tom Parker. It's hard to argue with those who say that rock and roll—for the masses—was officially born in the USA that night.

The Beatles took Cohn's maxim, kicked it through the goal posts of teen acceptance, and Beatlemania was invented. Paul was the cute one, John was the sarcastic one, George was the quiet one, and Ringo was the Ringo.

Those who think that this sort of simplistic way of looking at things is part of a bygone age can't have talked to a fourteen-year-old girl in the last 30 years. The Monkees, The Bay City Rollers, Duran Duran, New Kids On The Block, Take That, The Spice Girls and Boyzone all managed to offer four- or five-headed monsters, with each member attracting different groups of rabid fans drawn to his or her 'special' qualities. For instance, there's usually a cute one, a rebel, and one who is not so attractive but manages to bring out the mothering instinct lying inside every fan. One notable departure from this rule is Skyhooks—with the possible exception of lead singer Shirley Strachan, they were all the scary one (although, with Shirl's latest incarnation as overall-wearing TV handyman, he possibly qualifies these days).

Take New Kids On The Block. Millions did. Jordan was the heart-throb, Donnie was the bad boy, Jonathan was the shy one, and Joey was the cute little non-threatening pubescent one. Danny was the beefy, bull-necked one who had an underbite and looked like a trainee bouncer. But he still had a part to play. He looked normal, accessible, a reminder to all the readers of *Smash Hits* and *Countdown* that the five chaps from Boston were not gods. Danny was Ringo, basically. When John Lennon was asked if all the adulation from teenage girls affected him, he replied, 'When I feel my head start to swell, I look at Ringo and know perfectly well we're not supermen.'

But when you're talking about group identity, all pales in comparison with The Spice Girls. They could write a book on the subject. Well, they could get someone else to write a book on the subject and then put their names on it. They've managed to redefine the cute one/shy one thing into five distinct categories—Scary Spice, Baby Spice, Sexy (or Ginger) Spice, Sporty Spice and Posh Spice.

Apart from carrying on the time-honoured tradition of piecing together different personalities into a marketable group, they've made it incredibly easy for people to identify them and write about them. The tabloids couldn't believe their luck when it was revealed that Prince Harry's favourite group member was Baby Spice. In 1997, when Harry, his dad and Nelson Mandela were photographed arm in arm with the fab five, it was not only a PR exercise made in heaven, but one of the more bizarre meetings of pop and politics in recent memory. And that includes Boris Yeltsin trying to do the funky chicken.

One of the many slim volumes published soon after Spicemania hit town featured a quiz in which you could ascertain the kind of Spice Girl you are. (Incidentally, after doing the quiz I found out that I'm apparently a Sexy Spice, which means I'm proud of my looks and have 'bagfuls of confidence'.) You could also find out all sorts of revealing things about your boyfriend's personality, just by finding out if he was hot for Geri, or if Mel B got his juices flowing. The mind boggles.

The most difficult thing for the people involved in these groups is that the sum is not only greater than the parts, but generally speaking, the sum is the whole damn story, and the parts are useless by themselves. Actually, with their 1997 reformation album, The Monkees proved that even the sum of the parts won't work if (a) it's 30 years after the event, and (b) they decide to do all their own material and play their own instruments. Fans respond to the original magic of the machine, not the cogs and pistons.

Exceptions like George Michael—who managed to carve out a respectable solo career after being in a successful duo—are in a minority. And we must remember that Andrew Ridgeley was the other half of that duo, not exactly the most intimidating sparring partner, and quite possibly (this is just an informed guess) not the integral part of Wham's popularity. Few remember his post-Wham solo album, *Son Of Albert,* and those who do would gladly feign amnesia when asked about it.

And let's face it, if you had a gun put to your head and were asked to choose between the entire output of The Beatles between 1962 and 1970, and the complete post-fab Paul McCartney oeuvre, solo and with Wings, it wouldn't be much of a contest, would it? Anyone out there feel like choosing 'Mull Of Kintyre' over 'Helter Skelter'?

Why does pop music do strange things to people? Why do they get fanatical about it? Why do they give over large chunks of their life to obsessing over groups, collecting everything associated with them, tirelessly listening to their music over and over and over again, and following them around when they tour? Jon Savage, writing about the effect Kurt Cobain had on his fans, said,'This is one of the things that pop does: it gives a voice and a face to teens and twentysomethings trying to make their way in the world—a voice which you will rarely find in the mass media.'

Pete Townshend of The Who understood this perfectly. Even though he was older than his audience, and didn't move in their circles, he took on the persona of the young mod—edgy, speedy, trying to impress girls, looking for thrills, dealing with oppressive parents. He said 'I Can't Explain' was a song about a kid unsuccessfully trying to articulate what was inside his head. And 'My Generation', with Roger Daltrey stuttering his rage and insecurity, became one of the greatest generation-gap anthems pop has ever produced. A line like 'Why don't you all just f-f-fade away' doesn't look much on paper, but in the context of the song it says everything. You could also sing along to it at home and pretend that you were going to say 'fuck' but back out at the last moment. For a suburban fifteen-year-old in the mid-1960s that was subversive, and a cheap thrill.

Whether you believe the stuff people write in suicide notes is up to you, but Kurt Cobain claimed that he was miserable because he felt like he was letting down his audience. 'I can't fool any of you,' he wrote, perhaps understanding better than anyone that the fans know more about the star than the minders, the record company and the hangers-on.

But for all this high-minded talk of the psychic bridge between artist and audience, how do you explain the teen-pop fan's level of devotion? Were Bros speaking for their generation when they sang 'When Will I Be Famous?'? Were The Osmonds really talking about the impending apocalypse in 'Crazy Horses' and, if so, how come the kiddies loved it? Which part of what particular Zeitgeist were Sherbet tapping into when they released 'Howzat', a metaphorical blinder of a song which combined catching out an unfaithful lover with catching out an unwary batsman? And were Supernaut trying to do more than increase the demographics of their audience by claiming in their biggest hit that they liked it both ways?

The answer to all these questions is, of course, another question.

Who cares?

Courtesy of *Rolling Stone*

Say cheese—The Osmonds at their Sydney press conference.

FANSTORY

It's not always about the quality of the song. It's not always about the song, full stop. Nik Cohn put it nicely when he said it was about hyped mass hysteria and short-term collective insanities. And guess what? It's not always about the bands themselves.

Sheryl Garratt, who used to edit *The Face*, has written about being a Bay City Rollers fan. This was a girl who memorised such important facts as each Roller's inside leg measurement, just in case she ran into one of them on the street and they asked her, 'OK, what's my inside leg measurement?' She and her friends would sit around for hours, playing records, updating their scrapbooks and talking. But as she remembers it now, they talked a lot about themselves. The Rollers were an excuse to get together and share their feelings about any number of things. It made each of them feel less isolated, like they belonged to some sort of secret club. She recalls her first Bay City Rollers concert—everyone meeting up to get the bus to the gig, the long process of lining up and finally being admitted into the hall. And then the concert itself.

'We stood on our chairs and screamed. The Rollers were small, very small, down on the stage, and I don't remember what they played or even whether I could hear over the din. They weren't important by then, because what this was about was us. I'd never been that loud, that uninhibited before.'

Tony Hamlyn, an Australian Take That fan who you will meet later in this book, took this line of thought further when discussing the reasons he followed the band around hotels and airports and instore appearances. Basically, you become the star.

'You usually do all this with friends. You'll be in a gang and you'll all be together running around. It's almost like you're the pop group. It's like you're part of the entourage, because you're going where they're going and doing what they're doing.'

At the same time, there's a sense of exclusiveness in discovering a band or a singer who you believe is speaking directly to you about your life. For a time it feels like they're your personal property. One of the most poignant moments in 'The Beatles Anthology' documentary came when a young fan realised that the Fab Four were about to become a very popular group indeed. It had been announced from the stage that 'Please, Please Me' had just reached number one in the UK charts. A time for celebration? Not as she remembered it.

'There were about three rows of girls in the front, and every one of us started crying. It was a terrible night. We knew then—they'll go away and they'll get famous and they won't belong to us no more.'

That feeling of belonging has a lot to do with the whole fan process. And the feelings of betrayal, disappointment and despair—when our idols sell out, become public property, change their line-up, break up, or die—can be as strong as any disaster or heartbreak in a fan's own personal life.

The Ringo Factor

Sue Stafford

He's not the smart one. He's not the cute one. He's not even the quiet one. He's often the drummer. If not, he's probably the bass player. Sometimes, like the rest of the band, he can't play anything. Sometimes he's even a girl. It's the Ringo of the group.

Ringo Starr in The Beatles—the original and the best. He looked goofy, and many thought he was an idiot, but he'd occasionally come up with great one-liners. Phrases like 'a hard day's night' came from him. Some say he couldn't drum for toffee.

Bill Wyman in The Rolling Stones —also known as 'the boring one'. His biography was a meticulous diary which listed band receipts and sexual encounters with a singular lack of passion.

Peter Tork in The Monkees—constantly the butt of jokes from the other three Monkees. Managed to keep a gormless expression on his face for the band's entire career. Jokey opening credits sequence in TV show finds each Monkee looking upset when Tork's name appears underneath their mug.

Chris Partridge in The Partridge Family—he mattered so little to the overall make-up of the group that when the original child actor who played Chris in the TV series was replaced after the first season, there was no explanation given. Then again, there was also no public outcry whatsoever.

Derek Longmuir in The Bay City Rollers—his haircut made him look like a blond coconut, and his dopey grin was even dopier than the other fours'. Often mistaken for Bingo, the ape who drummed in The Banana Splits.

Clive Shakespeare in Sherbert—despite a cool surname, when he left the band and was replaced by Harvey James, fans didn't storm the record company offices. Harvey, you see, was a spunk.

Freddy Strauks in Skyhooks—looked like Red Symons's uncle. At one point he grew a beard. Seldom referred to as a spunk.

Craig Logan in Bros—also known as 'the little brown one' in teen mag circles, Craig was the one who wasn't blond, tall, chiselled, Aryan or a twin. Became romantically involved with Kim Appleby, of Mel and Kim fame.

Danny Wood in New Kids On The Block—had a neck like a tree trunk and a jaw like a lantern. Danny was often mistaken for a bouncer. Or a side of beef.

Brian Harvey in East 17—had an expression on his face like a constipated pug. Kicked out for drug use.

Gary Barlow in Take That—oh sure, now everyone says they love him, but it wasn't always that way for the guy once known as 'the fat one'. Obviously the musical director of the group—why else would they have let him in carrying those extra kilos?

Mel 'Sporty Spice' Chisholm in The Spice Girls—the one who doesn't wear tight skirts, and appears to still have her original breasts. Allegedly the most talented of the group.

Courtesy of BMG Music

Take That—spot the fat one.

Courtesy of Virgin Records

Scary, Ginger, Baby and Posh attempt to turn Sporty Spice into One-Armed Spice.

FANTALES

Clinton Meredith

Kiss

Clinton Meredith compared the piece of material with the pictures in front of him. It just wasn't quite there. The texture wasn't right.

'No,' he told his mother. 'That material's wrong. Take it back.'

At the age of fourteen, Clinton was taking costume-making very seriously indeed. He was, after all, preparing for the Kiss Army march of 1979. There would be a lookalike contest, and at stake was the first prize of being flown to Perth to see the first Kiss concert in Australia. He simply had to win. Choosing to emulate drummer Peter Criss ('none of that fancy metal work'), he and his friend Brian—who was two years older, but united in Kiss fandom—were quietly confident, but still unsure of what sartorial marvels other members of the Army might come up with.

Before Kiss, Clinton was already into the flash theatrics of groups like Hush, Alice Cooper and Sweet. Then he got a hand-me-down copy of *Kiss Alive!* It only had one of the two vinyl records inside, but that— along with the pictures of the band in their stacked heels and glittering costumes, surrounded by flames and the giant band logo— was enough to win him over completely. He remembers the very first time he placed the disc on the family hi-fi. 'It was like nothing I'd ever heard before. It was fast and heavy from start to finish.'

And now it had come to this—the Kiss Army march. It was just one part of three big events which had a huge impact on many teenage Australian boys around that time. The second was Kiss's appearance on the Sydney Town Hall steps, presented by the Lord Mayor. And the third was the concert itself.

'The tension and the excitement was unbelievable,' Clinton remembers of the morning of the march. 'We all squashed into Dad's 180B. My mum quite liked Kiss, and it didn't bother my dad that much.

I think he thought I'd grow out of it one day, but he's still waiting. It hasn't happened yet.'

The march started off at Circular Quay. The head of the Kiss Army was on the back of a truck, yelling through a loudspeaker. 'Remember, we are well-behaved people,' he warned. 'We are Kiss fans, not hooligans.' The Army advanced up George Street.

'Who do we want?' half the group would yell out.

'We want Kiss!' the other half would respond.

They sang snippets of Kiss songs at the top of their lungs, and got to know each other along the way. Finally they made it to Max's Roller Disco, which used to stand opposite where the Hoyts cinema complex currently resides. Once inside, the DJ started spinning Kiss songs through the PA system, and many of the fans took to the roller rink, trying out their moves to 'Rock And Roll All Nite' and 'Strutter'. Clinton and his mate didn't want to go through the trouble of taking off their platform boots, so they milled around with other fans who had also dressed to the hilt. Finally it was announced that the lookalike contest was to begin. Around 100 people assembled in the middle of the rink, and they were culled down to around 50, then down to 25. Clinton made the final cut. Now the finalists had to do a little act to a Kiss song.

'I went out there and went fucking stupid. I was jumping around and doing somersaults, spinning drumsticks on my fingers, and my mate Brian went for it too. And we won.'

Alas, a refueller's strike meant that Clinton didn't get to see Kiss at their first concert in Perth. He was flown to the Melbourne concert instead. He still recalls the strange feeling he got when he heard the whooshing sound of the lift that brought the members of Kiss up to the stage.

'I got this weird, tingly sensation. The only other time I've got that was at the start of the Kiss movie at the Ascot Cinema in Sydney on opening day. It was like a cold chill, and I got shivers down my spine. There haven't been any bands that have done that since.'

He pauses for a moment.

'I'm getting excited just talking about it now. Seriously.'

By the time Kiss were due to make their public appearance at the Town Hall, Clinton and Brian had perfected their outfits. Clinton's father drove them to the city in a long, white Ford that looked a little like a limousine. They parked underneath the Town Hall, and got a vantage point right at the front, near a police barrier. While they waited, newspaper photographers came up to them. Would they like to be photographed jumping off a wall? Of course they would.

By the time Kiss were about to appear, the street was packed. The Lord Mayor took the microphone and started talking about his love of Elvis Presley, probably in an attempt to make some connection with the crowd ('Hey, I'm a fan, too!') but not quite getting there. 'We thought, Get on with it! We just want to see Kiss!' says Clinton.

Finally, they appeared.

'They looked larger than life, and you could almost touch them. And you could actually hear them talking to each other. That was unbelievable to us. We were in shock, I think.'

They got more of a shock when Gene Simmons saw their outfits, pointed at them, then gave them a hand signal and stuck his tongue out. And they were about to lose it completely when Eric Carr, who had replaced drummer Peter Criss, leaned over the railing and addressed them directly.

'How come you didn't dress up like me?' he called out.

'Me and Brian nearly shitted ourselves,' says Clinton. 'It was a member of Kiss speaking to *us*. We just looked up and said, "Er, we didn't know what your costume looked like." And he laughed.'

After it was all over, they went back to the car, but a strange thing happened as they pulled out of the carpark. Kiss fans started pointing at them. Then they started running towards the car, crowding around it and bashing on the sides.

'Afterwards we realised what it must have looked like. A big white car with two guys in make-up sitting in the back. They thought we were Kiss.'

Clinton's dad yelled, 'Get off my car!', blasted his horn a few times, and cleared a path. Then Clinton Meredith, Kiss fan, hit the road.

Courtesy of Clinton Meredith

Clinton Meredith marching in the Kiss Army, 1980.

TAKING IT PERSONALLY

'Won't you tell your dad to get off my back
Tell him what we said about "Paint It Black"
Rock and roll is here to stay
Come inside, well it's okay.'

—Big Star, 'Thirteen'

'**I** don't usually take reviews or critics seriously, but …'
'Obviously, you have no background or education in regards to the art known as music.'
'The "helium-filled whispers", as you refer to them, are the most alluring and gentle voices to ever flow out of a human mouth.'
'If this album produced such a negative reaction in someone whose writing is so pedantic and unoriginal, I can only conclude that it would be a great one to buy!'

Ah, hate mail. As a music critic you tend to get your fair share, and if you don't, then you're probably saying that you like everything. All the above are quotes from letters that came to me as the result of one review of The Bee Gees' *Still Waters*. It's the most mail I've ever received from a single piece of writing. And it was all negative. Just in case you were wondering, folks in this line of work hardly ever get positive letters from readers. I think I've received two in the last ten years. Unless my editor has been protecting me from slanging matches regarding other artists, it proves that after all this time the brothers Gibb still have one of the more fervent fan bases around, willing to back them up with letter-writing campaigns.

The shortest bit of non-fan mail I've ever received came after a review of 1980s Australian band Crash Politics. It read simply, but efficiently, 'Go fuck yourself'. And the weirdest came from some guy in Queensland who was very upset about a review of country singer Shanley Del. He even made racist remarks about my surname. I found out months later it was actually a friend of mine playing a prank. He'd read some letters in my 'hate' file and modelled one of his own. It was scarily accurate in its tone.

Basically, the letters follow the same lines. They often start with something like 'I don't usually write into magazines, but I was so angry …' They invariably question the literacy/musical taste/qualifications/sanity of the reviewer. And they always, always, always quote figures and chart positions. 'If Celine Dion is so bad, how come she's a giga-platinum artist whose album has been in the Top 40 for the last seventeen years, blah blah blah.'

Of course, if the task of a music critic was to accurately predict chart positions and record sales, we would be called record company people. Unfortunately, we're meant to pass an opinion on something. And when that opinion is at odds with a band's fan base, there's usually an unfavourable reaction. The fans vote with stamped envelopes and Internet postings.

And I can totally understand it. I'm not immune to this behaviour myself. The only time I ever made the august pages of British music weekly *Melody Maker* was back in 1986, when, in a fit of right-on idealism, I sent a poison pen letter to the editor, damning Fred and Judy Vermorel, who had written a piece dismissing Live Aid as a bloated exercise designed to puff up the egos of rock stars and the western world in general. As recently as last year I fired off an e-mail to American glossy *Entertainment Weekly*, wondering about the point of a TV reviewer writing about new cartoons when he admitted that he doesn't really like animation much at all, and finds 'The Simpsons' completely unfunny. I suggested that if they were thinking of starting a restaurant review section,

TAKING IT PERSONALLY

they might consider sending someone who hates vegetables to write about the vegetarian establishments.

In the cold light of day, and with blessed hindsight, you think, Who cares? I was indignant at the time that at least pop stars with bloated egos were doing *something*, and Bob Geldof did seem to have his heart in the right place. But what did it matter if the Vermorels wanted to have a whine? And, sure, I think 'The Simpsons' is the probably the greatest cartoon in the history of the medium. So what if someone else doesn't get it.

At the time, however, when a nerve is struck, and you feel so right, so justified in your gripe, there's nothing more satisfying than getting it down, sending it out, and realising that, yes, you've stood up for what you believe in. You've made a difference.

Fans know what they like about a group, and often when the band changes a key element of their line-up they'll find themselves on the outer.

'Pete forever! Ringo never!' went the chant from diehard Beatles fans in Liverpool, following the announcement that Pete Best's place on the drum stool had been taken over by Ringo Starr.

Many a Bay City Rollers fan's world was rocked when Alan Longmuir announced that he was going to quit the band. What was even more shocking to the trusting public was that he revealed he had been lying about his age—he was, in fact, 26, and felt too old to be in the group anymore. The thought of The Rollers without Alan was apparently too much to take. Encouraged by pop magazines and the tabloids, fans gathered signatures—the reported number was 260 000—and Alan decided to keep flying the tartan and thumping his left-handed bass beside his toothy comrades.

Although Skyhooks managed to go on for a few years following the departure of guitarist Red Symons, when lead singer Shirley Strachan left the microphone they fizzled after one last album with new singer Tony Williams, due to lack of interest.

And, if pushed, even many devoted Take That fans admit that some of the magic left with Robbie Williams in 1995.

'They weren't Take That after that,' said the girl in the front of the line at a Gary Barlow instore appearance in Sydney last year. 'At the concert Howard said, "We'll be Take That as long as you want us to be Take That", but you knew deep down it wasn't true, so we were more prepared for the split.'

Oasis brothers bust-up brawl! Gender bender Boy George is heroin addict! Drugs found under bed of Aussie rock star and Lady Geldof! Spice Girl Geri in nude sex pic shots!

Over the years, the faithfulness of fans has been tested via the front pages of the tabloid press. Led by Fleet Street in London, mass-market newspapers can whip themselves into a frenzy over the behaviour of those on planet pop. Outrage sells, especially when those involved are admired by the masses. The media first realised this in 1958, after reporting that Jerry Lee Lewis was married to a thirteen-year-old girl. As a result, his tour of England was reduced to two concerts, and he scampered back to the USA with taunts like 'baby snatcher!' ringing in his ears.

Boy George went through a similar persecution when his heroin addiction was uncovered with glee in 1986. Ironically, up to that point his relationship with the gutter press had been a happy one. George sought them out and provided them with great copy about how he would rather have a nice cup of tea than have sex. He seemed to enjoy the media attention.

'I enjoyed it because it got me attention and a lot of fame,' George says today. 'I think all fame is about being loved and liked and being somebody but, like anything, it gets boring always pleasing people. When you go on television shows they don't want you to be political or serious, they want you to be fun.'

And he was fun. He was the cuddly, doll-like face of gay culture, a curiosity which the public at large could cope with. Unfortunately it all came to quite an ugly end. The group's popularity began to waver, George's romantic relationship with Culture Club drummer Jon Moss floundered, and the press went in for the kill. He was now officially fair game. The lowest low was probably when George's mother went to the door of her house on Christmas Day to find a paparazzi photographer on her doorstep. She asked him what he was doing there when he should be at home with his family having dinner. 'He might die,' replied the photographer.

More recently, the tabloids expressed their indignation over the lifestyles of ex-Take That member Robbie Williams and ex-East 17 member Brian Harvey, both of whom were busily disproving the squeaky clean, fan-friendly images of their bands. The tabloids have dug up every unflattering—and preferably unclothed—shot of any Spice Girl they can find. And they had a field day when Jarvis Cocker of Pulp ambled up on stage at an awards ceremony to interrupt what he saw as a piece of overblown, messianic posturing from Michael Jackson.

The tabloids must keep a shrine to Jackson, thanking whatever higher being it is they believe in for sending him to them. Here's someone who has somehow managed to fuel more freakish stories than the five Spice Girls put together. He sleeps in an oxygen chamber to maintain his youthful looks. He's desperately trying to buy the bones of the Elephant Man. His pet monkey wears nappies. He's attempting to turn into a white person via plastic surgery and skin pigmentation treatments. He's marrying Elvis Presley's daughter. He and Elvis Presley's daughter are separating. He's addicted to painkillers. He's marrying a woman no-one has ever heard of, and she's bearing his baby.

And on it goes. Each revelation has been received with a mixture of incredulity and morbid fascination.

Except when the accusations of child molestation arrived. All of a sudden this became serious.

How do the fans react to all this negative publicity? To find out, I went to hang out with them at the Sheraton on the Park in Sydney, where Jackson was staying during his 1996 tour. It's now a bit of a sacred spot for Jackson followers, as it was here that he married Debbie Rowe. On the way there, I got an indication of the view of the common man. What better way to find out what the public is thinking than to ask your taxi driver?

TAKING IT PERSONALLY

'I tell you what, I've got a lot of respect for black people, but here's a guy who's trying to be white,' he told me. 'He's had operations to straighten his nose and make him look Caucasian. This whole thing about a disease making his skin white is very convenient, isn't it? Why should he be ashamed to be black? That's how it appears to me. I'm not a racist, and most of my friends are non-Australian, but I think he's not setting an example for younger people to follow.'

Unsurprisingly, this wasn't the reaction I found when I started quizzing the fans on the footpath in Elizabeth Street. Jackie, 26, had travelled from England to follow the tour. She was indignant when asked about the criticism Jackson was receiving.

'If there is such a technology to bleach skin to such a degree, why is Michael Jackson the only one privy to such technology? Why would it be invented for him and not for anyone else? It's very obvious he has lost pigmentation. You can see that.'

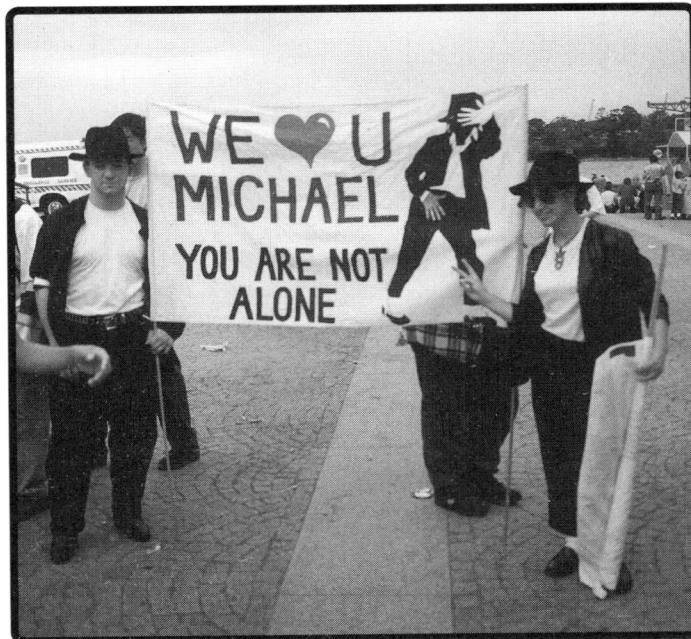

Michael Jackson fans fly the flag at the Opera House forecourt reception, 1996.

And as for the facial surgery?

'You go to Hollywood, and everyone's had a nose job. It is no big deal. If plastic surgery was free for everyone who wanted it, then everyone would have it. People can't afford it, so they criticise it. If it was available to them, they would have it. So what? He has a cute nose. If a white person has plastic surgery, fine. If a black person has plastic surgery, they're letting down their race. Michael wanted a different nose. It's got nothing to do with his roots and what his black brothers—quote, unquote—went through.'

It is worth pointing out that Jackie herself is black. I ask her about Jordan Chandler, the child Jackson allegedly molested.

'It's quite obvious. When the money was offered, they took it. If your child had been molested you'd go for criminal justice, you wouldn't go for settlement. People have been trying to build up a scandal about Michael for years and years and years.'

This line of argument comes up again and again when you broach this subject with Jackson fans.

'He loves kids. He's just that way. I can't see him doing that. I think those people who brought charges against him are just out for the money.'—Eddie, sixteen

'It's just publicity. People make a lot of money out of making stuff up about Michael Jackson. The whole thing with that kid was just to get money. He's always with children and none of them have reported anything, so it's a bit weird just one of them did.'—Rebecca, fifteen

'Why would the parents take money? You'd want the person in jail or dead.'—Gabriella, eighteen

Upstairs, on the first floor of the hotel, the Australian Michael Jackson Fanclub has set up temporary headquarters. The mobile phone rings every couple of minutes, and the small group of organisers is buzzing around looking very serious indeed.

Fez Lateef, the president of the club, has granted a short interview, but he says that he doesn't have much time. He has a cautious, vaguely officious air about him, and tends to answer most questions in the language of record company press releases, or perhaps cult members—'All his music is great'; 'He puts a lot of time and effort into his work and he's a perfectionist'; 'If I met him I'd thank him for his music, his dance and everything he's done for mankind through his music'.

He reveals that he's spent $4000 on this tour, but when I ask him what he does for a living, he fends me off with, 'That's personal.'

Lateef comes across like a politician when he's asked about the press concerning Jackson and young boys. He doesn't confirm or deny his belief in Jackson's innocence, and instead upholds the star's right to privacy.

'We just ignore it. We're fans of his music. We're not saying whether he does anything bad or not. It's none of our business. The media can write what they want. We're the fans. We don't judge him like that. It has nothing to do with us.'

Loretta Tolnay is more forthcoming. Many days of this tour she kept a vigil outside his hotel up to three o'clock in the morning. She is obviously passionate about Jackson, and scoffs at the rumours about his activities with boys.

'At first I just laughed and thought, How can anyone take this seriously? Granted, he's unusual. It's not normal for a man in his thirties to sleep with boys, but recently I babysat for a friend whose son is twelve. We stayed up watching horror movies, and afterwards he asked if we could sleep in the loungeroom, and we slept together. Of course there was nothing sexual. If we fall asleep and we cuddle, fine. It's the same with Michael. It's not about sex.'

When news of Jackson's drug use made news while the star was in Bangkok in 1993, Loretta took it personally. She felt concerned, then disappointed. She thought he would be stronger than that, and couldn't believe that he'd turn to drugs.

TAKING IT PERSONALLY

'Then I thought, No, what right do I have to be disappointed in this person? I have no idea what pressure he's under.'

Although she was (and is) an avid collector of all Jackson-related press, she stopped for four months because she felt the coverage he was receiving was biased trash. She has around 50 books on Jackson, and has read all but the five titles that focus on negative aspects, and she only bought them for the pictures. The one book she refuses to buy is Jordan Chandler's. 'Even the title, *Michael Jackson was my Lover*, makes me want to vomit.'

Loretta also resents the criticism of Jackson's surgery, and offers a psychological explanation for it. 'He was a cherubic kid, and then he got acne and people started talking. They said he was ugly. Then his dad would bring tramps to the hotels they were staying in and fuck them. People said he had a nose like his dad. He didn't want to look like his father. He'd look in the mirror and not feel happy. I don't begrudge him that.

'It makes me angry when people suggest that he's trying to turn himself into a Caucasian so he can sell more records. Sure, he's shrewd and calculating when it comes to marketing but I don't think he'd do something like that. He was unhappy with the way he looked and he wanted to change that.'

Loretta used to be more indignant about negative stories. She would ring up radio stations and write angry letters to newspapers. These days she has more of a sense of humour about things, but if she reads something particularly unsavoury, she will put pen to paper or pick up the phone.

She takes comfort in the fact that she saw him every day on the Australian tour, and witnessed crowds of people telling him that they loved him. 'Then I know that he has to go to bed feeling happy and things balance out.'

'The bass player and the singer—I hope the pair of them catch AIDS and die because I fucking hate them two.'

That's the charming Noel Gallagher of Oasis in 1995, eloquently discussing his fondness for the chaps in Blur. At the time, of course, Britain was in the midst of war. The Britpop war—Oasis versus Blur. At least, that's what the music press and the tabloids wanted everyone to think. Not since the days of The Beatles and The Stones had they been given such an opportunity to play two groups off each other.

There was Blur, the witty, playful, middle-class southerners who wrote canny pop songs that blended The Kinks and Madness. And there was Oasis, surly, rough, working-class northerners who wrote big singalong pop songs that blended The Beatles and, er, Gary Glitter.

Naturally the kids flooded the papers with letters, pledging their allegiance to one side or the other, and the whole thing came to a head on 7 August, when Blur's 'Country House' and Oasis's 'Roll With It' were released on the same day. When the chart came out the following week, it was Blur at number one, selling 280 000 in the first seven days, while Oasis made do with 250 000. The south had won the battle, but the north went on to win the war, as the second Oasis album, *(What's The Story) Morning Glory*, easily outsold Blur's *The Great Escape,* becoming a monster that even cracked America.

Now (as then) it all seems a bit silly. Oasis were obviously the commercial victors, viewed as world-beaters, while Blur were viewed on the world stage as an eccentric little British band whose fifth album took an abrupt left turn after a sabbatical in Iceland and a steady diet of Pavement albums. Still, this is probably not a good thing to say to a rabid Blur fan, who will tell you that sales don't mean anything, Oasis are thick, Liam was an idiot for marrying Patsy Kensit and, anyway, Damon is a spunk.

To get to the root of this whole band war thing, you have to go back to The Beatles and The Stones. Ironically, the two bands' musical styles and their geographical origins are exactly the opposite of the Blur/Oasis pairing. The Beatles were the working-class northerners, but their music (at least in the first half of the 1960s) was the lighter, the bouncier, of the two. The Stones, on the other hand, were Londoners from an art school background, but they were a rougher, grubbier proposition. It was a perfect set-up for head-to-head battle, but in reality the bands were quite fond of each other. They hung out together, they had a common love of American R&B, and The Beatles gave The Stones 'I Wanna Be Your Man' to release as a single in 1963.

Years later, in 1979, The Beatles would come up against a real rival. This was despite the fact that they'd broken up nine years before. It was also despite the fact that the name of this all-conquering beast was ... The Knack.

It says a lot about the role of the media in creating sensations and a constant thirst for the new that, following the success of 'My Sharona', daily newspapers in Australia ran reader surveys asking which band was bigger. The Knack, a power-pop band from Los Angeles, had shamelessly based their image

Courtesy of Rolling Stone

The Knack get their fifteen minutes of fame on 'Countdown'.

TAKING IT PERSONALLY

on the Fab Four—their first album was called *Get The Knack*, a title reminiscent of 1964's *Meet The Beatles,* and they appeared on the back cover uniformly dressed in pointy boots, white shirts and skinny ties.

The only difference was that The Beatles had a long career, which transcended their first flush of success, and eventually changed the face of pop music as we know it. The Knack were a one-hit wonder who disbanded after two years, and I say that with the affection of one who considers 'My Sharona' one of the greatest one-hit wonders in pop music.

Just four years earlier the same papers had pitted Abba against The Bay City Rollers, setting up phone lines for the fans of each band to ring in and register their votes. It's interesting to note that the media appeared to be on the side of the Swedes rather than the Scots. Journalists described Abba as talented songwriters with catchy pop songs and great looks. When referring to The Rollers, they simply emphasised the hysteria and hype.

All of this pales a little when compared with what happened in Margate and Brighton, England in 1964. Once again there were two distinct groups of fans at odds with each other. But this went a little deeper than the question of whose single would debut at number one.

Mods and Rockers had distinct styles, and their sense of dress and grooming set them apart from each other. Rockers wore leather and kept their hair long and greased back. They loved Elvis and rock music from the 1950s. They rode motorbikes. Mods had short, coiffed hair. They rode motor scooters (Lambretta, Vespa) and were very fashion conscious, wearing tailored suits and overcoats and natty shoes. They listened to American soul and imported ska/blue beat records from Jamaica.

On bank holiday weekends in 1964, these two groups came together and battled for 72 hours straight. 'It was a laugh,' said one mod after Margate. 'I haven't enjoyed myself so much in a long time. It was great—the beach was like a battlefield. It was like we were taking over the country.'

These were the ultimate fan subgroups. They granted you membership to a gang of people who thought like you, listened to the same music as you, and took the same drugs as you. And if that meant busting a few windows and beating up anyone who looked different, well, that came with the territory.

Here in Australia, the 1970s was an especially fertile time for fan wars. With that said, the rivalries were a lot cuddlier. You weren't just a Kiss fan, you marched in the Kiss Army. You either pledged allegiance to the perfect teeth and pleasant pop of The Osmonds, or the perfect teeth and pleasant pop of The Partridge Family.

But if you were a teenage Australian girl in 1975, all of this was pretty irrelevant. The most important decision you could make—apart from which shade of blue eyeshadow you would wear that

Courtesy of Rolling Stone

Skyhooks—ego obviously out of the question.

night, or if that poncho really went with that A-line denim dress—was which side you favoured in the Sherbert/Skyhooks debate. Once again, the bands themselves got along just fine.

'It was very much a fan-driven thing,' recalls Skyhooks' songwriter Greg Macainsh. 'We used to play it up a bit, but when we met up it was always OK. Shirley was pretty friendly with Daryl. We had a professional type of competitiveness, but it wasn't personal.'

Macainsh does remember that Skyhooks' guitarist Red Symons used to love telling the audience that he'd slept with Sherbert keyboard player Garth Porter, much to the delight of the crowd.

'I remember that,' laughs Porter, when reminded of the fact. 'It was pretty funny. I certainly didn't take any offence.'

Porter, now a record producer in Sydney, agrees that there were no personal hassles between the two bands, and points out that Sherbert gave Skyhooks their first Sydney gig, a support slot at the Opera House. 'There was no competition. We were just bands out there doing it. I used to read beat-ups in the music press about it, but it wasn't real as far as the actual bands were concerned.'

Macainsh feels that the bands were coming from two completely different corners of the music world anyway, so they were bound to appeal to two different audiences. 'They were a pop band who wrote love songs and that's not what we did. We used satire and humour. They were different ideologies.'

Remember, this was at a time when 'Countdown' was aired on ABC television every Sunday night, and a gullible thirteen-year-old could get the impression that bands lived together in the same house and borrowed each other's flares and platforms. Still, there were the requisite differences between the two groups. Skyhooks looked like characters from a cartoon. The band members dressed up in outlandish costumes—Red Symons looked like a transvestite pharaoh, Greg Macainsh resembled a technicolour pimp—and their songs were both outrageous ('You Just like Me Cos I'm Good In Bed', 'Smut') and lyrically concerned with urban Australian characteristics ('Carlton', 'Toorak Cowboy', 'Balwyn Calling').

Sherbert, on the other hand, were the dreamboats of 1970s Australian pop. 'You've Got The Gun', 'Summer Love' and 'Howzat' were slick productions that cruised through transistor radios as if they were weightless. Sherbert were glossy and hunky. You could imagine wanting to marry Daryl or Garth. Red and Bongo were a little bit too scary for that.

And like the north/south divide in the Oasis/Blur war, we had our own interstate rivalry in Australia. Sherbert was a Sydney band, Skyhooks were defiantly Melbournites.

Trudy Harris went against regional allegiances when, as a Melbourne girl, she became a Sherbert fan. She claims that it was never a contest, because for her and her friends, Skyhooks simply didn't exist. Their love of one band was so great that they refused to acknowledge the existence of others. She also feels that rather than being a north of the border/south of the border thing, who you followed was determined by your social group.

'Sherbert fans were more surfie-oriented, and Skyhooks fans were what we considered the sharps,' she

Courtesy of *Rolling Stone*

Sherbert—satin bomber jackets and unfeasibly wide flares a specialty.

says. 'At school, the social mix was very divided. You had different clothing which identified the groups, and the two never really mixed.'

So, while Trudy and her circle would wear Exacto windcheaters, corduroy jeans, desert boots and musk perfume, the suburban sharpie kids would wear tight little jumpers and vests, and feathercut their hair short at the front and long and wispy at the back.

'Even at school dances we tended to be divided and not mix. But there was never any persecution for being a Sherbert fan. I was probably persecuted more as I got older and I continued to go to see them.'

Peter Green is a friend of Trudy's, and their relationship has thrived despite the fact that he was a Skyhooks man. Unlike Trudy, he has fought on the frontline for his fandom. When he heard the band was coming to play in Wollongong, he was excited. But at the eleventh hour his young hopes were dashed when it was announced that the group had been barred from the city.

'Wollongong was the only place in Australia that stopped Skyhooks entering the area,' he says. 'They banned them from coming because they thought it was an R-rated show. It was a long time before they could actually play gigs there.'

What made matters even worse was the announcement that the group who would replace them for the night was Sherbert. Incensed, Peter made up a seven-metre-long Skyhooks banner, and on the day of the concert went to the theatre along with a mate, who had fashioned himself a hefty wooden placard. They made their way up to the roof, and started taunting the Sherbert fans on the footpath below.

'We were terrible to these poor girls. We were abusing them and saying, "Your band is a bunch of fucking wimps!" You had to take sides. Then the security people got us off the roof. We walked down there with this huge Skyhooks sign and there were hundreds of Sherbert fans waiting. They attacked us and ripped the sign to pieces. I remember this fat Sherbert girl running at my friend with her fists in the air ready to punch him, and he swung his sign and knocked her over and said, "Come on, who's next?"'

Reconvening to plot their next move, they decided to buy tickets for the Sherbert concert. They took along a couple of dozen extra friends, too—a few packets of frankfurts.

'The whole time we chanted "Skyhooks! Skyhooks!" and threw frankfurts at Sherbert.' He chuckles quietly. 'I'm embarrassed to think about it now. It was very childish. But at the time, it had to be done.'

'It had to be done'; 'You had to take sides'. It's the sort of language that wouldn't be out of place in a real war, which gives you some indication of how strongly people can feel about their fandom. Whether it's a criticism of your idol's talent, a questioning of his or her morals, or simply the media pitting one band against another, emotions run high when allegiances are tested. There's an intense level of emotional investment experienced by fans, and anything that threatens this bond is not going to be treated lightly. You don't want to be in the firing line when a fan turns around and retaliates, because the response is sure to be turned way up to eleven. Duck and cover.

The Other Woman

Hell hath no fury like a fan scorned.

♡ Within a week of Donny Osmond announcing his engagement in the 1970s, there were 11 000 ticket cancellations for the following tour. Some fans mailed back their Donny memorabilia, and others had ceremonial record burnings.

♡ When John Farnham was married in April 1973, hundreds of girls stormed the church. 'I was 23 and I got married—and pop stars didn't do that,' Farnham says. 'I was naive enough to think people were going to be happy for me, but that wasn't necessarily the case.' He says that older female fans still come up to him and tell him that 25 years ago they cried for a week when they heard he was getting hitched, and some even admit that they wanted his wife to die.

♡ Groupie Pamela Des Barres used to imagine what was between Paul McCartney's legs, something she referred to as the eighth wonder of the world. She would listen to the radio to hear if Paul 'was engaged to marry the creepy freckle-faced bow-wow Jane Asher. It drove me crazy. It was all I thought about.' She wasn't the only one. Asher would receive threatening phone calls from jealous fans, and anonymous letters detailing how they would cripple her, burn her, or throw acid in her face. When the death threats started, Paul pretended that their romance had cooled down, in order to deflect attention away from Asher.

♡ The most infamous 'other woman' was undoubtedly Yoko Ono, not only for the fact that she married John Lennon, but because she is still known in some circles as the woman who broke up The Beatles.

♡ In 1997 Liam Gallagher and Patsy Kensit appeared on the cover of *Vanity Fair* in a mock-up version of the 1969 love-in photos

featuring John and Yoko in bed. When Oasis cancelled their US tour, many fans blamed Kensit, calling her Liam's Yoko.

♡ Late in 1997 it was revealed that Darren Hayes, the singer from Savage Garden, had been married for two years. 'I always try to be available for interviews and promotions, but she is the only thing I don't share,' Hayes said. 'The day I saw her name in the paper for the first time I just felt really sad. It was like I lost a little bit of her.'

♡ 'Growing up, I was really jealous when Michael went to the Grammys with Brooke Shields,' says Michael Jackson fan Loretta Tolnay. 'I have all these articles and every picture of Brooke has my thumbnail scratched straight through it. I actually got scissors and scratched her face out. I remember Australia Day in 1987—I'd been in The Rocks with my mum. I picked up *TV Week* and I was eating a chocolate Paddle Pop on the train. There was a "behind-the-scenes" picture of the "Bad" video, and it said that his make-up artist was meant to be his new lover. I look in my scrapbook now and every picture of her has chocolate icecream all over her. I used to scratch pictures of Elizabeth Taylor, too, because there were stories that Michael had asked her to marry him. Back in 1988 I went to my school's swimming carnival. I was fifteen. There was a story in the paper that he was going to pay her to have his baby. I was so upset that by the end of the day I'd started menstruating, and I wasn't due. That's happened in my life about three times, but that was when someone I know had died out of the blue. When I found out he'd married Lisa Marie I was relieved because I was already living with my boyfriend and I thought it was good that he wasn't alone. I know now that I could never be Michael's wife, because I don't love children like he does, I'm not as selfless as he is. I'd want to keep him for myself, and he's not mine, he's for the whole world to share.'

Join the Army

Kiss fans should keep their day jobs. This was made obvious after I suffered through a karaoke competition at a Sydney Kiss convention at the Metro Theatre.

A series of self-conscious guys wander up to the microphone and tunelessly yodel their way through the lyrics to 'Detroit Rock City' and 'I Was Made For Loving You' to a synthesised backing tape that seems to have been recorded using a Casio organ and a Walkman. The singers all sound a bit like Peter Brady in the famous 'Brady Bunch' episode when his voice broke during the recording of the song 'It's Time To Change'. But not that good.

Unsurprisingly, it's two girls in the competition who come away with their dignity. Actually, the girl in Peter Criss face make-up doesn't have much of a voice either, but at least she puts a bit of life into her rendition of 'Shandi'. The obvious winner, however, is a big-boned girl who swaggers with confidence and looks totally comfortable both in her own skin and up there in front of a bunch of blokes who whoop and holler. She attacks 'Let Me Go' with scant regard for the lyric sheet.

Somehow, she doesn't get first prize.

'Now Gary's gonna come out and do something for us,' announces the MC.

'Cunnilingus?' shouts a very drunk, very hopeful girl who had earlier slurred her way through an abstract reading of 'Christine 16'.

Er, not exactly. Although Gary does do stuff with his tongue. He impersonates Gene Simmons. He struts around the stage, flexes his neck muscles, gives the sign of the horned beast with his hands, then finally chews up the blood capsules in his mouth and lets the mess all dribble down his chin.

Gene Simmons makes a point at the Sydney Town Hall, 1980.

Mirror Australian Telegraph Publications

'How does it taste?' I ask him as he leaves the stage.

'Not bad, really,' he says.

'I always go out to be noticed every chance I get,' he says later, after cleaning up a bit and taking a breather. 'I want to be just like Kiss. They go all out. I've already had about twenty people come up to me to take photos.'

Gary Messer is 28, and he's a storeman and packer. He made his Gene Simmons suit in 1992 out of motocross bike gear and 'the stuff that holds marble onto buildings'. So far the suit has served him well. He's won cash, a trip to New York, a 1973 tour program, and tickets to see Kiss in 1995 and 1997. He estimates that his collection of Kiss merchandise and memorabilia is worth $20 000, but his prize possession is a guitar which Paul Stanley smashed on stage in 1995 and then threw out into the audience.

As for Gary's own stage act, he also breathes fire, just like the God Of Thunder. Does anything ever go wrong?

'Once I had infected lungs because I inhaled kero. I was crook, but I still do it.'

Kiss can leave a bad taste in the mouths of some fans but still earn their undying devotion. Sure, there are the diehard followers who won't hear a bad word about them. These are people who think that schlocky Kiss albums from the 1980s are still godlike, even though Gene Simmons admits in interviews that the band basically lost the plot. But among the Kiss Army are folks who can see them for what they are, can criticise them, but at the end of the day still pledge their allegiance.

Anne-Lise Larsen is one of these people. She is the girl who should have won the karaoke competition. A classical cellist, Anne-Lise has the dubious honour of being able to say that Gene Simmons has played with her breasts.

'About 80 per cent of the fans here believe everything that Kiss say. I can see through it. When Gene says, "We're doing it for the fans", in fact it's "We're doing it for the money that the fans have." I even knew when the conventions came out in 1995 that it was the beginning of the reunion tour. It was a testing ground.'

As for Paul Stanley, she can't understand why a lot of female Kiss fans love him. 'He's got a lemon in his mouth and a stick up his bum. He walks around like he's Mr Universe or a god.'

Her favourite band is Kiss, but second comes Aerosmith. 'They're a much more musical band than Kiss—Steven Tyler is more talented than the four members of Kiss put together.'

It's a strange dichotomy, a love/hate thing. Despite all these put-downs, how can she still call herself a fan?

COME TOGETHER

'That's because they were the first band I got into. It's like your parents—you love them and hate them. Or your first love—you love them, you hate them, you want them back.'

For Anne-Lise it was love at first sight. She was in grade three, watching 'Countdown', when 'Rock And Roll All Nite' came on. The following birthday she got two cassettes—a Bay City Rollers album and *Kiss Alive!* She doesn't know where The Rollers album is now. She played the Kiss tape so much that it broke. For Christmas she got the vinyl version with the gatefold sleeve, which included messages from the four band members.

'I read Ace's message about being good onstage being like getting off, and "Thanks for getting me off every time". I didn't really know what it meant, but I knew it was naughty.'

When they toured in 1980, Anne-Lise was eleven. 'I used to think, they're only 27—by the time they're 40 I'll be 24 and we can get married and it'll be cool.'

She pleaded with her parents to let her go to the concert but they said no. She still hasn't forgiven them. Picture a morose eleven-year-old on a hot, sticky Brisbane night, sitting on her folks' patio listening to her favourite band in the world soundchecking in nearby Lang Park. The rain poured down in the evening, and drowned out the sound.

'I just sat there all night, crying and crying. I think a lot of people my age went through that.'

Mark Findiess is pissed off. He got a letter from Kiss, his favourite band. Well, not exactly from Kiss themselves, but from Kiss's lawyers. Mark produces a fanzine called *Sacrifice* about four times a year. He prints between 300 and 400 issues, and after printing costs, production and postage, loses money every time. Apart from the $25 membership fee, his sole source of income comes from selling bootleg concert videos. This is what has prompted the correspondence from the suits.

'I've sold one video in the last four weeks. I made $35, and in the same four weeks Gene Simmons probably made five million dollars. Gene Simmons doesn't understand that.'

Mark is 27, unemployed, and lives in Canberra. He has tattoos on all his limbs, including two Kiss logos. Unlike Anne-Lise, he managed to see the band the first time around in 1980, when he was ten years old. His memory of the event is hazy, but he vividly recalls the eskies piled up at the front gate, full of confiscated alcohol.

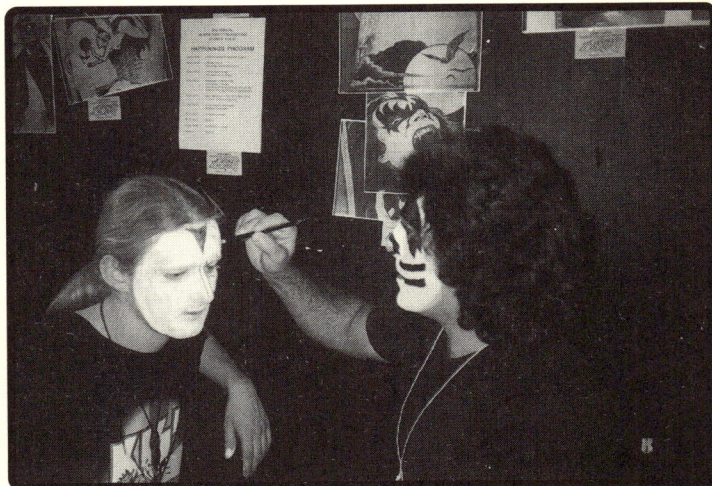

Barry Divola

Kiss and make-up—fans don the warpaint at a 1997 convention.

We meet at the Kiss press conference before their 1997 tour. He's angry about the lawyer's letter, and shirty about the band stepping on his toes, but he's here to see his heroes, so that's all been pushed into the background.

'I came here today and blocked that out, because I've waited almost twenty years for this to happen. To see the old Kiss today, you don't worry about the other shit.'

Four men in their forties are sitting on thrones, up on the stage of the Metro Theatre. Their faces are made up and they wear strange-looking boots with big heels. If you're a Kiss fan, you know the words of 'Do You Love Me?' off by heart, and realise that those boots are leather and their heels are seven inches high.

Immediately in front of Kiss (for it is they) are five rows of media. Behind them, the rest of the theatre is packed with fans, a few in full costume. One guy with kabuki make-up and a red cloak appears to be dressed as Gene Simmons imitating Santa Claus.

Anyone who has ever been to a press conference will tell you the drill. The questions dribble out slowly until someone who doesn't care puts in a sarcastic inquiry to prove they are cool and not too enamoured with the artist in the spotlight. Then the floodgates open. With TV, newspaper and magazine journalists caught between a rock (the members of Kiss) and a hard place (hundreds of rabid fans), this isn't exactly your regular press conference.

Everyone starts off with their own agenda. Lisbeth Gorr (aka Elle McFeast) gets a 50/50 response of groans and cheers for her leap up onto the stage to touch tongues with Mr Simmons. A 'personality' DJ, whose schtick is the impersonation of an Aussie simpleton, asks a question that none of us—let alone the four members of the band—can understand, as they can't recognise his words as belonging to the English language.

And then out they come. Questions about the band's age. Will they be using tapes to bolster their sound? Aren't they just doing it for the money? And, of course, a number of gormless inquiries about make-up.

The natives are getting restless. They boo the media. 'Let us ask some real questions!' one of them yells. Without wanting to bite the hand that publicises them, you can sense that under the pancake faces, the members of Kiss are loving this.

'Hey, listen,' Paul Stanley appeals to the masses. 'Unfortunately this is the media. Let's answer some questions from them, then we'll be glad to talk to you, because we know *you* paid for your tickets.'

Wild applause.

'We really do appreciate the media being here, and it's nice that you came,' adds Gene Simmons. 'But the people who put us here are our fans, and that's what counts.'

Wilder applause.

This is all great in theory. It's obvious that the media really don't have much of an idea about the Kiss phenomenon. A lot of them see the whole thing as a joke. Sure, the band probably is doing it for the money, but a lot of the fans realise that. The point is that they get a chance to see the original line-up, in original make-up, playing all the old songs. What's up with that?

Unfortunately, when the baton is passed over to the fans, they either gush effusively or make inquiries that are on a par with the media's feeble efforts.

'To add a bit of Australiana to the tour, why don't you call the band Pash?' is the first question.

Fortunately, Paul Stanley pulls out a good answer.

'You make us miss Norman Gunston,' he replies.

Towards the end, he manages to send the crowd on its way thinking they're the most important people in the world.

'We owe it to the fans. That's what it's all about. It's the grass roots, it's the people in the streets. No matter what anybody else says, the people speak, and they roar.'

Wild applause, cheers, whistling, hoots, foot stomping.

'You wanted the best, you got the best, the greatest rock and roll band in the world ... KISS!'

As introductions go, it's what they call 'hard to live up to', but in the end Kiss has very little to do with rock and roll. It's more of a circus. And let's face it, who doesn't like the circus? It's a week later, and the moment of truth is here, Kiss live at the Entertainment Centre.

So, let's make sure we've got everything.

Drum solo, check.

Guitar solo, check.

Second guitar solo, with 'impromptu' solo rendition of 'Shandi', check, check.

Bass solo with bass player hoisted 50 feet into air while spewing fake blood from mouth, check, check, check.

Ah, it's like punk never happened. I mean, we all love the fact that it paved the way for post-punk and new wave and, er, new romantic but, hello, aren't the Eagles still touring? And, hello, didn't The Sex Pistols get back together? It's all a cabaret, old chum.

In every single interview, Kiss go on and on about value for money, and giving people more bang for their buck, and complain about the grunge generation who just whine at their audience about how depressed they are. But when push came to shove ... well, they delivered, actually. In spades, with explosions, fire, and flashing guitars on top.

Plus a drum riser like an elevator, and a couple of cherry pickers, one of which malfunctioned, leaving Paul and Ace embarrassingly trapped above the audience in the dark when they should have been backstage counting down exactly how many seconds to wait until returning for an encore.

Sue Stafford

Living dolls—Ace, Gene, Paul, Peter.

Sometimes even the most well-oiled machine gets a little gremlin in it. A few of us started calling out the names of Spinal Tap songs. At any moment we expected an undersized model of Stonehenge to descend to the stage.

Taped to the floor of the stage next to each microphone was a sign with the words SYDNEY, AUSTRALIA boldly marked. Because we all know that '_____, _____ (insert name of your town and country here) rocks our world!' and '_____! I can't hear you!' and, furthermore, 'We love you, _____!'

It was shameless rock cliché after shameless rock cliché. And it was immensely entertaining. And I laughed a lot.

'If a band ever charges you a lot of money to come see them and they don't give you value for your money, you give us a call and we'll come back down here,' Paul shouted towards the end.

Perhaps he was thinking of running for minister of consumer affairs, rock division. Everyone under this roof would vote for him.

'You look great! You look wonderful!'

A woman Geoff Stevula has never met has just walked up to him and started giving him compliments. Geoff isn't famous. He's 32 years old and he works for a food manufacturer. He's standing outside the Entertainment Centre. He also happens to be dressed and painted up like Paul Stanley.

'Thanks a lot,' he replies to the woman. 'Have a good night, OK?'

Geoff has taken two weeks off work to follow Kiss around Sydney, Melbourne and Brisbane. He's spending $2000 in a fortnight, and treating the whole thing as a holiday.

'You'd have to be a fool to say they're not doing it partly for the money,' he says. 'But it's like Kiss have said themselves, they'd rather make sure they can get along with each other. If they hated each other they couldn't do it—it wouldn't last any longer than a couple of months.

COME TOGETHER

'The fans are what make this the biggest. For myself, Kiss is just one huge party band. They sing about girls, sex, having a good time. There's so much bad news out in the world today. People get a chance to come and see a band like this, let their hair down and have a great time for two hours.'

Geoff's financial commitment might seem outlandish to the average person, but compared to Motormouth (possibly not his real name), a 31-year-old warehouse worker, it's positively frugal. He is seeing eight concerts around Australia, and has spent $6000 on concert tickets, flights, accommodation and merchandise. He's been painting his face and dressing up as Gene Simmons since the age of nine.

'I've always carried the flag—they're the biggest and the best,' he says.

This is an eerie occurrence you notice when talking to fanatical Kiss fans. They spout lines like 'the biggest and the best', phrases that the band have been hammering for years. I point out to Motormouth that even Gene Simmons admits a lot of their work in the 1980s was substandard. How does he feel about that?

'That's his opinion. I don't agree with him.'

Have you ever met them?

'Yeah, I had a heart attack.'

Did you have a chat?

'Oh, God no! How could I have a chat? What do you say to the gods? They're bigger than Jesus Christ.'

Walking around the crowd, it's hard to equate the atmosphere here with that of a metal gig. It's more of an outing, a carnival. Sure, there's more denim and leather and mullet haircuts per square metre than your average control sample of human beings, but there's also a distinct lack of aggression or cooler-than-thou attitude. Folks in their thirties and forties rub shoulders with eleven-year-olds. People sit around drinking, comparing notes on shows they've seen already. And dotting the crowd are those who have made the extra commitment by dressing up as their favourite member.

Two enterprising girls have brought along a make-up kit, and are painting faces for ten dollars. One of them is saving up to go to South America. She would have been a toddler when Kiss first toured, seventeen years ago, yet even she has fond childhood memories of the band.

'I was sitting on top of my grandma's roof listening to them,' she says. 'My mother used to roller-skate to "I Was Made For Loving You", and I recall that vividly.'

She stops for a moment, taking her attention away from the guy she's making up to look like Ace Frehley, a make-up sponge clutched in her fingers.

'Every time I hear that song, that's my recollection—my mother skating, and my nanna's rooftop.'

TWIST AND SHOUT

'You drive us wild, we'll drive you crazy'

—Kiss, 'Rock And Roll All Nite'

My strongest memory of The Beatles cartoons, apart from the jokey bit where Ringo unplugs his drum kit and the whole thing deflates, is the screaming girls. They're drawn as a quivering mass that makes a noise like a jet engine as it scuttles through alleys, up and down staircases, and through traffic. The Beatles frantically race away from the many-headed beast.

I always thought that was strange. It puzzled me as a kid in the same way that I couldn't figure out why the men on 'Gilligan's Island' would always run a mile when Ginger started getting all sexy with them. Most guys dream of being in a band at some stage in their lives, and a large part (if not all) of that has to do with attracting women. Here they were being pursued by what looked like the entire female population of England, and they were running away. Why didn't they want to get caught?

Well, maybe because they would be ripped apart.

John Lennon recognised the compromise he had to make for his success. As he said to his chauffeur when fans mobbed his Rolls Royce one night in 1963, 'They bought the car. They've got a right to smash it up.'

The Beatles certainly entered uncharted territory with regard to mass adulation. It was the first time, but by no means the last time, that the word 'mania' was added to the end of a group's name to try to convey the extreme nature of the reaction they elicited from the public.

But then came the 1970s, and things really went quite silly indeed. Hysteria distinguishes that decade as surely as platform shoes, fondue sets, bad haircuts and the juxtaposition of colours like brown and burnt orange. Sure, it's always dangerous to categorise trends into neat groupings of ten years, but there was something about that time which made it strangely appropriate for large groups of teenage girls to scream, weep, rip at their hair, tear up concert hall seats, faint, and receive medical attention. Even when, in retrospect at least, many of these groups were not exactly God's gift to womankind.

Three families were largely responsible for kick-starting the phenomenon—The Jackson Five, The Osmonds and The Partridge Family. The first two were real families, and the third lot were just pretending. But, come to think of it, when you consider that the Osmonds were a bunch of toothy Mormons who lived in a family compound, and the Jacksons would become one of the pop world's most infamous hot-beds of gossip, rumour and weirdness, the Partridges looked pretty damn normal. Until Danny Bonaduce went and beat up a transvestite prostitute he'd picked up on a highway in 1991, anyway.

The three groups presented an appealing image for an audience that was dubbed with a new name—weenyboppers. These were kids—mainly girls—between the ages of about eight and fourteen. Like a set of dolls, these pop groups came in different sizes and ages. The older members could play instruments and lead dance routines; the younger ones were cute (with the possible exception of Jimmy Osmond, who was once memorably described as a small constipated toad on Methedrine) and had all the energy. But it became pretty obvious early on in the piece who the star attractions would turn out to be. Donny Osmond, Michael Jackson and David Cassidy would be transformed into teen idols in their own right and take up valuable wall space in bedrooms for a few years in the first half of the 1970s. Their public appearances would be accompanied by hysterical scenes.

At the end of 1973, 8000 fans turned up at Heathrow Airport to greet The Osmonds. A railing collapsed and bits of concrete rained down on the crowd below, injuring over twenty kids. There were reports of girls producing knives from their bags when police tried to control them. By the time the family got to Australia in 1975, they were demanding 50 security guards at each concert, size-able crash barriers at the front of the stage, and guards outside their hotels on 24-hour duty.

David Cassidy recalls the sound of thousands of fans screaming Partridge Family songs outside his London hotel room window in 1971. When the fans were en masse, he sometimes feared for his safety, and he could feel an almost violent edge in their wild eyes and piercing screams. He claims there were only two places he had to himself when he was a pop star—when he was asleep or in the toilet.

In 1975 and 1976 canny proprietors of haberdasheries around Australia must have had a very good time. If they had played their cards right and stocked up on tartan, they would have anticipated the flood of teenage girls who would buy material and create scarves, jackets and, most significantly, pants that ended somewhere around the mid-calf area. These were called Roller Strollers, a perversely ugly fashion statement in an era not fondly remembered in fashion circles as the prettiest of times. Yes, The Bay City Rollers were about to invade our shores.

Formed way back in 1967, these Edinburgh lads had managed to transform their bubblegum singalongs into a British phenomenon by the mid-1970s, via the aggressive managing style of Tam Paton, who named the band by sticking a pin at random into a map of the USA, and landing on Bay City, Michigan.

'They call it Rollermania—and it's the wildest teenybopper mind-blowing thing to hit the pop scene in a decade,' trumpeted one news report from London, sounding quaintly out of date but accurately identifying the bedlam which would surround their upcoming Australian tour. Another London reporter posted a story warning us what to expect. He said that a Rollers concert was like a Roman circus, gravely recounted the number of injuries, reported the death of a policeman from a heart attack, and blamed the band for inciting hysterical reactions in their fans. He even named some of their security staff—Paddy the Plank and Big Mike—perhaps in an effort to give the impression that they sounded like thugs or mafia minions.

There was no need to fan the flames. Rollermania was well and truly under way. Tickets went on sale in November 1975. In Perth 2000 girls turned up to get seats, and in the crush a policeman was hurt and fans collapsed from overexcitement. From Adelaide, we saw pictures of barricades and policemen on horses taming the 3000-strong crowd who came to pick up $5.70 tickets. And this was weeks before anyone got a chance to catch sight of the band's chipmunk grins and boofy hairdos.

Mirror Australian Telegraph Publications

Bay City Rollers fans proudly displaying the tartan.

After the Scots landed, they were in the newspapers on a daily basis, usually under headlines bearing the words 'chaos', 'hysteria' and 'frenzy', and featuring stories detailing the numbers of girls who were treated for bruises and fainting spells.

Just about every concert would have to be stopped when the crush of fans threatened to injure those at the front of the stage. The areas outside were dotted with girls flat on their backs, the big cuffs of their Roller Strollers flapping, striped socks showing, sneakers pointed towards the sky, and looks on their faces that were a strange mix of reverie and heat exhaustion.

'Stop dicing with death—please!' the Rollers—or more likely the press release from their manager—said in an interview. 'If you can't control your emotions there is going to be a very serious accident.'

TWIST AND SHOUT

They told their fans to keep cool. They could shout if they liked. They could wave. They could even scream. But they should keep those emotions under control. 'Uncontrolled emotions can be disastrous,' they warned, sounding like Sunday school teachers.

Ah, but uncontrolled emotion is the stuff of teen band success. Once that goes, then the group is over. And emotion inside the Rollers' camp wasn't exactly cool, calm and collected, either. While they were in Australia, Woody collapsed from 'exhaustion'. Later Eric Faulkner would be treated for an overdose, and it would be revealed that they all regularly took prescription drugs to cope with the stress. By 1976, members were leaving and the Scottish slide was under way. Their 1978 album, *Strangers In The Wild,* didn't even chart in the UK. At the end of that year, bass player Alan Longmuir recalled the response in Australia as being the most volatile while he was in the band.

'We really haven't seen anything like them, and we've seen them all,' he said of Australian fans. 'It was our experiences down there last time we toured that prompted us to get our own security force. Those kids clawed at us. You could be killed if a lot of them got hold of you.'

Around the same time, John Paul Young bought a shirt made out of silk scarves for $35. It was a lot of money to spend on an article of clothing in the mid-1970s, especially for a guy who wasn't really famous yet. He got to wear it once, and that was on 'Countdown'.

'Totally unbeknown to me, Molly had geed the audience up and as soon as I got out there, they went ballistic and started yanking and tugging at me,' he remembers. 'I was just horrified because my professional self …'—he lets out a self-deprecating laugh—'… was being undermined. I thought, Jesus Christ! I'm here to sing! Leave me alone!'

He was trying to do a live vocal over a backing track, but the kids ripped the cord out of the microphone. Young was dumbfounded and frantically looked around for the floor manager, hoping for some advice. The next thing he knew, he had been dragged off the stage and was lying on the ground. The cameras lost him under a sea of pubescent girls.

By the time he got backstage he was totally confused. He didn't know what had happened or why. A couple of months earlier he had been doing casual work, welding for

ABC Archives

Mark Holden—carnations not pictured.

49

a security-grille company. Now he was a major lust object. Didn't he realise that as a pop star he would be treated as a piece of meat?

'I suppose so, but I'd still rather it didn't happen. Adulation is one thing, but going ballistic is another. It's like, are you here to be entertained, or are you here to rip somebody's clothes off?'

In the 'Countdown' audience's case, they voted with their claws.

Mark Holden, the man who has handed out more carnations than Interflora, also came in for his fair share of pawing. Formerly a long-haired university student from Adelaide, he was remodelled as a clean-cut romantic figure who sang the lovey-dovey confections 'Never Gonna Fall In Love Again' and 'I Wanna Make You My Lady'. He only played seven live concerts in his career, but his 'Countdown' appearances always ended up in a tug of war with the fans.

Holden thinks times have changed as far as hysteria is concerned. Last year he made an appearance on the ABC TV youth program 'Recovery', and happened to be scheduled for the same show as silverchair. As he arrived, he noticed about five or six kids at the front gate.

'We used to get escorted into "Countdown",' he recalls. 'There would be two, three, four, five hundred kids out the front every time you went there. It would be pandemonium. And none of us were as big as silverchair are.'

As Devo once put it, 'Freedom of choice is what you got, freedom from choice is what you want'. There's a hell of a wider choice of music in the 1990s than there was in the 1970s. The pie is being cut into thinner and thinner slices. And pop music itself has a lot more competition from television, movies and video games. Perhaps the most telling statistic in this regard is the star who has pulled the highest turnout for an instore appearance in Australia. Take That? Janet Jackson? Savage Garden? The honour goes not to a singer or group, but to Gillian Anderson, the star of TV program 'The X-Files'.

'We want Sherbert! We want Sherbert!'

By the mid-1970s, Garth Porter had grown used to hearing that sound, six or seven floors below him, as he woke up in yet another hotel room. If fans approached him in ones or twos, there was no competition for attention—he could simply talk to them, sign an autograph, and pose for a photo. But eventually the chance of being accosted by just one or two fans became a remote luxury for Garth, Daryl, Tony, Harvey and Alan.

'As terrible as it may sound, when there were a whole bunch of fans, you did everything you could to avoid them, because it just got out of control. It would just get crazy.'

For Porter, the most frightening experience occurred when the band had finished playing a concert at Festival Hall in Melbourne in 1975. At this stage they'd taken to hiring armoured security vans to transport them everywhere, as the limousines they had previously used were badly damaged by crowds bashing on the panels. There was a gap between the back door of the hall and the van parked by the kerb, and the security people had lined the path to keep back the fans who were hanging around waiting for a glimpse of the group.

'On this particular occasion I'd forgotten my clothes bag, so I zoomed back to the dressing room to get it, then I flew back out the door,' Porter remembers. 'But by that stage the other guys were in the van and the security guys had all moved on. I got halfway there and I ended up having to crouch in this foetal position. They were just all over me, screaming and pulling and yelling. I actually felt a big piece of my hair being ripped out.

'It was very frightening because there was just nothing I could do. It was like being in the middle of a rugby scrum, except probably worse because it was totally out of control. Eventually security realised what was happening and they cleared a path back to where I was. I was put in the van very shaken and dishevelled and scratched. It was a very scary moment.'

Not long afterwards, Skyhooks were playing a concert on the banks of the Yarra River, separated from the crowd by the muddy water of Melbourne's main estuary. But as they played, they noticed that the numbers on the opposite bank seemed to be thinning. Fans had realised they simply had to cross a nearby bridge in order to get closer to their idols. By the end of the show, the area behind the stage was swamped with Skyhooks fans. The band had a caravan where they changed into their stage outfits, but now there was a sea of people between them and their sanctuary.

By the time they made it back to the caravan, the kids were banging on the aluminium siding and rocking the whole thing backwards and forwards. Finally a police van had to be backed up to to a window, and the band crawled into the back and were driven away. Greg Macainsh recalls that it was the first time he'd been in the back of a police van, and he hasn't repeated the experience since then. At the height of Skyhooks' popularity, he remembers being frustrated with the fact that they couldn't hear themselves on stage over the screaming.

'I've got a tape of a gig we did at Myer Music Bowl and it's just constant screaming through the whole show. We used to play by watching each other, and somehow we all finished the songs at the same time.

'It's a strange thing to have 5000 people chanting your name. It's not a normal human experience. It's not something you can just dial up when you want. Hysteria is the fans' own projection of their feelings. It's got nothing to do with what you're actually doing, and it's got nothing to do with listening to the music.'

If it's 1982 in Melbourne, then it's time for Duran Duran mania. At radio station 3XY they've had a bright idea: let's have a press conference in the basement. It was announced on the air so a certain number of kids could be let in. The organisers had no idea of the response they would get.

'It was the scariest thing I've ever been through,' recalls Michael Matthews, who at the time was looking after the group as promotions manager at EMI. 'I remember watching footage of The Beatles and thinking it was great, but being in the middle of it is frightening. I had security there but I didn't inform the police. There were kids everywhere. They were pushing on the plate-glass windows at the front of the radio station and we were scared they might go right through it.

'We had to get the hell out of there so we went down through the basement and through these cages. But you couldn't escape them. They were grabbing you and hitting you. They were frenzied. Our clothes were torn. There's nothing uglier than a bunch of girls who want to tear you apart. These girls were savage. You could see in their faces that they were crazy. It looked like *Children of the Damned*.'

What does he think would have happened if they got to the band?

'If they got to the band they would have ripped them to pieces, like a flock of seagulls going for the last chip.'

'Some fans were hysterical when Michael Jackson arrived,' said the 1987 TV news report. Then the camera focused on a distraught fourteen-year-old girl, tears streaming down her face and a look of utter disappointment filling the screen.

That girl was Loretta Tolnay. She had been waiting three years to finally see Jackson in the flesh. She thought she'd missed her chance when she heard news reports about his accident on the set of a Pepsi commercial in 1984, when his hair caught fire and he suffered multiple burns. A couple of years later, when she read that he used an oxygen chamber at night, she was concerned again. She used to cry at the thought that he might die before she got a chance to meet him.

So, finally, she was at the airport ready for his plane to touch down. She had a really good position near the arrivals gate, but as time wore on, more and more fans streamed in, and photographers, newspaper reporters and television crews started jostling for a vantage point. The plane was delayed. Finally, after all the waiting, Jackson arrived—through a different door.

There was a manic rush, and the tumble of bodies meant that Loretta found herself on the ground when her idol waltzed through. Weighed down with a stuffed toy, a camera, multiple badges all over her jacket, a free album from the record company, and a complimentary six-pack of Pepsi, she felt terrible. She felt even more terrible for the girl who was trapped beneath her on the floor.

TWIST AND SHOUT

'On the news footage you can see me get up and shovel up all my shit. I asked the other girl on the ground if she was alright, and she was like, "Go after him!" It was like, "Save yourself!" I went straight after him but security are obviously trained to recognise people like me. I must have had that look, because three of them grabbed me and held me there until the van took off. When they let me go I ran down the street after the van, but then I just stood in the gutter and cried.'

Despite her distress at the airport, watching the footage on television made her really proud, because under her name at the bottom of the screen it said 'fan'.

'It was like, Bob Hawke—Prime Minister. Loretta Tolnay—Fan,' she says.

Loretta got to see Michael Jackson twice in concert that year. She cried the first night because she couldn't believe she was really seeing him. She cried the second night because she knew it would be a long time before she would see him again. In fact, Loretta got so worked up that she started hyperventilating, and the ambulance people gave her a paper bag to breathe into.

'I know other people would think, You poor deluded girl, get a grip on yourself, but it means that much to me. I want Michael to know how much he affects me. I couldn't control it, even if I wanted to.'

Losing control is what it's all about. Why does it happen? Well, it's obviously got something to do with the music. But add in elements like image, hype, peer-group influence, sheer pubescent energy and a genuine desire to let oneself go, and hysteria is a perfectly understandable phenomenon. Anyone who has been to a big sports event, a rally or a concert will tell you that a mass of people congregated for a single purpose is the ideal forum for the expression of extreme emotions. It not only reinforces that behaviour, but positively encourages it.

'Who's got the power?' Alice Cooper asked in 'Department Of Youth'. 'We have!' yelled the kids in response. 'And who gave it to you?' he added. 'Donny Osmond!' they screamed. Remember, Alice, crowds can easily turn against you, too.

Ritual de lo Habitual

Like the wild animals of the jungle, audience members at concerts tend to exhibit behaviour which falls into set patterns. Sure, your average Billy Joel punter isn't into bullying his way past security to scale the stage, grabbing the piano-pumping maestro around the neck and blubbering, 'I love you, man!' before taking a running jump and landing in a sweaty mess across the laps of the staid patrons in the front row of whichever entertainment centre the Joel-meister happens to be filling for ten nights in a row. But a certain number of ritualistic moves are widespread enough to gain entry into any pop sociologist's list.

Sophie Howarth

1. Cigarette lighter aloft during the ballads

We're about halfway through the gig. The band has come out firing on all cylinders, and we've been through the obligatory album tracks. Now it's time for the slow one. The lights go down. The acoustic guitar comes out. The drummer lightly swishes his ride cymbal. The singer has an expression on his face that suggests someone nicked the last beer out of the rider. And one by one, out they come. Everyone who owns a Bic disposable has hit the flint, and now they're being held at arm's length above their heads as they sway from side to side. Whether it's Metallica doing 'The Unforgiven' or John Farnham doing … well, anything, really … the combination of melancholy minor chords and the smell of lighter fluid will forever be mingled.

2. Air guitar

Popularised in the mass media by three dynamic doofus duos—Bill and Ted, Wayne and Garth, and Beavis and Butthead—this one is a public display of the almost exclusively male solo bedroom activity which involves cranking really loud music on the stereo (usually something like AC/DC, Deep Purple or Nirvana), standing in front of a mirror, and making movements with your hands that suggest you have suddenly become a mime and are playing the blistering guitar solo/fuzzy power chords emanating from the speakers. A special sub-category of this ritual involves standing with a gaggle of mates in front of the lead guitarist at a gig and imitating his every move. After the gig these guys will corner the hapless musician and discuss string weights and pick thickness with him for anything up to three hours.

3. The girl up on the shoulders

A special favourite at outdoor festivals. The most incredible things about 'hoisting the chick' are that (a) the guy offering the lift will invariably be shirtless, (b) the girl will invariably do the 'slow motion

Mirror Australian Telegraph Publications

air pump' with alternate fists, and (c) even though there are 10 000 people in a field, it will invariably take place directly in front of you, blocking your vision of the stage.

4. Crowd surfing

Possibly pioneered by Iggy Pop, who would stride out across the upturned palms of an audience and then smear peanut butter across his bare chest. This has become a standard audience ritual at rock gigs in the 1990s. Using the support of a mate, hoist yourself up out of the packed mosh-pit. (Note: If the crowd is too sparse, you will land on your head immediately and be ridiculed by your peers for being an idiot.) Relax your body as fellow pit dwellers hand you across the crowd. As you lurch dangerously close to the security guys at the edge of the stage, attempt to wriggle away from their outstretched hands. When you are finally deposited behind the barrier after losing this battle, race back out into crowd and repeat.

5. The stage dive

(a) Drink many beers.
(b) After taunting security all night, finally break the defense line by clambering up on stage.
(c) Wave meekly at bemused band, then turn to face the crowd with an idiot grin on your face.
(d) Spread arms out wide, as if acknowledging their praise for your talented move.
(e) Run as soon as it looks like the roadies are about to break your out-spread arms, and leap off the edge of the stage head-first into the audience.
(f) If they catch you, you may wish to crowd surf for a time. If they don't, proceed to St John's Ambulance people.

6. Throwing stuff up on stage

With Tom Jones it was women's underwear. With punk bands of the 1970s it was spit. The fans have paid their money, so why shouldn't they chuck stuff at their idols? Some bands found that certain songs would result in particular items being hurled in their general direction. After Skyhooks released 'Smut', a song about a guy masturbating in a darkened cinema while holding a packet of Twisties, the band found themselves showered with oven-shrunk Twisties packets. Weezer would sometimes have to dodge cardigans when they broke into 'Undone—The Sweater Song'. And following the Foo Fighters' video for 'Big Me', which parodied Mentos mints ads, they became moving targets for the little disc-shaped lollies hurled from the crowd. At any outdoor festival, where it invariably rains, mud becomes a favourite projectile. Perhaps Donita Sparks of L7 was seeking revenge for all this when, at the 1992 Reading Festival, she reached between her legs, removed her tampon and threw it into the crowd. Now *that's* performer/audience interaction.

FANTALES

Annette Walsh
Sherbert

I first heard them on the radio with 'Can You Feel It Baby'. I was eleven or twelve. I would have heard it on 2SM. I went out and bought the single because I loved it. Soon after that they had their first pin-up in *TV Week*, so I knew what they looked like. Then I carried on from there, buying every single—'Free The People', then 'You're All Woman', and so on.

My sister and a couple of girls at school were into it as much as I was, but they didn't stick with it. I'm divorced now, but most of those people from school are married with kids. All my friends are people I've met through ads in magazines and at concerts. Virtually all of my friends are Sherbert and Daryl Braithwaite people. I've got one friend in Newcastle who I've been writing to since I was twelve. Others I've met along the way, some from when Daryl made the comeback in 1989 with *Edge*.

In the beginning I used to swap around my favourite member. One week it would be Clive, the next week it would be Garth, then it would be Daryl. My sister and I gave each other nicknames. My nickname was Tony and my sister's nickname was Daz. To this day we'll still sign our Christmas cards to each other like that. It stuck.

I liked the whole band, but people say Daryl is the gentleman of rock, and he really is. He's a really, really nice person. He has plenty of time for the fans and he always comes down to talk to us if he sees us at a table.

Back in Sherbert days it was way too hard to meet them, with the armoured cars and bodyguards and all that. When Sherbert ended and he went out solo and did a lot of clubs there weren't many people there. Sometimes we'd be there and there'd be only twenty people in the audience, so that was when you'd be able to talk to him.

I was very nervous the first time I met him. It took me a while to

Peter Green (left) and Annette Walsh.

get out of that. We hung around and said hello after the shows, and maybe got an autograph and a photo. We'd go to everything. If he had eight shows in Sydney, then we'd go to eight shows. We'd even go up to Newcastle.

The first time I saw Sherbert was at my high school in 1973. Bands used to come out and do lunchtime shows back then. They only had one album at that time, and I was just so excited. One of my girlfriends actually got all their autographs, and I paid her five dollars for them. That was a lot of money. I remember standing up on the second level watching Daryl drive away in his white Torana—the number plate was CIZ 085. I was really thrilled. I copped a bit from some people for loving Sherbert. I sat there in the second row and sang every song as they sang them.

In the 1970s, the Hordern Pavilion used to be my second home. And there were the free 2SM shows at Victoria Park. I had excellent parents. My mother is 65 and she comes to stuff with me now. When the tickets would come on sale for the Hordern shows, my parents would drive my sister and I out at one or two in the morning and we'd wait at the roller-door gates until nine in the morning, and then everyone would run to the ticket office. Then they'd come back and pick us up. Same with the Victoria Park shows, they'd drop us off really early in the morning so we'd be down the front and then we'd meet up afterwards. I've been really lucky to have such great parents.

I hated Skyhooks. Sherbert were it, Skyhooks were no good. I must admit, a few years later I bought *Living In The 70s* and I love that album. I think it's excellent. And when they did their reunion tour a few years ago, I went and I thought, Geez, I was an idiot back then. But back then, it was the thing to do—you loved Sherbert and hated Skyhooks, or the other way around. When the King of Pop would be on, I would sit in front of the TV and I would cry if Daryl and Sherbert won and I would cry if they didn't. I would go down to the newsagent every Monday and buy five copies of *TV Week*, and send in five nomination forms, filled with Daryl and Sherbert. The next week, I'd do the same thing. We just had to let them win.

Sherbert were more of a nice band. Their image was softer, whereas Skyhooks were out to shock. They didn't shock me, but you just hated Skyhooks because they were rivals of Sherbert. I love

Skyhooks music now, but back then I wouldn't have dared go to a Sky-hooks concert. That would be betraying Sherbert. I was a Sherbert person.

I'm dedicated to things. I don't give up. Daryl deserved his success. But now he's getting ignored, and he has no record company—we're really mad about that because he is one of the best talents in this country. We think he deserves a chance, but we don't want him as big as someone like John Farnham. You can't get anywhere near John Farnham. We can still see Daryl and talk to him and he knows we'll always be there. We just live for when he comes back to Sydney. It just makes us so happy.

I still dream about Daryl. I'll be somewhere and I'll run into him. Even my mum dreams about Daryl. My friends, too. I wanted to marry Daryl when I was younger. Everyone liked Garth because he was the best looking, but Daryl's the one who took my fancy. I think he's better looking. I will never give up on him. Never.

At the Hordern gigs it was often Sherbert, John Paul Young and TMG [Ted Mulry Gang]. I grew up with the three of those bands and I really reckon they made me the person I am today. I wouldn't want to have grown up without those bands. They've had a very big influence on my life. I'm just so lucky that I can still see them today. I will never give up on the bands I love, and I know I'll be like this until the day I die. I'm 38 now but I still feel like I'm eighteen. I don't feel any different to how I felt back then.

Peter Green

Skyhooks

The first time I heard Skyhooks I was literally forced to hear them. I was at school and I was about thirteen. There was this guy called Clarence and his brother was connected with bikie gangs. A lot of bikers and skinheads really liked Skyhooks early on. Clarence had a cassette and he used to harass people into listening to it, believing that his music taste was 100 per cent it. At the time I was into glam stuff like Slade and Suzi Quatro. I wasn't really listening to much

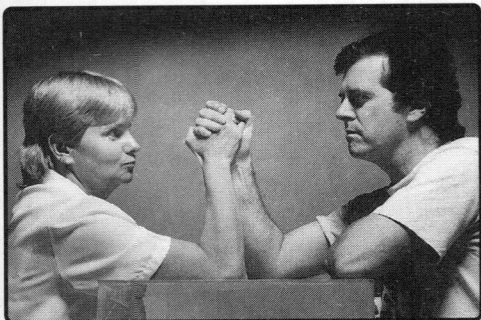

Sue Stafford

Australian stuff. So we were forced to listen to *Living In The 70s*. I heard the title track and 'You Just Like Me Cos I'm Good In Bed' and 'Smut'—I got quite embarrassed as a thirteen-year-old boy hearing that.

The lyrics caught me straight away. And the sound of *Living In The 70s* was unique. There aren't a lot of Australian albums that sound like that. That's why it continually does well in those readers' polls and lists of great Australian albums. Shirley's voice was totally unique, and on that album Red Symons's guitar playing was very good. But it was Macainsh's lyrics that caught me off-guard. I guess we'd been listening to music relating to overseas cities for so long that it had been accepted. To hear songs about Melbourne was really different, even though I was this kid in Wollongong—I didn't know anything about Carlton or Toorak or Balwyn.

After my first Skyhooks gig, I realised they were getting big, and I met people who were excited about the band too, and it was the beginning of the gang thing. As the years went on we linked up with hundreds of people. We used to go in convoys to gigs, and we'd fill up the first four or five rows. Girls would come with us to the Bondi Lifesaver because they knew we wouldn't hassle them—we were there for the music.

As far as the Skyhooks/Sherbert thing goes, the main reason I like Skyhooks is because of the incredible songs. The songwriting standard is so much better than Sherbert's, without a second thought. Skyhooks have their full catalogue out, but Sherbert have one 'Best Of' out there. *Living In The 70s* is still in the top-twenty best-selling albums, but you never see a Sherbert album in there. There was a good feeling around the band and they had a good sense of humour. I used to actually go and see Sherbert sometimes, and enjoyed some of the shows, but the passion wasn't there as it was for Skyhooks.

Look, if I was an actor I would always want to play the villain because it's a better role—Sherbert were like their name, a bit sickly and nice, whereas Skyhooks were a bit rude and crude, and understood what music was about and had longevity. I don't think Sherbert had longevity. *Howzat* is a fine album and I've always loved 'Slipstream' and 'Summer Love', but I don't think they hold up as well in the 1990s.

FANTALES

I can never ever remember any Sherbert fans in Wollongong. It's like Adelaide is a Cold Chisel town. I really think Wollongong should have been transported to Melbourne many, many years ago, and made an outer suburb somewhere between Oakleigh and Dandenong. The city fathers in Wollongong banned Skyhooks from coming into the city limits. I could never understand how they were going to police that— like, were they going to arrest them if they were caught in Nowra? I thought that was strange.

Sometimes you have to make the statement that you are a fan. Today I can honestly still say I'm a big fan. Last year we set up the Skyhooks Web site. We work for a lot of other bands now and I was thinking that it might be time to move on. But the one thing about Skyhooks is that there's an external family around the band which still exists.

I had a bit of a dysfunctional family. Wollongong is renowned for high divorce statistics. My parents were going through a shaky patch. At the time I was an only child and the music actually got me through a very tough time. It was a great escape, and I made a lot of new friends. We used to hang out, and many of them were going through experiences where their parents were getting divorced. My parents ended up working it out and getting it together, whereas most of my friends' parents didn't. My dad's dead now, but both my parents always encouraged me in the area of music. My father had a really big record collection, and my mother still buys CDs by young Australian artists. I remember my mother bought the first Blondie album before they were really popular. If there was a gig 50 or 60 miles away she would always drive me.

In late 1976 we thought we'd take over the fanclub because we'd been getting a lot of mail from fans wanting photos and information. We decided to do our own thing. We'd put little ads in *RAM* and get a hundred letters. The existing fanclub had all these different people running it and it always ran at a loss and wasn't very good. We sent off for t-shirts and they never arrived. So we decided to do it ourselves. Skyhooks really lit the fuse for me. They gave me a job in the industry. If it wasn't for Macainsh's encouragement, then I wouldn't be doing this now.

63

BANDS AS FANS

Daniel Johns from silverchair

I don't think I've ever really been obsessed with anyone, but probably the band I've been into more than anyone else would be Black Sabbath.

I first heard them when I was really little—like, eight or nine years old. I obviously didn't have any money to buy my own albums so I used to play my dad's old LP records, and one day I put on *Paranoid*, probably because the cover caught my eye or something. That combination of intense heaviness with real dark lyrics sounded like nothing else I'd ever heard and it still knocks me out even now. Ever since then they've been the ultimate rock band for me. I never get sick of listening to their early stuff. Even after all these years, songs like 'War Pigs' still sound great, I reckon.

We were actually lucky enough to meet Ozzy Osbourne in 1997 when he came to one of our gigs in America. We were all really nervous when we heard he was coming, but he turned out to be a really good bloke. We told him we play 'Paranoid' live sometimes, and he said, 'Really? So do I.' He was smoking this big cigar, so while we were onstage we knew he was out there watching us because we could see this constant orange glow where he was sitting in the balcony. It was pretty intimidating!

Then on my eighteenth birthday his daughter, Amy, gave me this great plaque as a present. It's a multi-platinum award for sales of *Paranoid*, and it's signed by all the members of Sabbath. It's probably one of my favourite possessions.

I'm definitely still a big Sabbath fan … always will be.

Cute, real cute,
Marie

ALL YOU NEED IS CASH

**'Money, money, money, must be funny
in a rich man's world'**

—Abba, 'Money Money Money'

You know you've really made it when you're 25 centimetres high and made of plastic. The Beatles, Kiss, Donny and Marie, Cher, New Kids On The Block and The Spice Girls have all been replicated in moulded polyurethane, packaged in a cardboard box and, sold to the masses. Even Peter Andre has been frozen in time in a curious shade of orange and, much like in real life during the first half of the 1990s, two carefully placed strands of hair hang over his eyes. Strip off his shirt, and there is the famous Andre six-pack, plastic stomach muscles which will withstand the ravages of middle age and never be covered with flab.

Merchandising, product tie-ins and repackaging are cornerstones of pop, and the advent of the doll is just one of the more extreme arms of the many-tentacled beast. Ironically, the second Beatles movie was originally going to be called *Eight Arms to Hold You,* and it is at the Fab Four's pointy-toed boots that we must start our tale.

> *Journalist*: Do you resent fans ripping up your sheets for souvenirs?
> *Ringo*: No, I don't mind. So long as I'm not in them when the ripping is going on.

By 1964 The Beatles had become a licence to make money. Anything that vaguely had a whiff of Fabness about it would sell. The epitome of this was when two Chicago businessmen bought the sheets and pillowcases from a hotel in Kansas City where The Beatles had slept. They paid $1000 for the privilege, a move which might sound like complete folly. But what they did next was to cut up the linen into one-inch squares, and sell each piece for a dollar. There were 160 000 pieces. Do the maths.

Almost 25 years later, I was working as the feature writer at a pop magazine. Just before I joined, they had run a competition to win the bedsheets which had been used by members of Bros while they stayed in Sydney. The response was overwhelming. Soon afterwards, the publisher and a few of his cronies popped out for a long lunch. On returning late in the afternoon, one of the cronies swaggered up to my desk.

'Isyapassportuptadate, Bazza?' he garbled.

'Excuse me?' I answered.

'Is your passport up to date?'

'Er, yes. Why do you ask?'

He put a finger to the side of his nose and gave me a knowing lock.

'Don't worry. You'll find out.'

It turned out that over their alcohol-fuelled meal they had hatched a plan to send me to Europe in order to follow Johnny Diesel (back then he hadn't reduced his monicker to just the name of a fuel). My brief was to wait until he got a haircut, race into the barber after he left, scoop up the hair from the floor, and whisk it back to Australia so we could run a competition.

Fortunately, by the next day all that remained of the idea were the hangovers

ALL YOU NEED IS CASH

'I'm totally into kitsch. The day they made a Duran Duran board game was a very happy day for me. The only thing I regret they never made was Duran Duran dolls. We were speaking to someone about it once but it never quite happened. It's a shame, that.'

—*Nick Rhodes, Duran Duran*

'If it has the Krusty symbol on it, then it must be a quality product,' Bart Simpson once said about all the merchandise that was endorsed by his favourite TV clown. 'Krusty wouldn't lie to us.'

The same logic goes into the marketing of most pop bands these days. Many of them advertise caps, t-shirts and pullovers in CD booklets, all bearing groups' logos. And it all started with The Beatles. Rings, lockets, badges, combs, sweaters, jackets, aprons, toy guitars, cigars, matchboxes and even icecream were all fair game if they had The Beatles' image stamped on them. There were reports in 1963 that a factory in Bethnal Green was having trouble keeping up with the huge demand for Beatles wigs. They just couldn't churn out those black plastic things fast enough. Soon enough there would be no need to pretend you had a mop top; instead teenage boys started to let their hair grow long, in imitation of their heroes.

Of course, all of this has little—if anything—to do with the music. But with a teen-generated phenomenon, this is exactly the point. Now, a Beatles cigar might be a sought-after item that will fetch a high price at a collectors' fair. Then, it was just something you had to have because 'they' were pictured on the cigar band. It was another way to make contact, another relic to savour, another week's pocket money that you'd devoted to them.

'Yes, I have time for you! Donny has time for you 24 hours a day when you wear this exciting personalised, jeweled watch designed especially for Fan Club members! Just think, every time you look at your new watch, Donny will smile back at you! Order now—$15.95'
—*an advertisement for the official Donny Osmond watch, 1974*

Sue Stafford

ALL YOU NEED IS CASH

Annette Walsh was member number 59 in the Sherbert fanclub—when you realise that the club ended up being 10 000-strong at its peak, it's an indication of how early she got into the group. In the beginning she would write off to the club and they would send her posters for nothing. They were just wrapped that someone was showing such enthusiasm for this new group. Soon enough things changed, and the merchandising arm kicked in—calendars, stickers, badges, t-shirts, mirrors and the infamous satin bomber jackets ($30) were all up for grabs.

The 1970s marked a turning point in the financial lengths a fan would have to go to in order to be a completely devoted follower. Now there were so many more opportunities to show your love than by simply buying each album and going to the concerts whenever the group came to town. Kiss wrote the book when it came to market diversification and gimmickry, and they continue to do so. In fact, Gene Simmons would turn 1995 interviews into a sales pitch for *Kisstory*, the definitive, must-have Kiss tome.

'It's a monster coffee-table book,' he informed me, even though I hadn't asked about it. 'It weighs in at over four and a half kilos. It's like trying to pick up a bowling ball. It's a coffee-table book where all you need is the legs of the table. The measurements are about a foot and a quarter long by a foot wide, 440 pages, each copy in its own hard-shell case, each copy numbered and signed by the band ...'

Sue Stafford

71

Sue Stafford

And so on and so on. *Kisstory* sold for $270 at the merchandising stalls during the band's 1997 tour.

'Yeah, it's a fair bit of money, but it's worth it because I love this band,' said one guy who I talked to at the Sydney concert after he had plonked down the cash and was carefully stowing his prized possession into his backpack. 'This is like the ultimate book for Kiss fans, and it's a memory of tonight, too. It's just a grouse thing to own.'

Are these kinds of marketing initiatives fleecing the fans? Of course. But it's a two-way street, and the diehards love owning everything. Go to the Internet and try downloading a list of Kiss merchandise from just one collector. Seventeen pages later, you'll be marvelling at the fact that someone would willingly pay $20 for an empty doll box, $550 for a bedspread, and $295 for a 15-inch piece of green material, which was apparently Peter Criss's tail for his *Dynasty*-era stage outfit. Here you can buy guitar picks, backstage passes, drumsticks and photocopies of tour itineraries. These items are important because they are associated closely with members of the band, and in some cases have been used by them. It's encouraging to know that the Kiss condoms for sale are sealed. Presumably they have not been preloved by Gene or Paul.

It wasn't always so easy to get a Kiss condom. In 1978 Clinton Meredith was a rabid Kiss fan just entering high school, but everything related to his favourite band would come to Australia months after the American release, and a lot of it was hard to find. When he went to the USA for the first time in the Christmas holidays that year, he went with his father to a record shop, and headed straight for the K section. There, like a holy grail for the twelve-year-old, was a copy of *Alive II*.

'I looked at it and thought, What is this? It wasn't even released in Australia yet, and no-one I knew had even heard of it. When I brought it back it caused a ruckus. I was telling these guys in fourth form about it and they were ready to beat me up.'

They told him to stop lying. There was no such thing as *Alive II*. They were bigger Kiss fans than this little jerk, and they'd never heard of it, so what was he talking about?

'The next day, I brought it into school, and from that day I was untouchable.'

It was also his first brush with the value of merchandise. Inside *Alive II* was a sheet of tattoos. His new school buddies were so impressed by this that they offered to buy them. He off-loaded two for five dollars each, and regretted it soon afterwards. It took fifteen years to find another sheet. And it cost him a lot more than ten bucks.

> *Me*: What do you think was the most bizarre piece of Kiss merchandise?
>
> *Paul Stanley*: Well, the dolls certainly weren't anatomically correct.
>
> *Me*: You'd want to change them slightly?
>
> *Paul Stanley*: Well, if I changed mine, it would have to be more than slightly.
>
> —*a conversation with Kiss's Paul Stanley, 1995*

Kiss pinball machines and original covers of the *Yesterday … And Today* album (featuring The Beatles draped with raw meat and holding headless dolls) are excellent ways of parting fans and their money. But many fans will tell you it's the music that matters. With that said, they can't get enough of collectors' items, even if the record company is repackaging the same material in slightly different sleeves. There might be different edits or mixes, the artwork might be changed on a re-release, or they may be offering extra tracks. Maybe there's a bonus poster, or an extra CD of live tracks. Sometimes there's no difference whatsoever in the music, it's just that you have to have all the different formats—seven-inch single, twelve-inch single, CD single, CD album, EP, cassette. Others will go so far as collecting exactly the same album printed in different parts of the world, or on different labels, even if the track listing is identical from region to region.

Matthew Hancock, who followed Australian guitar-pop band The Hummingbirds, cites the example of their first single, 'Alimony'. He owns this song in nine different incarnations—the original Phantom single, the CD single, the CD single re-release, the rooArt picture-disc release, the rooArt seven-inch vinyl, the version on the first album, the twelve-inch rooArt remix single, the LP version on twelve-inch vinyl, and the Phantom Records test pressing, of which only 25 copies were ever made. That's a lot of money to spend on what is essentially three and a half minutes of pop music.

'I have this friend, alright, and she's a gynaecologist in Hollywood, and she scored this for me from the lab where she works. It's a Madonna pap smear. I know it's kind of cloudy, but it's a Madonna pap smear. It's got Ciccone on the top—that's like a medical label, Ciccone. Check it out, I know it's kind of disgusting, but it's like, sort of getting down to the real Madonna … Do you think maybe you'd be interested in buying something like this? It's like a high dollar item. It's one of a kind. Chance of a lifetime.'
—from the movie Slacker, written and directed by Richard Linklater, 1991

There's nothing stopping a fan following their idol around the city, the country, or even the planet. Apart from money, of course. But the more dedicated treat their holiday time as a chance to pursue a performer on a tour. And all their cash will go towards the quest.

Sam Pickard saved for two years, working overtime at a record store, in order to travel around America for six weeks. In that time she saw Bon Jovi play fourteen shows, attended a fanclub weekend with 400 other devotees, enjoyed a boat cruise with the band, got photographed with them, experienced a soundcheck, went to the premiere of the film *Moonlight and Valentino* in which Jon Bon Jovi starred, and even got to see the singer's house. ('I'd never do that again,' she says. 'It was really intrusive.') The whole jaunt cost $10 000. Was it worth it? 'Of course.'

When international bands come to Australia to undertake promotional tours or concert tours for a couple of weeks, some fans can go through thousands of dollars flying between cities, catching taxis, buying gifts, purchasing concert tickets and putting themselves up in the same hotels as their idols.

Brett Price used one of his old obsessions to fuel another. Originally a fan of Bros and New Kids On The Block, he went on to follow Take That with a passion. New Kids became his money-maker. Through connections, he had obtained limited-edition releases and got them autographed, then sold them to fans. He remembers off-loading one picture disc for $500. The exercise funded his trip to London in 1993, when he spent $6500 following Take That on tour.

'Originally I was going to live over there, but Take That took up everything,' he says.

Was it worth it?

'It was worth every cent,' he replies without hesitation.

Journalist: What will you do when Beatlemania subsides?
John Lennon: Count the money.

Hello Cleveland!

'Check one, two … check one, two!' My, my, the things bands say to their fans when they're up on stage.

'I was talking to someone backstage earlier and they said that a lot of you people out there like to take the taste of alcohol.'—*Paul Stanley of Kiss*, Kiss Alive!

'Hello tree people! I'm singing for you, too.'—*Neil Diamond*, Hot August Night

'Ever get the feeling you've been cheated?'—*Johnny Rotten of The Sex Pistols, live in San Francisco, at the band's final performance*

'Here's a song Charles Manson stole from The Beatles. We're stealing it back.'—*Bono of U2*, Rattle & Hum

'I ain't taking shit off today.'—*Madonna, Live Aid*

'The ones in the cheap seats clap your hands. The rest of you just rattle your jewellery.' —John Lennon, Royal Variety Performance, 1963

'I'd like to say thank you on behalf of the group and ourselves, and I hope we passed the audition.'—*Lennon again*, Let It Be

'I don't believe you.'—*Bob Dylan's riposte to a fan who yelled out 'Judas!' at the infamous 'Dylan goes electric' show in 1966*

'It's kinda weird up here. You gotta keep your bodies off each other—unless you intend love. And you need people like the Angels to keep people in line.'—*Grace Slick at Altamont, where Meredith Hunter was beaten and stabbed to death as a result of the Hell's Angels' loose interpretation of 'keeping people in line'*

'Can anybody here play the drums?'—*Pete Townshend of The Who, in San Francisco, 1973, after Keith Moon was 'taken ill' mid-performance*

'Either those cats cool it, or we don't play.'—*Keith Richards, Altamont*

Bono in front of his own little world.

75

FANTALES

Claire Isaac

Duran Duran

It wasn't exactly cool to join the choir at Turramurra High School. But one day in 1983 there was a sudden, mysterious influx of new recruits who had never before shown any interest in singing. The school's music teacher was married to a guy who wrote jingles and TV themes, and the girls of Turramurra High were going to be chirping the tune for a bubblegum commercial. Basically, it involved lots of la-la-la's, and the closing line 'the flavour lasts a long, long time'. There was going to be lots of free bubblegum in it, and the chance to hear your voice on television.

But for Claire Isaac and her friends, this was chicken feed. The real attraction was the fact that they would be recording the song at EMI's 301 Studios. And Claire knew who was going to be there at the same time. Five guys with English accents were putting down tracks for an album with the unlikely title *Seven And The Ragged Tiger*. Duran Duran were in town.

The first time Claire heard about Duran Duran was when she was twelve years old. Her family had just moved to Australia from England, and she was an Adam & The Ants fan. One of her friends wrote to her from England and told her that she had become a peacock punk, and that she was in love with a group who had just released a single called 'Planet Earth'. Slowly, the pictures of Adam and his various Ants on Claire's wall started to get some competition. Soon enough the king of the wild frontier was overtaken by Simon Le Bon and his band of puffy-panted, floppy-fringed cohorts.

'They came out here in 1982 to tour, and that's when it went completely crazy,' Claire remembers. 'I was fourteen by then. I went to my friend's house first, and we got so hysterical that her mother refused to drive us. We were so strung-out. I was so overcome that I left my

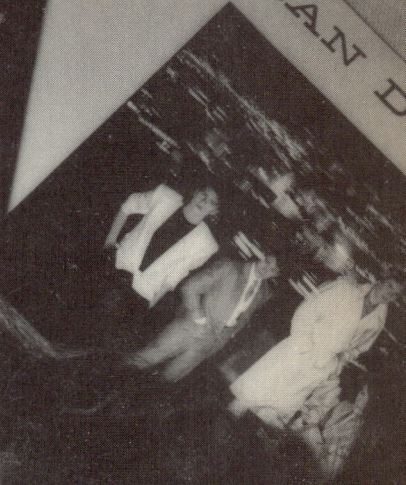

Claire Isaac meets old romantic Simon Le Bon in 1983.

ticket at home and I had to get my mum to drive around with it because I was in tears. At the concert we screamed the whole time, and we stood on the seats and our whole row fell over. I thought we were all going to die. I twisted my ankle. I had the day off school the next day because I was so tired and emotional.'

That week the band was interviewed on 2SM, and Claire went along with loads of other girls to try and catch a glimpse of them. She got a photo of the top of Simon's head, along with his autograph and 'a scribble' from Nick Rhodes. Later, a friend who had done work experience at a newspaper showed her some press photographs from that day, and after blowing up a section of one picture on a photocopier, Claire saw herself and her friends in the crowd. She noticed two things. 'We had looks of pure adulation on our faces. And I was wearing tragic new romantic clothes.'

But that was nothing compared with the following year. A friend breathlessly turned up to Claire's house with the most unbelievable news. She had been at the State Library with her father, and there on the steps doing a photo shoot were Simon, John, Andy, Nick and Roger.

They found out that the band was recording their next album at 301 Studios, and that day after school they got the train into the city and waited outside. They made the pilgrimage every day after school, and spent the entire weekend hanging around. Claire got into trouble from her mother for neglecting her homework. She used to wind her watch back so that she'd have an excuse for turning up late at home. What did they do when they actually saw a Duran Duran member emerge from a car at the studio?

'We'd take photos of them, get them developed the same day, and bring them back the next day to get signed. You were always trying to get the perfect picture with your favourite member. If they said your name without being reminded, then that was the ultimate. If one of them said, "Hello Claire," you were in heaven forever. Unless your name wasn't Claire, of course. We'd even see their girlfriends in town and we'd try to be really good friends with them, in the hope that for some reason they'd like a teenage girl trying on make-up with them.'

Didn't they ever feel jealous of these women, who were taking the place of every red-blooded teenage girl at the time?

'It was never really a sexual thing with Duran Duran for me. I had crushes, but I would never want anything to happen because it would have spoilt the whole illusion. We didn't want to have sex with them. We wanted to spend time with them and sit down discussing what they thought of the latest Thompson Twins album.'

Soon enough the fans discovered that the band was staying at the York Apartments, near the Harbour Bridge. This became a new vantage point. They had rules about what you shouldn't do—don't scream, don't chase them, don't grab hold of them. The fans didn't want to ruin their chances of having contact with them again.

Claire's most obsessive moment from this time? She doesn't even hesitate—it was definitely when she ripped a piece of lined writing

Sue Stafford

paper from one of her books and rubbed it on Nick Rhodes's car, leaving a smudge of dirt on the page for posterity. She still has it.

After the band went to Melbourne to rehearse for a few weeks, and then returned to Sydney to start their national tour, everything had changed. Now they were staying at the more upscale Sebel Townhouse, and stories about them were in the newspapers. Claire and the diehards at 301 and the York Apartments suddenly had lots of competition.

'We were really pissed off with all the fans who came along later. You couldn't get near the band anymore, and security was really tight. And all these girls would just scream. We got so used to seeing the band every day before, that we'd feel ripped off if that didn't happen.'

FANTALES

Claire's obsession with pop music continues. She went on to work for *TV Hits, Smash Hits* and *Hit Songwords*, and got a buzz interviewing New Kids On The Block, East 17 and Take That. And her love for Duran Duran changed as a result.

'I got a bit sick of them being arty wankers. The reason they were big in the first place was that they were a perfect pop band, but like they all do, they get too serious and ruin it. By the time I got to interview them, they were serious rock stars who cared about their art.

'But of all the bands I've loved, Duran have meant the most to me, I know that sounds really daggy, but it's true.'

Meanwhile, back at that bubblegum commercial, the girls have finished doing all those la-la-la's, and Claire is hanging around the jukebox in the studio foyer with her friend Julie, trying to look inconspicuous. Finally, their loitering pays off, as Simon Le Bon and Roger Taylor wander in. They have a long chat to Simon, and Roger gives them a drumskin that he has signed.

'They even signed and drew pictures on these white t-shirts we'd brought along. It was just me and my best friend standing there digging each other in the ribs because we couldn't believe it was happening. We floated all the way home. It was the most amazing day of our lives.'

COPYCATS

**'Oh, how real those roses seemed to me,
But they're only imitation, like your imitation love for me'**

—Marie Osmond, 'Paper Roses'

Allegedly, Oasis once returned to their rehearsal room after taking a break down at the pub, and found a note taped to the door. It bore the following words: 'Find some riffs of your own.'

This story begs the question—what do you stick on the door of the rehearsal room used by an Oasis tribute band?

Tribute—something given or spoken as a testimonial of respect, gratitude or affection. So much for dictionary definitions. Respect, gratitude and affection mightn't be the words etched on the hearts of every member of a tribute band. Ten years ago, this phenomenon was about as widespread as Internet access. Now it seems that everyone bar A Flock Of Seagulls has spawned their own copyists. Jagged Little Pill, an Alanis Morissette show, managed to get off the ground when the Canadian singer/songwriter only had one major album to her name.

When you talk to these bands, and those behind the scenes who put them together, a general code emerges, a pattern of words which is repeated over and over like a mantra.

1. We are not a covers band.

   The words 'covers' and 'band' are truly dirty when put together in that order. Covers bands are shoddy, makeshift, throwaway outfits that are a complete waste of time and money. Tribute bands are completely different.

2. What we're on about is entertainment.

   Basically, we're just there to put on the best show we possibly can, and give people a good time.

3. People want to see this kind of thing.

   Everyone's bored with original music. That's why the live scene is dying.

4. We're not taking work away from original bands.

   Hey, if they were any good, they'd be successful.

5. We're accomplished musicians and we put on a good show.

   I've been playing guitar since I was ten, mate. I've been in bands since I was fifteen. I've paid my dues. This is the only way you can make money playing music. Oh, and …

6. Yeah, of course, we're big fans of the music.

   Well, that and the work's there.

Paul looks cheeky as he nods his head in time to the bass riff he's playing. John chews gum and tilts his head back as he reaches the high notes. George has his mouth half open as he concentrates on a lead break. Ringo shakes his head as he swishes the ride cymbal and grins amiably at the young girls down the front of the stage.

COPYCATS

We're crammed into a long, low-ceilinged room, but it's not Liverpool, it's not the Cavern Club, and it's not 1963. It's The Rocks in Sydney, it's an art gallery, and it's 1997. It's not The Beatles, but The Beatnix. The group's manager, Tony Dean, has organised Beatlefest, a weekend exhibition of memorabilia, videos, photographs and collectibles. 'I used to be in the band when I was thinner,' he says, patting his stomach.

As expected, there are people like Tony standing around tapping their feet to The Beatnix—men in their forties who have been flicking through the racks of rare vinyl and staring intently at a copy of the infamous *Yesterday … And Today* cover. But some of them have brought their kids along, and they're getting into it, too. One sandy-haired five-year-old stomps around in a little circle as the band breaks into 'Get Back'. And those teenage girls up the front—they weren't even born when John Lennon was shot, yet they're sitting there cross-legged and with big smiles on their faces, wrapped in the four guys wearing Sgt Pepper suits.

All these folks are watching a band attempting to play note-perfect renditions of songs from a band that broke up over a quarter of a century ago. Not only are they not the original Beatles, but they're not even the original Beatnix. That post-Fab Four split with Tony Dean at the beginning of 1996. They're now called The Beatels.

Of course, neither The Beatnix nor The Beatels are alone. Britain boasts The Bootleg Beatles, Silver Beatles, The Cavern Beatles and Sgt Pepper's Band. There's Abbey Road from Spain, Clube Big Beatles from Brazil, and Help from the USA. Meanwhile, in Sweden, the geographically monickered Liverpool and the spoonerism-friendly Lenny Pane battle for the attentions of Beatles devotees.

Wherever folks don rose-coloured glasses and have access to rear-view mirrors, the tribute band thrives. And Australia is a real leader in the field when it comes to imitation. A few tribute bands from our shores have even gained a modicum of popularity overseas. It's ironic that Britain became a stomping ground for The Australian Pink Floyd Show, when the original band is not only from England, but still occasionally lumbers out onto the road itself. The Antipodean version would advertise their shows with parodies of famous Floyd album covers, substituting an inflatable flying kangaroo over Battersea Power Station for the inflatable flying pig on the sleeve of *Animals*.

Another really successful parody was Bjorn Again, who even had the good grace to come up with a clever name, a rarity in a genre that either uses lame bastardisations of original names (The Bleach Boys, Creedence Clearwater) or just bungs a song or album title on the top of posters (Love Cats, Throwing Copper).

In their heyday during the early 1990s, Bjorn Again would only do interviews in character. They spoke in dodgy Swedish accents that came via Melbourne. And in those accents, they patiently explained to interviewers that they weren't in fact a tribute to Abba.

'There was a plane crash and we all woke up on this desert island and couldn't remember anything about our past, apart from all this music in our heads,' guitarist Bjorn Volvoeus earnestly told me. 'This guy called Lasse Wellabalsam was fishing and recognised us. He said we were a huge Swedish pop group. He put us in a studio and suddenly we found that we could all play and sing.'

Volvoeus and songwriting partner Benny Anderwear locked themselves into a cottage in Rooty Hill and nutted out classics like 'S.O.S.', 'Mamma Mia' and 'Ring Ring'. When they added the girlish harmonies and flashy costumes of Agnetha Falstart and Frida Longstokin, the combination was dynamite. The secret of their success? Benny was more than willing to impart his knowledge.

'It works as long as it's good fun, with a good clean beat and a good strong tune, and it has to be about love.'

When asked about future plans, Benny and Bjorn revealed that they were starting work on a musical, possibly called *Draughts* or *Chinese Checkers*. Although they never made good on their threat, they did release one album before imploding, along the way becoming a favourite of many 'real' bands; they even appeared at the 1992 Reading Festival, at the request of headliners Nirvana. There's nothing weirder than seeing a field of people moshing to the words 'you can dance, you can jive, having the time of your life'.

Kiss were asking for it, really. When they decided to take off the make-up in 1983 and release a series of albums, some of which even bass player/God Of Thunder Gene Simmons has referred to as 'complete crap and waste of time', they left a huge chunk of fans still thirsting for the face paint, the fire-breathing, and the good old days of 'Detroit Rock City', 'Strutter' and 'Rock And Roll All Nite'.

Into that vacuum rushed a slew of tribute bands, multiplying like the hundreds of groupie Polaroids collected by Simmons. Some would only perform material that covered the broader territory Kiss performed on their live albums. Others would only play songs recorded by the original line-up. And others again would play 'make-up' material, but perhaps feature a Vinnie Vincent (who replaced Ace Frehley) or Eric Carr (who replaced Peter Criss).

This sort of thing is so widespread, and it's taken so seriously in Kiss circles, that there's even an Internet site set up to review Kiss tributes from around the world. Contenders have to send in two live shows on video, and be dissected by a panel of judges.

What does the original band think of all these clones?

'Some of them are just great,' says singer/guitarist Paul Stanley. 'I think it's such a tremendous compliment to have people re-creating a certain moment in the band's history, and to do it in a way that's really studied.'

Stanley, a man not renowned for his strong sense of irony, went so far as to have a tribute band play at his birthday party in 1992. He was astounded to be standing there watching a guy imitate his every move, right down to the onstage patter that he has spouted over the years.

'I have a lot of our shows on videotape, and clearly some of these bands get twentieth generation bootlegs of them, because you hear the same raps I used.'

Imitation may be the sincerest form of flattery, but in the case of Kiss, it may have sparked something in the minds of the original members. In 1996 Simmons and Stanley decided to bring the
long-departed Criss and Frehley back into the fold for a reunion tour, donning the make-up one more
time, and playing all the songs that the fans had been demanding for years.

The tributes had become a conduit for something else—a band imitating itself from a time twenty
years ago, in a galaxy far, far away.

Imitation interrogation

The substitute Liams, McCartneys and Barnesies get plonked in a
chair and asked the hard questions. Are tribute bands murdering
original music? Do they get asked for autographs? What about the
groupie situation? And if a Blur tribute band and an Oasis tribute
band met at an airport, would they have a fistfight?

Courtesy of Southbeat

Patrick Loughrey—Liam Gallagher in Oasis tribute band, Noasis

Is this the ultimate act of fandom or purely a business opportunity?
It was put together three weeks after Oasis cancelled their Australian tour in 1996. It's purely a business opportunity. I wouldn't
do any other tribute band, but this sounded like fun. I'm a fan,
though. I've got their stuff.

You now play Liam, but you used to be Noel. What happened?
He (the former Liam) lost it. He started living it. He was a very
rude man. He even had a blond girlfriend, his Patsy.

What were your first gigs like?
We botched it on stage constantly. The bass player was terrible,
he'd roll up to gigs vomiting and we were very sloppy. This was
November 1996 to January 1997—the summer of discontent.

Then what happened?
I was fed up with Liam's antics. He'd kick me fair up the coit on
stage, and he wasn't joking. He'd spit water at me too, and roll up

late. After that night I decided to get a whole new band. I should have always been Liam anyway, because I'm a vocalist. I've never seen or heard from him since. We've had a few members. A guy who used to play Bonehead would get really drunk every night and piss the bed. We've had four drummers, including hired drummers like the guy from Swoop, three bass players, two singers, two Noels and three Boneheads in the last six months.

Aren't you taking work away from original bands?
Kids out there don't want to hear original Australian fuckin' bands. Not out there. They want covers and drinking and dancing and fun. Out in the suburbs, that's what they want. If people wanted to see original bands, then original bands would be doing really well in this country, and they're not. If they do well it's because they've been doing it for years or they're like Powderfinger, who have been lucky with a lot of airplay.

Do you want to be in an original band eventually?
Sure, absolutely. I've bought a really good four-track and I've got a billion songs in my head. I've got ten pretty good tunes.

Don't you get sick of playing the same songs every night?
'Champagne Supernova' is a pretty boring song. But no, the Oasis songs we do in our set are pretty hardcore, angsty songs, apart from three or four ballads for the fans.

Do you find you get your own fans who follow you around?
A few backpackers are familiar faces who come to all the gigs. Some of them nicked our backdrop. They come up to you and expect you to be from Manchester and you say, 'I'm not, I'm from South Australia.'

Do you ever listen to Oasis at home for enjoyment anymore?
I bought the 'Wonderwall' single the other week. I was looking for 'Master Plan', this song that all the backpackers want us to play, and it's a B-side of 'Wonderwall', so I got that.

What's your favourite Oasis song and one you can't stand?
'Don't Look Back In Anger' gives me the shits. [*sings in a bored manner*] So … Sally … can … wait— over and over again. It's just such a contrived lyric. I've always loved 'Morning Glory' because of the sheer brute noise of it and Noel plays it really well and does a good harmony in it because we've worked together for years.

Do you get asked for autographs?
Yeah.

Doesn't that make you feel weird?
I already am. So it won't change me much.

COPYCATS

Is it more like theatre than being in a band?
Yeah, you have to sing like someone else and put on the act and be like a lad. You have to act like a total pillock on stage.

What was the deal with appearing in the KFC Real Meal Deal ad?
The song was written and recorded and I went in and did the vocals at the studio in the Opera House. I had to sign a disclaimer saying that I got a certain amount of money and after that I wouldn't claim any more money from it. It literally took me fifteen minutes. I had to sing three different prices for the 'chicken fillet burger chips and a Pepsi', one for New Zealand, one for country areas and one for the city. [*sings*] 4.75 with chips and a Pepsi, 4.95 with chips and a Pepsi. Four seventy-five was really hard to sing.

Do you get any groupies?
I'm not allowed. But there are lots of really young girls wanting to give us hugs all the time and sign everything. They're so young and they get so excited. You're doing the songs they love, and they're having fun.

Is there anyone in the band who actually dislikes Oasis?
The last bass player. He couldn't stand any music later than 1970. He was into lounge, Neil Diamond and Elvis Presley. But he had fun and he liked to party.

If there was a Blur tribute band would you start a war with them?
Oh yeah, for sure. There should be one. I like Blur, actually. I like their style, like The Kinks and Small Faces. Geezer!

Would you wish any members of a Blur tribute band to get AIDS?
No. We'd wish them the flu.

Steven Shipley—Paul McCartney in Beatles tribute band, The Beatels

Why The Beatles?
Well, I'm a fan. The music was very strong, and it still is today. You play to crowds who are between eighteen and 45 and they all get into it now as much as people who got into it 30 years ago. It still sounds fresh, and I don't feel that it's become dated.

You don't play left-handed like McCartney?
I wanted to play guitar left-handed, but when I went to my first guitar lesson at the age of ten, the teacher said, 'Well, the first thing we'll do is teach you to play right-handed, because later on you'll have dramas if you're a left-handed player.' I've been looking for him ever since to sue him. He ruined my career.

Is this more of a good gig than the ultimate act of fandom?
I'd say it's a good gig. If it was purely a fandom thing, I'd probably not be in it and they'd get some-one left-handed to get the real look, but our sound is really convincing. We do sound like The Beatles. We hope people come to see us, shut their eyes, and think it is The Beatles. If you're going to a trib-ute band and you go and do it half-cocked, then you're just ripping people off. You have to get as close to the mark as you possibly can. And the other thing is that it should be a band that's gone. As far as The Beatles or The Doors are concerned, they're bands that are gone and will never come back, but the following is still strong. If people want to go and relive it, fine. Let them relive it.

Aren't tribute bands killing original music?
There's probably some point to that argument but I really believe that we don't sway anybody to not see an original act. We're just another choice in the marketplace. If they chose to see us then that's the choice that the punter made, not anything we forced them to do. And maybe it's a reflection on the current state of original music. Ten, fifteen years ago you would have gone to see The Angels or Cold Chisel or Midnight Oil or Matt Finish or countless great Aussie acts, but nowadays they just aren't there.

Don't you ever get sick of playing the same songs every night?
I think if I was playing the songs of any other band I would, but with The Beatles, it's so varied and it's such strong material and you always get good feedback from the crowd that it always seems like a fresh experience. If I was playing in a Clash or Sex Pistols show, after five months I'd be thinking, Oh God, not this song again! There's too much variety in The Beatles to get bored—'Michelle' to 'Revolution' to 'Strawberry Fields' to 'Love Me Do'. They were all done by the one group.

Do you ever listen to The Beatles for enjoyment anymore?
No, it's more to be analytical and work out what's going on if we decide to do a new song. There are over 300 Beatles songs and we've got down about 120. We always like to pick a new song and throw it in and we have to work it out. It's not just enjoyment then, but it's a labour of love. But every now and then I'll throw on a Beatles album and just listen to it for the pleasure. I loved watching the Anthology documentary because of that. We've probably all become bigger fans by learning all these songs—it opens up your eyes to how good they were as songwriters.

Favourite and least favourite songs?
That's very, very hard. It changes from month to month. If you're in a rock 'n' roll mood you walk around singing 'Helter Skelter' to yourself, and if you're a bit melancholy you walk around singing 'Yesterday'. They're two songs that are right at the top of their fields—one of the best ballads you'll ever hear and one of the best bits of heavy metal you'll ever hear. Occasionally we'll do 'Act Natu-rally', a country and western number that Ringo sang—you do it in a rock venue and think, This might not come off here. But you do it and they get right into it.

COPYCATS

Do you have your own obsessive fans?
We have a couple of fans from Melbourne and they'll drive up to Sydney every couple of weeks to see us. That's pretty excessive in the ways of fandom. Even if we're just doing one show, they'll come up for the weekend. That's a hell of a long way to drive to watch an hour and a half of music.

Do you sign autographs?
Sure. We sign our real names and then in brackets we put who we play, just so they know who it is.

Do you find that strange?
Sometimes. You realise they're not fans of yours, really, but in some circumstances they are your fans because they see the show a lot, and they think no-one does it as good as us, so if they're never going to see Paul McCartney play with The Beatles, we're the closest they're going to get. So they might as well get our autographs. There are kids out there who never saw The Beatles, but they still love the music, and they want to be a part of the fandom.

Do you get groupies?
Well, there were in the past, but we're all settled down and married now. There was a scene a few years back, but nowadays with the diseases, you have to be very careful, and we've all got serious situations happening now anyway. Is twenty minutes with a fan worth a lifetime of regret?

What's the closest you ever got to The Beatles?
The first live show I ever saw, at the age of fourteen, was Wings in 1975. I slept outside the Hordern Pavilion for a night and was first in line to get a ticket at eight o'clock in the morning, so I got a front row seat. That was a huge buzz seeing Paul McCartney that close up.

Paul Lockwood—Rick Brewster in Angels tribute band, Mr Damage

Why The Angels?
I grew up on 'em. I used to see 'em when I was a kid. I'm 29 now. Everyone likes The Angels and everyone knows the songs.

What's the history of the band?
Basically, mate, it was just a bunch of guys who got together through a jam night at Uncle Buck's in Penrith. They have it every Tuesday night. We got talking and got together on a few Angels numbers and the pub was pretty impressed so they gave us a gig. This was around February 1997.

How many different line-ups have there been?
We've had three different guitarists. One guy just didn't have his heart in it and wasn't learning the material fast enough, so Richie from No Exit (another Angels tribute) played with us for a couple of months.

What's the feeling between tribute bands who cover the same group? Competitiveness? Animosity?
It depends who you talk to in the bands. I don't personally feel anything like that. It's a big city and a big country. Other guys in the band feel differently—they think other bands are the competition and they shouldn't be helped out in any way. That happens in all bands, I think—that animosity. I don't see any problem with helping out other people.

Aren't tribute bands killing off original music?
Mate, I've been playing guitar since I was a kid. I've been in original bands. I released a CD single in Tassie, and it's hard to get work. You need other avenues. You can play guitar at home or sit in the garage with your mates but, at the end of the day, if you want to get work then this is an avenue to get out there. When we eventually want to promote our own material we'll have some credibility as peformers.

Is this more of a good gig than the ultimate act of fandom?
Well, I've always loved The Angels, but I'm not that fanatical about them. It's an opportunity for us to make a little bit of money, but I do enjoy playing their music.

Don't you get sick of playing the same songs every night?
Rehearsals can get a bit tedious, playing the same stuff over and over, but once you get up onstage, it's grouse. The crowd usually gets really into it.

Favourite and least favourite Angels song?
'Eat City' is one that I don't really like playing—I don't get to do much in it. I don't really look forward to that one. As far as the best songs, I really like 'After The Rain' and 'Take A Long Line'. They really get the crowd pumpin'.

Do you ever listen to The Angels at home anymore for enjoyment?
I listened to them for six months straight, but now I don't listen to them as much as I used to.

Were you ever fanatical about them?
I used to go to all their shows—the Hordern Pavilion, Lidcombe Oval, Brookvale Oval—they were always on with Rose Tattoo and Avion and bands like that.

Have you ever met them?
No. Our lead singer actually took our bio when he went to see them at Panthers on the Lounge Lizard tour and he got it signed by Doc Neeson. He basically wrote 'Get fucked'. And Brent Eccles wrote 'Phone APRA now'.

Do you get asked for autographs?
Yeah. It's phenomenal. I can't understand it. We're just a bunch of blokes playing other people's stuff. People treat you like you're gods. The posters don't last. We'll put them up and they keep getting taken. It's weird. But it's an ego trip.

COPYCATS

What about groupies?
Yeah. Probably more than when I played in original bands. Not that they do anything for me, because I'm married, mate. No good to me. You get offers. Down at Bateman's Bay last weekend we were offered sexual favours for Mr Damage caps. Basically a head job for a hat. It's weird. It's a twenty-dollar hat. Twelve years ago, when I was a single man, I would have brought a lot of hats. Plenty of girls want to take their gear off for you. A couple of the guys had a bit of an ego problem. They thought they were rock stars and the heads started to swell. But it's like, 'Hey mate, you better come down to earth, because you're not a rock star, you're in a concept band.'

Mick Bazley—Jimmy Barnes in Cold Chisel tribute band, Circus Animals

Why Cold Chisel?
The music, and Jimmy Barnes's style of singing. He's the best singer in Australia, and probably one of the best in the world. I never saw Cold Chisel, but when I was about fourteen I saw the video for 'You Got Nothing I Want' and I thought it was just great. Now I'm 32.

What's the history of the band?
We've been together for three and a half years. I'm the one original member.

Have there been many line-up changes?
We've had three or four bass players and eleven keyboard players.

Aren't tribute bands killing off original music?
It's hard to get work in an original band, so you don't have much choice. In concept and covers bands you can make more money, and in the meantime you can do originals in your spare time.

Don't you ever get sick of playing the same songs every night?
It can get a bit repetitive sometimes, but it pays the bills, and I do enjoy it.

How close are you to the Barnes persona?
I drink a bottle of vodka on stage and I've got the beard growth, except mine is more four-day. It's a challenge to do Jimmy Barnes 'cause you need a pretty strong voice and a good scream and you've got to be pretty wild on stage.

Courtesy of Southbeat

Is this more of a good gig than the ultimate act of fandom?
I enjoy doing this, and if I didn't I wouldn't do it. But at the same time it gives me some income.

Do you ever listen to Chisel at home for enjoyment anymore?
Sometimes. You hear it on the radio a lot anyway.

Is there much rivalry between Chisel shows?
There's competition, definitely. Sometimes they get a venue before us or undercut us price-wise. It can get difficult. We're all doing the same thing. I've seen their guys at our gigs and I've been to one of their gigs too.

Favourite Chisel/Barnes songs?
'Working Class Man'.

A song you're not so into?
'Forever Now'. I'm just not a big fan of it. It's a radio song. But it's too reggaeish.

Do you sign autographs?
Yeah. They usually want posters signed. I don't understand it, really. I'm not him.

Do you get any weird fans?
One bought me a bottle of vodka and wanted me to drink it in front of them.

What about groupies?
It's out there, but I'm nearly married so it's a bit hard. I got a lick on the face last week. We tend to do the gig and go home.

Tribute Bands We'd Like to See

Why limit yourself to slavishly aping the music of one band, night after night? After all, there's got to be a fanbase out there for some cool combinations.

♡ *Toto Recall*—'Africa', 'Roseanna' and, er, all those other great hits, sung by a guy with gigantic pecs and an Austrian accent.

♡ *Blonde On Blondie*—the songs from Bob Dylan's classic 1966 album performed by a Debbie Harry impersonator.

♡ *Stylophone Council*—the Paul Weller portfolio painstakingly picked out on the dinky instrument promoted by Rolf Harris in the 1970s.

♡ *R.E.M. Speedwagon*—a band adept at following up 'Keep On Loving You' with 'It's The End Of The World As We Know It (And I Feel Fine)'.

♡ *Metal As Anything*—'Live It Up', 'The Nips Are Getting Bigger' and 'Too Many Times' assayed in a heavy metal style.

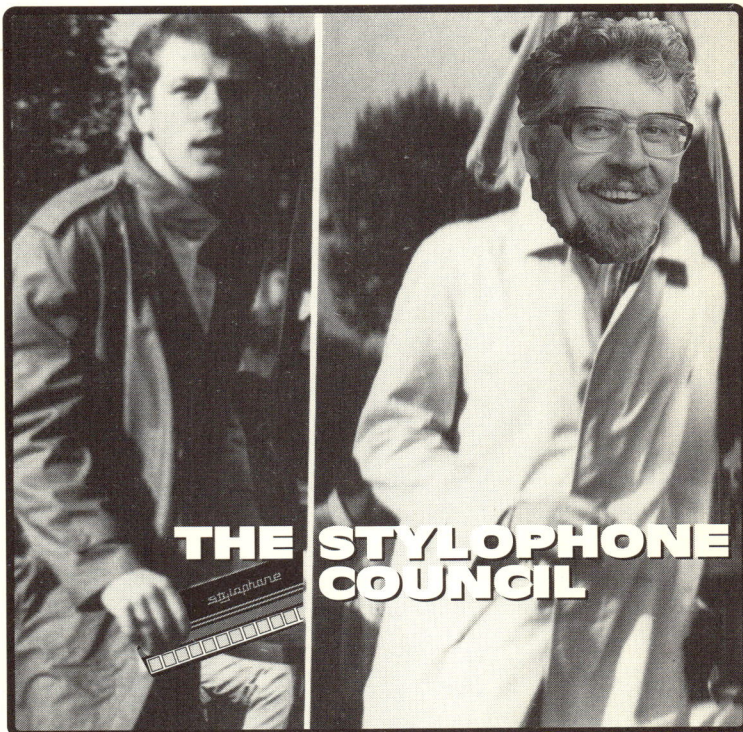

Paul McNeil

THE STYLOPHONE COUNCIL

stylophone

♡ *The Motherfuckas And The Papas*—imagine Snoop Doggy Dogg having a go at 'California Dreamin' ' and you've got the general idea.

♡ *Boyz II Menswear*—silky four-piece harmonies wrap themselves around the tunes of the saddest exponent of short-lived British new wave of new wave movement.

♡ *Men At Björk*—interesting juxtaposition of a woman who comes from Iceland (which is near the top of the globe, non-geographers) and a band whose biggest hit was 'Downunder'.

♡ *Cypress Hillbillies*—a banjo-pickin', tobacco-chewin' duo who attack 'Hits From The Bong' with gusto.

COME TOGETHER II

Mamma Mia, Here We Go Again

Four men in their thirties sit in front of a hushed assembly. They have something in common, and everyone in the room wants to hear about it. They've all seen something that the rest of us will probably never experience.

'I just broke down in tears the next day when the whole thing came back to me,' says one. 'I took two days off school because I couldn't cope with it.'

'They were so clear,' marvels another. 'After seeing all the pictures of them on my wall, they were three-dimensional and wearing white, and they just jumped out at you.'

Philip Morris

The Swedes meet some perfect Australian children on their 1977 tour.

'Seeing them that close was extraordinary,' agrees another. 'They looked beautiful all dressed in white. They just looked like angels.'

Near-death experiences? Dramatic religious conversion? Abduction by aliens? Bad acid trips? None of the above, I'm afraid.

All of these guys are recounting their first glimpse of Abba in the flesh.

It's weird. This is a celebration of the twentieth anniversary of Abba's 1977 Australian tour. It's a 48-hour event in a four-star hotel, where videos will be shown on a constant loop, 'superfans' will relate their experiences, and later we can all go to a disco that plays nothing but Abba. But that's not the weird thing.

Where are the women?

I'd turned up thinking that 80 per cent of the crowd would be female but, in fact, that percentage is male. John McKechnie is 39, which means he was nineteen at the height of Abba fever. Didn't he cop any flak for being that deadly combination of (a) a guy and (b) an Abba fan?

'Not really, because it seemed that everyone was an Abba fan back then,' he says. 'Between 1979 and 1983 were the really tough years because everyone hated them and made fun of them. Going into a record store to ask about *Voulez Vous*, which took a long time to come out, people would just laugh at you. Now, of course, it's cool to like them again.'

A lot of that probably has to do with the 1970s revival, the success of films like *Muriel's Wedding* and *The Adventures of Priscilla, Queen of the Desert*, and the realisation that it was cool to celebrate dagginess. And it seems that the gay community has had a large influence in reintroducing disco in general and Abba in particular to the mainstream.

'Without wanting to blow my own trumpet, we sort of heralded it,' John says. 'In 1987 we had a ten-year anniversary convention, with a disco and a show, and that made it into the press and onto radio. From that, the Unicorn Hotel [in Sydney's Paddington] started hosting Abba nights.'

John also mentions DJ Maynard F# Crabbes, who started flying the flag soon afterwards. He's happy that the end result was more people hearing Abba, but still feels that Maynard is a bit of a bandwagon jumper.

'We original Abba fans were a little put out, because Maynard made it sound daggy. That's not what we were on about. But we got over it, and it's fine.'

It's strange walking into a world where the three hottest topics of discussion are as follows:

1. Why didn't Abba tour Queensland? The general consensus is that it was the state's conservative politics, and the fact that Benny and Frida were, in the parlance of the time, 'living in sin'.
2. In which song did Frida slip over at the Sydney concert? 'S.O.S.' was widely reported at the time, but the conventioners claim it was in fact 'Waterloo'.
3. Even the most rabid Abba fan will admit that the strange mini-musical in the concert, called *The Girl With The Golden Hair*, was confusing at best, and crap at worst.

COME TOGETHER

Annie Wright was 21 in 1977, and she worked in promotions and publicity at RCA, Abba's record company. She's today's guest speaker, but as she's interviewed and then quizzed from the floor, it's obvious that the fans know more about the tour than she does. After all, they've been poring over the details for a couple of decades. She does tell us that as she was a young blond woman and she emerged from the same hotels and fleet of cars as the group, she was often mistaken for Agnetha and besieged by fans. And she gets a good laugh when she talks about the anxiety in the Abba camp when the rain wouldn't let up before the first Sydney concert.

'I was ringing Alan Wilkie [a weather forecaster] daily. I thought he had a special link to God. Everyone was going, "Have you talked to Alan? Have you talked to Alan?"'

'The fans haven't changed'—a fan comments on a video that shows a 1970s Swedish TV audience, all wide lapels, bad haircuts and goofy looks.

'There is so much more to National,' the band sings to the tune of 'Fernando', as part of an Australian TV advertising campaign. On the screen they vacuum and make orange juice, listen to a stereo through giant white headphones, and put batteries into a toy donkey. There are only so many hours of Abba videos you can take in, and a few people are now milling around outside in the sun, taking a break.

One of them is Kim Jeffery, who has seen just about everything ever filmed of the group. She has a collection of 55 videos devoted to them. Kim has travelled to Sydney from the Gold Coast, where she and her husband run a sheet-metal business.

'When I go home, after "my life"—cooking the dinner and looking after the family—I sit in the office and write to people about Abba. I have a network of Abba fans in Spain, Holland, Ireland, Scotland and Sweden.'

Is your husband an Abba fan, too?
'No. Midnight Oil.'

And what does he think of your fandom?
'He accepts it, but he doesn't want me to advertise it to our friends. He gets embarrassed.'

Abba broke up a long time ago.
'That's right, but I don't look at it as if they've broken up. I still watch their videos and it feels like they're still here today.'

Is this group of people at the convention like an extended family?
'I think so. We're all different people from all walks of life, but we've got one thing in common. We all fit in here.'

Around the walls of the convention room are tables stacked with Abba collectibles and merchandise. There are calendars, swap cards, t-shirts, purses, bags, magazines, keyrings and solo albums. But my two personal favourites are the ones where you can almost get Abba under your skin—separate Frida and Agnetha spray colognes, and Abba: The Soap.

A common symptom experienced by those who saw Abba in 1977 is lingering confusion. The cause of this is *Abba: The Movie.* Most big fans have seen it many, many times, and their real-life experiences as teenagers have blurred with the events of the film, which is basically lots of concert footage, some behind-the-scenes stuff, and a doddery plotline involving a DJ (played by the guy in 'Hey Dad … !') who is under orders to get an interview with the group at any cost. A couple of the inner sanctum are actually in the movie, usually in crowd shots, and often for only a split second. Nevertheless, this seems to hold some cachet in this company.

'During the day a film crew came along and got us to yell out, "We want Abba!"' remembers a fan called Luke who was at the Melbourne Town Hall when Abba were given a civic reception. 'I thought it was for the news, but nine months later I was sitting in a theatre watching *Abba: The Movie,* and there I was up on the screen. That gave me quite a fright.'

The band's arrival at the Town Hall seems to be a holy moment for these fans, as it offered a chance for fans to get closer to the group and see them somewhere other than on stage.

'The most vivid moment was when they got halfway up the stairs to a landing, and they all stopped and turned around and waved,' Luke tells the rapt crowd. 'That was amazing, to see them side by side as I'd looked at them so many times in pictures.'

At that moment, when all his dreams were coming true, Luke suddenly realised something.

'I was bawling my eyes out, but I couldn't quite understand why.'

COME TOGETHER

Frida had a bouquet of flowers, and she started picking flowers out of the bunch and dropping them into the crowd below. Although Luke didn't catch one, a friend of his had scored a couple, and gave one to him.

'I remember I had this flower stuck under my t-shirt because I didn't want anybody taking it, so I was walking around doubled over, bawling my eyes out. I remember this woman coming up to me and she said, "What's wrong, darling? Did someone kick you in the stomach?"'

Luke looked up at her through his tears and bleated one word—'Abba!'

And then he hobbled away.

I'M YOUR GREATEST FAN

'Don't push me 'cos I'm close to the edge, I'm tryin' not to lose my head'

—Grandmaster Flash & The Furious Five, 'The Message'

The only problem with looking for attention is that you just might get it. If it's true that one of the main reasons any of us are put on this earth is to leave some sort of mark so that future generations can say, 'Hey, I remember John Citizen, and he was a good bloke who did this, this and this', then for the rock star, this need is magnified a hundred times.

Despite the protestations of Eddie Vedder, pop music by definition is meant to be popular. And as with anything that's popular, it attracts all sorts of people to it like a magnet. Some of these people are obsessive. Some of them have problems. Some of them have very serious problems indeed. Some of them have trouble dealing with reality, and feel that an artist is speaking to them alone through their songs. They reason that if only the artist could meet them, then they would understand that there was a common bond between them.

Some of them are under the impression that they should be famous themselves. If you don't really have any talent, or you don't get the right breaks, then the easiest way to do that is to either stalk a famous person and hope that some of their fame rubs off on you as a result, or kill them, so that you'll become famous by getting rid of a famous person. It's kind of like an exchange program for unstable folks.

And then there's emotional blackmail. This can take the form of threats, demands and accusations. In the mid-1970s, members of Skyhooks had become accustomed to walking out their front doors to find girls on the front lawn. Drummer Freddie Strauks lived with his parents, and his mother used to make the fans cups of tea if her son wasn't home. Red Symons once woke up in the middle of the night to find two fans at the end of his bed, watching him and his girlfriend sleep. More worryingly, he was once sent a photo of his toilet, taken by a fan who had broken into his house.

For a few years Greg Macainsh wouldn't even travel into the city because of the hassles and attention it generated. Things took a darker turn when one fan got his phone number. She told him where she was, and said that if he wouldn't agree to meet with her, she would kill herself. He told her to calm down, and explained that he couldn't meet with every fan who asked him.

'A couple of hours later I got a call from the cops asking if I knew this girl,' says Macainsh. 'She was in the hospital and she'd cut her wrists.'

Macainsh still believes he did the right thing by not giving in. At the time, the band was being accused of corrupting the morals of their fans. Six songs from their debut album, *Living In The 70s*, were not allowed to be played on commercial radio. Journalist Mike Willesee confronted them in a television interview with accusations of sleaziness, and the band hit him with the line that they did their own thing, and their audience was free to make up their own minds. When Willesee started citing examples, including the song 'Smut', which is about masturbation, Shirley Strachan turned to the audience and said, 'Well, you all do that anyway, don't you?'

'The point is that we had to make a choice, and we decided that we weren't responsible for what people did, otherwise you'd go crazy,' says Macainsh.

In the 1980s Peter Farnan would often walk out of his house to his EJ Holden and find a fresh

A rare shot of Boom Crash Opera with their hands not up in the air—Peter Farnan is far left.

rose stuck in the broken radio aerial. He jokingly says that he'd like to think that it was a silent, loving tribute to a great rock guitarist. Farnan was—and still is—in Boom Crash Opera. There was a time when they were regularly mobbed on 'Countdown', and boasted a strong teen following.

Farnan says that lead singer Dale Ryder was the major recipient of underwear and dirty videos, but 'at one point even I had to revert to a silent phone number and make sure I wasn't followed home'. And Farnan even had his own obsessive fan. From 1987, she started writing him long letters, and she sent them for five years. They included flowery poetry that alluded to Arthurian legend and the story of Robin Hood and Maid Marion, casting herself and Farnan in the lead roles.

'Eventually I tried not to read them. My girlfriend would read them and say, "Look, this person is putting a lot of effort into this." She got a computer and started using Old English typefaces. Gradually the letters became longer, and the poems were like these huge muddled concepts.'

Soon bottles of champagne and baskets of fruit would arrive at the record company for him.

'Afterwards, she wrote that it was about time she revealed who she was. She just wrote, "It's me, Suzy." *[Farnan doesn't want to reveal her real name.]* I had no idea who it was. A few weeks later I got a letter from a friend of hers who said Suzy was really hung up on me. She sent a photograph of Suzy, but I still had no idea who it was.

'She would write things about the way I looked in her eyes when I was singing. She was convinced I'd made eye contact. My performance skills must be fantastic because all I can see when I'm up there is bright light.'

Eventually Suzy went on a holiday to Britain, and kept writing from there. She actually went to Sherwood Forest, supposedly the spiritual home of her relationship with the guitarist from Boom Crash Opera.

'Later the letters tailed off, probably as the sales of *Fabulous Beast* tailed off, and a bit of the intensity with the band tailed off, too. It's actually a bit scary telling you this and knowing it will end up in a book, because it will show that I've noticed her more than I intended to let her know I did.'

The more you talk to bands, the more you realise that just about every musician has at least one story to tell of an overly obsessive fan who worries them a little. Kamahl might seem like an unlikely candidate, but when he was riding the success of his 1970s hit 'The Elephant Song', he became a target for a woman whose daughter ran his Dutch fanclub. Apart from making one pause to wonder at how boring the music scene in Holland must have been at that time, it also proves that if someone as seemingly benign as Kamahl can arouse the attentions of the obsessed, then anyone can. Even Olivia Newton-John. She was once stalked by Ralph J. Nau, an American man who was charged with axing his eight-year-old stepbrother to death in the late 1980s. He was also obsessed with Sheena Easton, which goes some way towards explaining how he ended up in a mental institution.

The path from fan to stalker is full of cracks. A failed relationship can trip someone over into unhealthy obsession. The stalker may be under the false impression that a star is in love with him or her. Others harbour paranoid tendencies and believe that a certain famous person is evil, or that the star has wronged them or society in some way.

Janet Jackson had to file for a restraining order against one fan who showed up at her door claiming to be her husband. Along with his further boast that he was Jesus Christ, this was plainly not true. Madonna also had trouble with a guy claiming to be married to her. Todd Lawrence climbed a fence and rang the doorbell of her LA home to inform her of the fact. He was sentenced to a year in prison in 1994, but the following year, a more distressing chain of events occurred with a different stalker. Robert Dewey Hoskins broke into Madonna's home, allegedly telling guards on duty that if she refused to marry him, he would cut her throat from ear to ear. He was shot while reaching for a weapon. In January 1996 Madonna was forced to appear in court to testify. Her comments to the jury say something about the nature of the relationship between stars and stalkers. She said that it made her sick to the stomach to be in the same room as a man who had threatened her life.

I'M YOUR GREATEST FAN

'I feel it made his fantasies come true,' she told them. 'I'm sitting in front of him and that's what he wants.'

❀❀

'SILVERCHAIR SONG A SCRIPT FOR MURDER'

silverchair's manager, John Watson, still remembers the day he walked past a newsagent with lead singer Daniel Johns and caught a glimpse of that newspaper banner. In August 1995 an American teenager, with the help of a friend, had killed his parents with a gun, then drowned his five-year-old brother. By January the following year, when the case came to court, the boys' lawyer had a list of motivating factors he wanted the court to consider in support of his argument that the boys had diminished responsibility. Among these was the fact that they had played the silverchair song 'Israel's Son' during the day of the killings.

Even though the possibility of using the song as evidence was thrown out pretty quickly, the attempt illustrated how a band can become public property. A song written by a fifteen-year-old schoolboy in Newcastle was being used as a scapegoat in a murder trial halfway across the globe, simply because the accused was a fan and his lawyers could see a loophole.

Perhaps it was their measured exposure to the public and their tender ages at the start of their career, but for some reason silverchair attract more than their fair share of

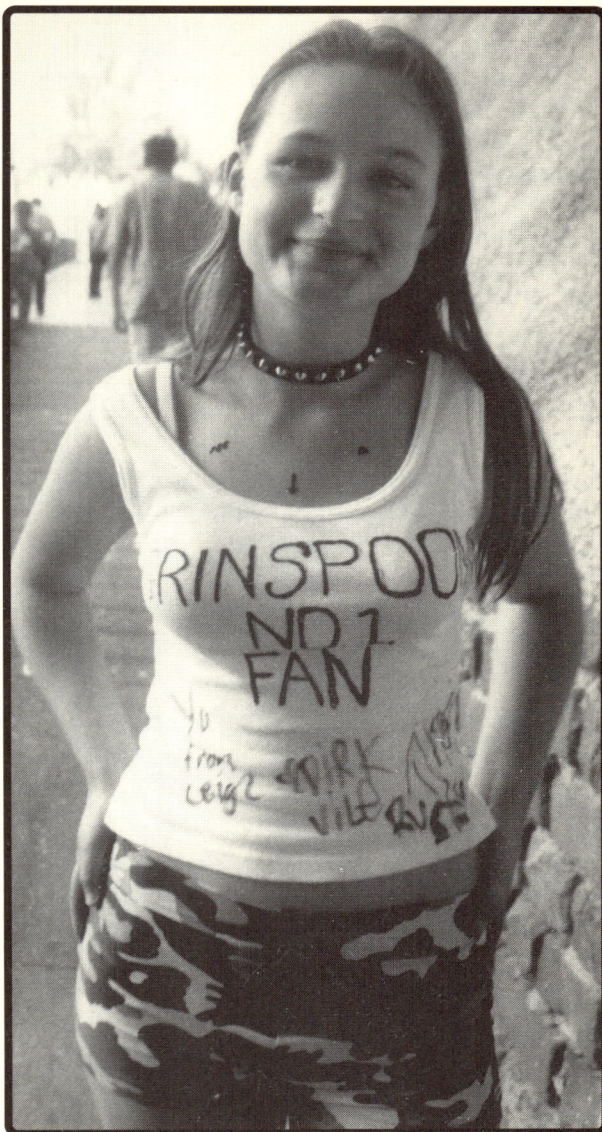

Sophie Howarth

107

obsessives. John Watson admits that there is what he calls 'a Mrs Robinson thing' surrounding the band among women in their thirties and forties. One Sydney woman complained to police that Daniel Johns was stalking her, and wanted him subjected to a restraining order. When she was pressed for particular incidents and dates, it turned out that silverchair were in New York at the time.

'I tend to get the kooky stuff sent to me,' Watson sighs. 'I don't want to talk about it too much because that just encourages it, but you do get the occasional person who has an unhealthy obsession.'

One incident he will recount is the time a guy rang the management office from Dallas and demanded to speak to Daniel. He sounded depressed and agitated. 'I've got a gun here and the clock is ticking—you'll have blood on your hands if you don't get him,' he said.

Watson tried to talk him down. Daniel was just a teenager, he explained. He didn't have the answers to the guy's problems. He gave the caller some phone numbers he could ring for professional help. Even though Watson took the threat seriously, he sensed something melodramatic about it. Sure enough, five minutes later a girl called. She too had a Texan accent, and she was in tears.

Philip Morris

She was having Daniel's baby. Now things were getting slightly suspicious. One Texan rings threatening to commit suicide, and five minutes later another claims to be pregnant, and it's all silverchair's problem.

'I'm like, "Oh really, when did you get pregnant?" ' Watson continues. 'She named a particular show the band had done in Atlanta, and I remember I had been with Daniel literally every single minute. Even the quickest operator couldn't have had time to do this. It was implausible, and in hindsight quite funny. But there are others we take more seriously because they're not healthy.'

Some encounters are not just unhealthy, but life-threatening. While there may be a case for someone claiming that they want to kill Ace Of Base because their music is annoying, jaunty Europop, this wasn't on the mind of a fan who burst into the home of singer Jenny Berggren's parents in Goteborg, Sweden, in April 1994. Berggren confronted the woman and asked what she wanted. She apparently replied that she was fascinated by Ace Of Base and wanted to meet them. She then demonstrated her fascination by dragging the singer at knife-point into her parents' bedroom, where Berggren's mother, after suffering cuts to her hands, managed to disarm the woman. They restrained her until the police arrived, but Berggren later told reporters that she felt sorry for the attacker and that, just before the police took her away, the woman gave her a hug, as if she regretted what had happened.

If Björk is a spikier pop phenomenon than Ace Of Base, then it's only fitting that her stalker story is downright weird, and more than a little creepy. It involves eleven videotapes and a hollowed-out book. The story goes that Ricardo Lopez, a 21-year-old fan from Florida, had been videotaping himself over a period of nine months. Included in the collection was footage of him constructing a bomb. Concealed inside a book, it was designed to spray acid in the face of Björk when she opened the package. The last videotape shows Lopez putting a .38 calibre revolver to his head and pulling the trigger while listening to 'I Miss You', a song from Björk's 1995 album, *Post*. Apparently he wanted to let the singer know that he wasn't happy with the fact that she was romantically involved with a black man, jungle-music pioneer Goldie. The bomb was intercepted at a London post office.

Others haven't had the good fortune of a slow postal service. Largely unknown at the time in pop music circles, Selena hit the headlines when she was gunned down by the president of her fanclub at the age of 23. Known as the Tex-Mex Madonna, she was a star in the Mexican community, and when Yolanda Saldivar launched the singer's fanclub in 1990, it soon boasted a membership of 9000. As a result, Selena also entrusted her with the running of a couple of boutiques that sold memorabilia and her own line of clothing. In early 1995, however, Selena's family believed that Selena's greatest fan was embezzling funds. The singer and her husband turned up at Saldivar's motel room and took away business records. Fatefully, Selena returned the next day to get some missing bank statements, and was shot in the right shoulder by Saldivar. The bullet cut through an artery, and she bled to death.

'People will come up and ask for an autograph or say hi, but they won't bug you,' John Lennon once told an interviewer about his life in the Big Apple.

How wrong he was. On 8 December 1980 Mark Chapman put five bullets into him. Only hours beforehand he had met Lennon and asked him to sign his copy of *Double Fantasy*. Chapman was obsessed with Lennon, and in his imbalanced mind felt tormented by the fact that the songwriter preached peace and love, but had somehow sold out by living a comfortable life with his family.

'I just shot John Lennon,' Chapman told the police who arrested him, a copy of J.D. Salinger's *The Catcher in the Rye* tucked under his arm. This was a stupid thing to say for two reasons. First, it was highly incriminating. And secondly, it would give Dolores O'Riordan an idea for a very annoying Cranberries song sixteen years later.

Chapman got what he wanted. He got rid of what he saw as a hypocrite. Before he pulled the trigger Mark Chapman was nobody. Afterwards, he was the guy who killed a Beatle. The fan got famous.

Stalking Etiquette

Anyone can yell their head off, scream their idol's name repeatedly at the top of their voice, let fly with a series of blinding camera flashes, and then fall into a blubbering heap on the footpath. But, strangely enough, this isn't the best way to form any sort of workable relationship with your idol. In fact, it isn't even the best way to form a distant relationship with your idol. No, the truly sussed fan has a code of ethics. Here, three superfans offer their handy hints on the rights and wrongs of idol worship.

Loretta Tolnay (Michael Jackson fan)
♡ Get to know hotel staff. Introduce yourself and be upfront.
♡ Befriend the security staff who travel with them. Don't be pushy and aggressive and demanding. Be polite and make conversation. Talk about them—everyone else is only interested in who they're working for. They can make it hell for you or make it really easy.

Sam Pickard (Bon Jovi fan)
♡ You have to be in the right place at the right time. I've had so many fluke meetings. I ran into them in the street one day. I've had Jon call my hotel room by complete accident.
♡ I read. All the newspapers tell you where they're staying at some point. You lodge stuff away.
♡ Be friendly. Be genuine.
♡ Don't get in their face or invade their space. Don't grab them or try to get something off them.
♡ If you ask for an autograph or a photo and they say no, just accept it.
♡ Don't sleep with the road crew.

Julie Ledger (Bros/Take That fan)
♡ If you're following their van in a car, you don't pull up alongside and take photos. The whole idea of following them is to find out where they're going to be next. When they get out at the next stop, then you can hopefully get some photos. To lean out and

Mirror Australian Telegraph Publications

scream and yell while they're driving is a bit embarrassing. I know it's a bit funny following them, but if you don't know the itinerary, what else are you going to do? If you want to have a chance to talk to them with no-one else around, then you follow them. But if you do silly things they're not going to want to talk to you or respect you.

♡ Don't run inside the hotel lobby and take heaps of photos, especially if you're not staying in the hotel. And don't crowd them in the hotel, because that's their personal space. They're paying to stay there, so you shouldn't invade their privacy.

♡ I can't stand it when girls scream in bands' faces. That's too much. I can't deal with it. I can understand it, though. When I was younger, if Bros had stood next to me I would have lost it. But you learn as you get older.

♡ If you're a true fan, you stay with them, even after they've broken up. I still know what Bros are up to.

FANTALES

Sam Pickard

Bon Jovi

Sam Pickard has been pushed, slapped, kicked and spat on. She has had her hair pulled, and her arms scratched and burned with cigarette butts. She has had cans and rocks thrown at her and been called a slag.

It's tough being a Bon Jovi fan.

Especially when all the above persecution has actually come from other Bon Jovi fans.

'They're full-on,' she says. 'Bon Jovi fans are hardcore and so bitchy. It's all very buddy-wuddy when everyone wants information, but as soon as someone gets close to the band, that's it. They're real arseholes.'

Sam is someone who has got close to the band, so she has suffered as a result. She owns Sweet Oblivion, a CD collectibles store in Sydney. Three years ago she organised a Bon Jovi convention. That same year she followed the band around the USA for six weeks. In 1993 she did the Australian tour for the album *Keep The Faith*. She collects everything to do with the band, even underwear used to promote the *Slippery When Wet* album, which she admits is really bad, but loves anyway.

It all started back in 1986 when she was eleven years old and heard 'Living On A Prayer' on the car radio. The DJ didn't back-announce the song, but she couldn't get it out of her head. Then she heard 'You Give Love A Bad Name', and found out that this was the same band who did the song she loved so much. From that point on, she was hooked.

Growing up in the tiny town of Woombah, near Coffs Harbour, the nearest record store was one and a half hours away, and she would

often make the trip to catch up on Bon Jovi's new releases. She wrote into the penpal pages of *Smash Hits* and *Countdown*, wanting to get a hold of all their records and videos.

And finally, in 1987, the *Slippery When Wet* tour came to Australia. Sam missed the whole thing.

Sue Stafford

'I got myself into such a state about the tour that I gave myself an asthma attack and had to go to hospital for the entire time they were here. I didn't see anything. I was devastated.'

It wasn't until November 1989, when the band toured behind the *New Jersey* album, that Sam got to see them. She spent thirteen hours on a train to Sydney, went straight to the Sebel Townhouse and waited outside to catch a glimpse of the group. For the next three days she hardly slept.

'We saw them the very first day. Jon came back from a jog, and I couldn't believe it. I ran across the road and nearly got hit by a car. The security guards came out and everyone got palmed off. I ducked underneath and there he was standing in front of me on this step, all sweaty with his hair under a baseball cap. He had on grey jogging shorts and a blue singlet. He looked lush. I just started crying. I couldn't do anything. Then he was taken away and I just collapsed and cried for another three hours.'

Sam's fandom has remained constant and along with that dedication has come problems with boyfriends.

'They don't get it. It's insecurity on their behalf, but it's made relationships really hard. It's like they want me to make a choice. That would be like asking a boyfriend who is a surfer to give up his surfboard.'

And then there are those fans who cause bodily harm at concerts if you've got a good seat, or throw things at you if you've been interviewed on television about meeting Jon.

'It causes break-ups in friendships with other Bon Jovi fans, too. There is only one of my best Bon Jovi buddies who has never done anything wrong by me, and I think it's because he's male. All the rest have been girls, and they've just screwed me.'

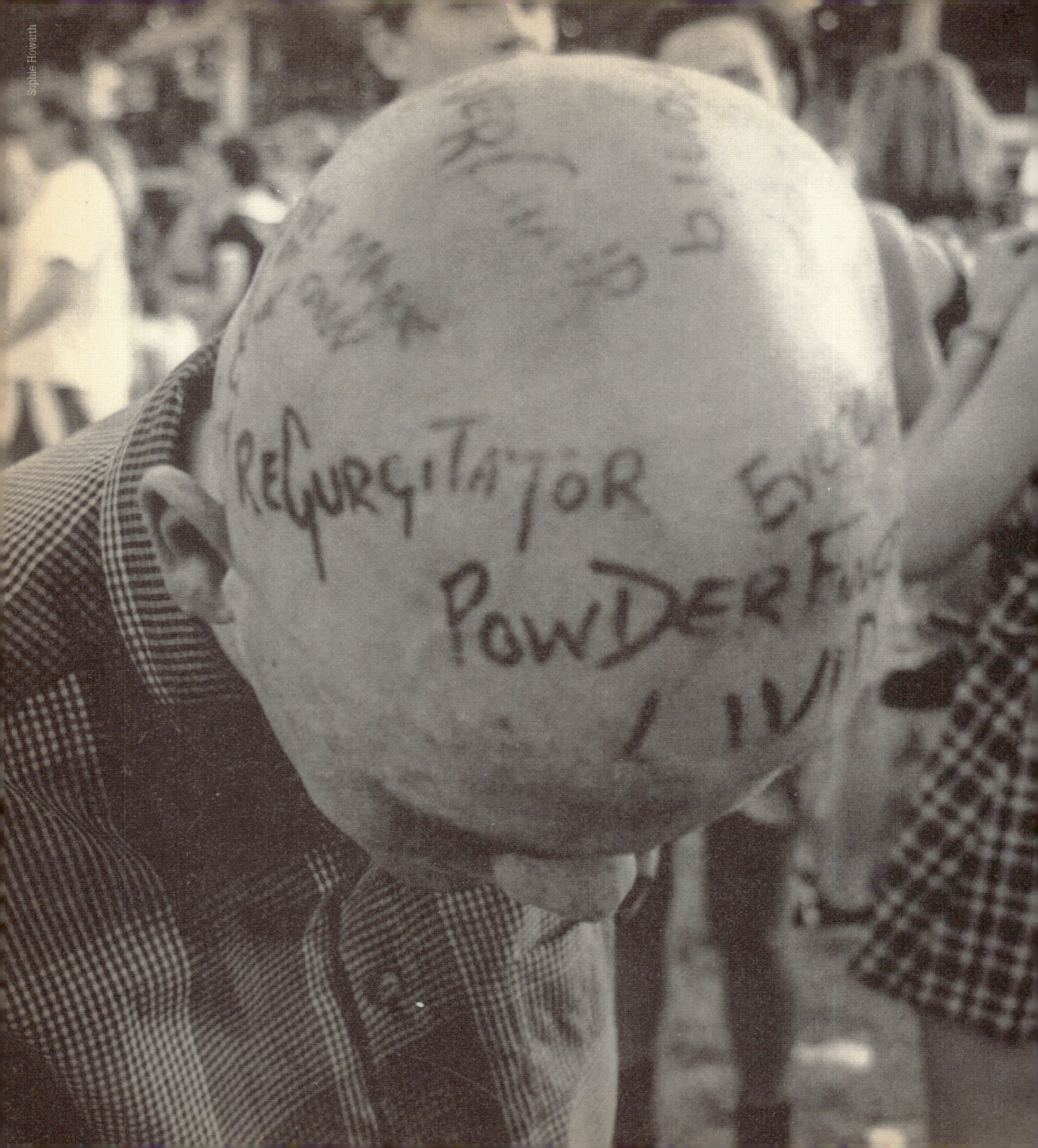

READ ALL ABOUT IT

'And someone asking questions and basking in the light of the fifteen fame-filled minutes of the fanzine writer'

—Billy Bragg, 'Waiting For The Great Leap Forward'

'This is a chord,' wrote the folks behind an English fanzine called *Sideburns*, back in 1976. They drew a diagram of an A chord for guitar.

'This is another,' they continued, illustrating the way to play an E.

'This is a third,' they concluded, drawing a G.

'NOW FORM A BAND,' they demanded at the end.

It was all very 'spirit of 1976'. By that stage of the decade, music was resembling Jabba the Hutt from *Star Wars*—a bloated beast that was all-powerful but not particularly appealing. The message sent out by bands like Genesis, Yes, Supertramp, The Eagles and Fleetwood Mac was that in order to be in a band, you needed to be either a musical wizard, live on the west coast of the USA, or have enough money to imbibe mountains of cocaine—in the case of Fleetwood Mac, preferably all three.

In 1976 things came to a head when punk broke in the UK. The immediate triggers appeared to be the brutal approach of The Ramones, the decadent rabble of The New York Dolls, and the no-frills, pared-down style of Television and Patti Smith. If you looked in a rear-vision mirror, then the primal sounds of The Velvet Underground and The Stooges were lurking somewhere in the foundations of punk bedsit city. The combination of bored English youth, unemployment and the willingness for change was enough to set things alight.

The message in that piece from *Sideburns* was simple. You don't need training. You just need attitude. As everyone from Bachman Turner Overdrive ('it's easier than fishin' you can be a musician') to Radiohead ('Anyone Can Play Guitar') has pointed out, pure gut-level rock has little to do with education, access to a huge bank account, or truckloads of flashy equipment. Following The Sex Pistols, punk bands sprouted like mushrooms in shit, and within six months something very big was happening.

In tandem with the music came fans who wanted to express what was on their minds. They wanted to document the scene, to talk about (and with) the new groups which were forming every week, to report on the gigs and to let others know about the way it was affecting them and why it was pushing them into action. Of course in 1976 the mainstream media was no place to do this. Besides, the fans had no access to that forum. So, in the spirit of the times, they did it themselves.

One of the first English fanzines from this era, and certainly the most influential, was *Sniffin' Glue,* edited by Mark Perry, who called himself Mark P. to avoid unwanted investigation by the dole office. It had been predated by *Punk* (first issue, December 1975), a US zine put together by Legs McNeil and John Holmstrom in order to write about the emerging scene at CBGB's, a bar in the Bowery area on the Lower East Side of Manhattan. *Punk* was a more professionally assembled thing, but the spirit of *Sniffin' Glue* was the same—highly personal writing, unlimited enthusiasm, slapped together in a rough but loving fashion using whatever was at hand and photocopied for distribution. And it had a burgeoning scene to document. It was the opposite of glossy magazines that followed trends and kept a close eye on advertising revenue. It was another world. And it started an avalanche.

READ ALL ABOUT IT

The word zine comes from fanzine, which in turn is a bastardisation of fan magazine. You have to go back to the 1930s to find its roots in the science fiction nuts who would put out small, roughly put together magazines full of fiction, articles, letters columns, editorials and reviews of sci-fi books and films. *The Comet, Time Traveller* and *Science Fiction* (edited by Jerome Siegel and Joe Schuster, who went on to create Superman) were a few of the better known titles. In the 1960s comic books got the same treatment, via zines like *Alter Ego* and *Batmania.* But it was the punk movement that created the basis for the zine explosion which would grow exponentially throughout the 1980s and on into the 1990s.

'All you kids out there who read *SG*, don't be satisfied with what we write,' Mark Perry told his readers in the pages of *Sniffin' Glue.* 'Go out and start your own fanzines.'

And they did just that. Adrian Thrills of *48 Thrills,* Jonh Ingham of *London's Burning* and Jon Savage of *London's Outrage* would all eventually become music journalists and/or authors. The editor of *Bondage,* Shane MacGowan, went on to front The Pogues.

Zines provided a voice for people who had previously thought they couldn't be heard. Once they got going, they wouldn't shut up. In 1981 a young, shy Mancunian chap put together a booklet about his major obsession, The New York Dolls. He had penned a few things for a fanzine called *Kids Stuff,* went on to contribute live reviews to *Record Mirror,* but was rejected by the *NME* when he persistently asked for work. His name was Stephen Patrick Morrissey. Now he has fans who write zines about him in England, the USA, Canada, France, Spain, Japan and Italy. The fan became the star.

Over in the USA, in the wake of *Punk* came *Flipside, Forced Exposure* and *Maximumrocknroll*—zines which kept on keeping on throughout the 1980s due to their coverage of hardcore and underground music. In the mid-1980s something new started happening, led by a title called *Nancy,* which was put together by a librarian in Ohio. These little volumes started taking on a much more personal bent, and the subject of the zine became the person who put it out. At the same time, music became just part of the contents list—you could be obsessed with trashy TV, old magazine advertisements, teen movies or junk food. Anything became fair game to write about. You didn't even need to concentrate on pop culture, although being from a pop-culture obsessed generation meant that it nearly always impinged on the lives of these writers. In 1988 Pagan Kennedy started publishing *Pagan's Head,* which documented her road trips, her haircuts, her memories of childhood, her friendships, her erratic career path and, eventually, the illness which resulted in the removal of one of her ovaries.

Here in Australia, two of the most influential zines from the first half of the 1990s were *Lemon* and *Eddie.* The former taught other fanzines that they should be outspoken and shout about the music they care about; the latter showed them they could write about anything that interested them and package it in a pleasing way.

Lemon was run by Louise Dickinson, a straight-talking chick who loved loud music, in-your-face opinions and her dog, Arlo. All of these featured in a mag which ended up having a glossy cover, a professional layout, occasional free seven-inch singles and a devoted readership of 5000, a remarkable figure for an independently produced Australian publication. She even courted notoriety when she reviewed a single by female duo Club Hoy in 1993.

'"Don't be silly, put a condom on your willy"?' she wrote, quoting from the song in question. 'Christ! These girls need a good raping.'

The resulting furore went well outside the normal realms of the zine audience. First the pot got stirred in Sydney's free weekly music press. Then Club Hoy's record company sent her an accusatory letter, pointing out that they were advising other companies not to provide *Lemon* with product to review in future. Then the Australian Women's Contemporary Music Association got in on the act, and the story was deemed big enough to appear in the *Sydney Morning Herald,* highlighting a piece about sexism in the music industry. After that it became fair game for the tabloid current affairs programs, with pieces airing on both 'A Current Affair' and 'The Today Show'.

In *Lemon* #16, Louise printed both the positive and negative letters she received during this period, and revealed all the emotions she was going through at the time. She admitted that what she said was a dumb thing, but also pointed out that *Lemon* was a fanzine with a bad attitude and a foul mouth, and that her readers realised this. It was never meant to be for regular consumption.

'It was fair enough that they drew attention to the offensive nature of the review—I can deal with that,' she wrote in her editorial. 'But attention/hysteria from the mainstream media whose viewers would ordinarily never come in contact with *Lemon*? And talk of law suits? Full on—jeez, get the world in perspective, y'know.'

As I had written up an interview with Sonic Youth's Kim Gordon for that issue, Louise sent me a copy, along with a letter thanking me for the contribution. Part of what she wrote in that letter said a lot about the whole process of producing a zine.

'Due to the fact that zining is a shitty, low-down, dirty, thankless, money-gulping, stressful task, I have no immediate plans for another *Lemon*, but given a few months I'll probably be at it again.'

She would only do one more issue, as she died in 1995 after overdosing on antidepressants, following the death of her mother from cancer.

Lemon paved the way for younger zine writers into the 1990s. Damien Power, who puts out the stylish *Spleen 2,* said as much in one editorial. 'In December 1992, when I was thinking about starting a zine, I wrote to several zine publishers for advice. Louise wrote back saying, "Don't do a fanzine, it's horrible, thankless work! You'll regret it, believe me." Horrible thankless work, maybe, but it was work she loved. *Lemon* was an inspiration to me, and I'm sure to many others.'

Eddie Greenaway, who published twelve issues of *Eddie* between 1991 and 1996, says that producing a zine is totally a labour of love.

'I've never really made any money from it, and I don't think you really can if you're sticking to the true ethos of self-publishing. But I still think it creates a lot. The number of people we've published is phenomenal and many of them have used what they've written for *Eddie* as references to get work or get published elsewhere.'

Although music is an element of the *Eddie* make-up, Greenaway was conscious of avoiding a narrow focus—he wanted to draw together diverse interests, such as history, sport, comics and what he refers to as 'loungeroom culture'. He also was against the idea that zines had to be slapdash.

'We wanted to have a magazine aesthetic and a zine attitude. We wanted to highlight the fact that you could integrate the art and text and make it look good as well. We didn't want it to be throw-away.'

In order to provide a focus for himself and his contributors, from issue four Greenaway introduced a theme for each issue—Bad Luck (featuring a John Hewson dartboard centrefold), Love, Sport, Law & Order. The two most popular issues were Sleaze (sex and porn) and Music (which came with a compilation CD of indie bands). He also made each release an occasion by having launch nights.

For a while Greenaway tried to get funding from arts councils, but found the process demoralising. The final straw was when the Australia Council told him that they were sorry, but they didn't fund comics. He feels that this is indicative of the lack of knowledge in the mainstream about zine culture. He also feels that the mass media often misunderstands what zines are on about, while at the same time magazines such as *Max* and *Ralph* have taken some of their irreverence and attitude from the zine world, and events such as the 1998 youth project *Loud* have co-opted many of the ideas wholesale.

Bitter? Maybe a little. But he views the whole *Eddie* experience as a positive one.

'We wanted to question things, to be a window on culture and preserve a moment in time and show where people were at. People have asked for advice on starting up a zine, and I tell them it's fucking hard work, but be realistic about what you want to get out of it and write about things that interest you and you'll have an incredible learning experience.'

Lemon and *Eddie* used to be exceptions, but now independent music stores' shelves are full of locally produced zines. Some zero in on particular artists or scenes. *Spleen 2* and *Spunk,* for instance, are more professionally produced than your average 'photocopier and a stapler' zines, and they cover underground music on small independent labels. The advent of Britpop spawned a few independently produced publications (*Britpack, Chester*) trumpeting the talents of Oasis, Blur, Suede and, er, Menswear.

Melbourne band The Fauves even had the audacity and humour to produce *Shred,* an irreverent zine about themselves. *Shred* swung between lambasting other bands (rejoicing in the break-up of skivvy-wearing popsters The Sharp, faking an interview with the much ballyhooed Mantissa) to mocking themselves (photocopies of bad reviews, unflattering photographs, sending up their own lack of success).

More recent zines have combined *Eddie*'s eclecticism with the confessional approach of the so-called perzines (personal fanzines). Here, the cardinal rules of straight journalism—not using the first person; being fair, balanced and objective—go completely out the window. These no-no's are the whole point of these zines. And the more interesting ones go about it with abandon.

Here's the introduction to the first issue of a small Sydney fanzine called *Makeout*:

We've grown up—we pay rent, we have jobs, we can go to the pub—except it doesn't feel like we have. It's like we're still 15 and we're just pretending. As if we want to act like adults, FUCK THAT! If being a kid means you can shop at Toys R Us, read *Dolly* and sing along to your favourite group in your bedroom, then that's us forever! It's all about heroes, and we still have them pinned to our bedroom walls. Maybe it's a little different to when we were fifteen. We're more realistic. We know they live in the real world. Not 'Beverly Hills 90210'. But this makes it even better. We have realised that our heroes don't have to be the ones magazines sell us.

The entire premiere edition—two folded A4 sheets—was devoted to Graham Coxon, the guitarist from Blur. For their follow-up issue, they asked people to write about someone or something that inspired them. The fiftysomething mother of one editor wrote about how much she admired the ethos of straight-edged, fiercely independent US band Fugazi. She wrote:

The more I think about Fugazi and their little effort amidst the huge mess of the music industry, the more I realise that somehow I have focused onto the core of my own beliefs, the ones I use when I make life's decisions, e.g. if you believe in something strongly enough, be it an ideal or an action, eventually you will achieve that dream.

In these zines the creator decides on her own heroes. Sometimes those heroes are pop stars, but sometimes they're friends, the support group around the creator of the zine. For the readers, the hero often ends up being the creator herself, as she articulates her obsessions and thoughts, and gives her audience a sounding-board for their own lives.

Another contributor to *Makeout* #2 admitted that despite the fact that the whole concept of pop music was demystified for her through correspondence with her favourite bands, talking to them after shows, and even having them around at her house, she couldn't completely shake the starry vision of fandom. 'I know I should be snubbing the music-makers and just falling into the music, but that's a bit hard,' she wrote. 'It's a bit hard coz they're rock gods in my teenage eyes.'

There's a link here with the pop scrapbook. Or, rather, a giant leap forward from the pop scrapbook. The meticulous process of collecting, cutting out and pasting down pictures and articles from established magazines and newspapers into large scrapbooks is a coming-of-age thing for many people obsessed with pop music. There's the scouring for new information, the never-ending quest for unseen photo shoots, the embellishment of each page with borders of love hearts, the creation of a cover, and the carefully printed annotations, like the number plate of Daryl Braithwaite's car, or noting the dates of 'Countdown' appearances by Duran Duran.

These scrapbooks are personal. For the owner, they are an achievement borne of hard work, and concrete proof of the depth of their fandom. It is something you can share with your close circle of friends who share your obsession. Zines have many of those same characteristics, but with one very big difference—the creation comes almost entirely from within. A bower bird will collect any blue object for its nest, regardless of its value—it can be a jewel or a piece of plastic. Scrapbook compilers are the bower birds of the pop world—they want everything bearing the faces of Sherbert or Duran Duran or New Kids On The Block or Take That. When a zine creator uses mass media sources, however, it's often for ironic purposes—laughing at the hypocrisy of advertisements, wallowing in the kitsch of TV soap operas, defacing pictures of mainstream musicians.

'I'm sure my commercially oriented journalism skills will be useful—after all, zines are about making money, aren't they?' wrote the editor of *Are You Normal?,* sarcastically alluding to her tertiary studies in journalism.

'I was thinking fashion pages, style barometers, make-up tips, heaps of advertisements. I know there's a market … but for your sake (my much loved readers) I decided against it. I'll stick within the realm of this self-destructive planet of rock, real people, cheap alcohol and the good ol' Australian music scene.'

In zines, the mundane and the sublime stand side by side. In the Lismore zine *Spammy* one of the editors lists his current favourite things in the introductory letter, a flip mish-mash of teenage (albeit cool teenage) obsessions:

'I do believe, for today, that I am in love with: Cibo Matto; Buffalo Daughter; the new Muffs LP which took a while to grow on me but now I'm most fond of; Luscious Jackson on vinyl; Kate Johnson; *Who* ads on SBS; my Tamagotchi virtual pet; cute one-cup coffee plungers; London; my Italian classes; and convalescence.'

Later in the issue, he writes an incredibly personal piece about being gay. He introduces it with his reservations about revealing his thoughts in the pages of *Spammy*:

'I'm kinda scared about including this piece on my being gay, becus [*sic*] I'm paranoid that someone from my school will see it, someone who doesn't understand and doesn't care, and they'll tell someone and it will get out, or rather, it will be verified that I'm gay and then life at school will be worse than it already has the ability to be and it will just roll on from there, but I'm going to put it in cus I want to, and if I can't be confident, without hesitation in my own zine, then where, right?'

Where, indeed. Perhaps Queensland zine *My Life As A Megarich Bombshell* puts the mundane/sublime thing in even starker terms when editor Marisa tells us that an old flatmate once told her that there is a Kylie Minogue song for every occasion. That might sound like a fun idea in a frivolous sort of way, but she concludes, 'Pop music may be mass-produced and formula, but its simple clear emotions can have common resonances in us all.' Does that sum up the whole pop process, or what?

Later in the same issue she reminisces about her total devotion as a teenager to the lead singer of Transvision Vamp, Wendy James. But it's not done in some gooey, nostalgic manner:

When I was sixteen years old, Wendy James was my total idol. She was outspoken, she had attitude. She appeared on 'Hey! Hey! It's Saturday' with her wrists bandaged and she said she'd slit her wrists over Bros, who were also in the country at the time. She could even make sarcasm appear clever and witty. She was intelligent, she said what she wanted. She bleached her hair blonde and left the bumps in it you get when you've had a ponytail. She was sexy and sexual and smart and pissed off and funny, and through that sixteen/seventeen-year-old period she was exactly what I needed and wanted. I hadn't bought *Smash Hits* since I was thirteen and Simon Le Bon [Duran Duran] broke my heart by getting married, but suddenly I started buying all the pop magazines again.

Anyway … then when I was eighteen, her bubble burst and she faded into obscurity (as pop stars do). That was okay for me, because by then I didn't need her anymore. But I feel kind of bad for her 'cause she could have been so much more. Eight years (almost nine) have gone by since I first saw her, but I can't look at her through anything but adoring sixteen-year-old eyes.

In a way, we've come full circle, and we find ourselves back at that English fanzine from 1976. After all, Wendy James knew better than anyone that all you needed was three chords and plenty of front. That do-it-yourself attitude is exactly what fanzines are about. Fans know their subject, even if that knowledge may at times be outrageously subjective. Through zines, they have found an outlet for what's inside them—their opinions, their likes, their dislikes, their dreams, their secrets. At the same time, zines are like those square spaces that are cut into hoardings surrounding a building site—they provide a window through which outsiders can catch a glimpse of what's going on behind the flow of daily life.

Spice Girl/Partridge Girl

'Girl power!' yelled The Spice Girls. 'Pretty flower,' whispered Susan Dey, better known as Laurie, the ever-grinning, not-very-good-at-miming-playing-the-keyboards member of The Partridge Family. Female role models in pop have changed slightly over the last 25 years. Let's compare what Susan had to tell readers of a Partridge Family annual and *16 Magazine,* and what sort of advice The Spice Girls have for their sisters today.

Sue Stafford

Partridge Girls

- For a well-balanced meal, she always includes protein and vegetables.
- She has naturally long eyelashes.
- She doesn't like wild, funky outfits that are daring.
- She cares for her hair with good habits to keep it clean and shiny.
- She doesn't pout when she can't have things her own way.
- 'When I was twelve years old, I entered an unbelievable "dream world". It was as if one day all I cared about was horses, puppy dogs and tomboy stuff—and then the next day I was all gooey about real-life guys, teenage idols and romantic poetry. Fortunately, when I went to school I was able to leave my day-dreaming behind.'

Sue Stafford

Spice Girls

- Emma's ambition is to be able to eat 100 donuts in ten minutes.
- Victoria told one interviewer that she looks 'crap' without any make-up on, and first thing in the morning no-one would recognise her.
- 'I don't want to be a nice girl. I want to be a hot, sexy bitch.' (Emma)
- Q: What do you always bring on tour?
  Geri: My skipping rope, so I can train and tie people up. And my electric toothbrush. That's got a dual purpose as well.
  Q: For those lonely nights?
  Geri: Exactly. And you don't have to say you love it in the morning.
- 'But y'know, if Oasis are bigger than God, then what does that make us? Bigger than Buddha? Cos we're a darn sight fucking bigger than Oasis.' (Mel C)
- 'Lots of people dream about having sex with somebody of their gender. Me too.' (Geri)

FANTALES

Julie Ledger, Tony Hamlyn and Brett Price

Bros/Take That

Take One—The Family

Julie: We used to have big Bros get-togethers. We had this group called The Family. It was based around these fans from Springwood in the Blue Mountains. There were seven or eight of them and they were obsessed. They were so dedicated. That's how I met Tony in 1990. We clicked instantly.

Tony: There's this excellent photo of Julie and me the first time we ever met, and we're completely animated in conversation.

Julie: I wrote him a letter and I think he thought I was a freak. I found out he was a poofter (*laughter all round*), then I realised everyone was gay (*more laughter*). That was fine. It was really funny.

Take Two—They literally changed my life

What about New Kids On The Block?
Julie: God, it was so wrong to like them. We loved Bros so much and they took all the Bros fans away. Bros tried so hard. They literally changed my life. I came from a family where my father was too much in love with my stepmother to care about me, and my stepmother was such a bitch. I had a terrifically traumatic teenagehood and to fall in love with pop music around that time, where Bros were going, 'We love our fans', and you literally knew that they really, really did …

Left to right—Brett Price, Julie Ledger, Tony Hamlyn.

Tony: Talk to anyone who was a Bros fan and you'll see it. It goes deeper than possibly any other band I've known, because it was such a personal, intense thing. They really pioneered that thing where they touched the fans and we were part of the whole thing.

Julie: Matt and Luke's mum would walk out of the house and tell the fans what they were doing every single day.

Tony: Matt would stand outside a hotel for hours, not even signing autographs, but just chatting with fans, and it was more interactive, you felt like you were part of it, not just watching it.

If you didn't have Bros back then, what would have happened to you?
Julie: I would have killed myself. I honestly had a really awful time. I'm fine now, but it was terrible. That was my escape. It made me feel like I had something to connect with.

Tony: And you get to meet all these other people who feel the same way. That's why we were so loyal. Bros didn't have a hit for years and we were all still meeting up and writing to each other and ringing each other. We were still close.

Tony and Brett, did pop music fill a gap for you, too?
Brett: The whole pop music scene helped me to deal with my sexuality. My father was away a lot so I didn't have a father figure in my life. Bros was a major obsession at the time. It was different with Take That.

Julie: It was different. When I was into Bros it was my life and I could never have met them—I would have broken down, cried and lost my mind—and I'd still lose it.

Tony: After that it was Brett who got into New Kids first.

Julie: He got into everything first.

Tony: All of us have contacts at certain record companies who will give us certain things or tell us certain things, but for some reason, no matter how annoying or forceful Brett is, they will always give Brett what he wants and he will always get it first. We can't believe it.

Julie: They give him stuff to make him shut up.

Tony: But we denied liking New Kids for a long, long time …

Julie: Because we wanted to be faithful to Bros.

Take Three—You've got to have a favourite

Julie: Brett had a video of Take That doing 'It Only Takes A Minute', and we literally watched it over and over and over again. I even took photos of the screen.

Tony: We sat there till three o'clock in the morning and we were screaming into pillows. And we picked favourites. That's the rule. You've got to have a favourite.

Brett: I liked Gary for the first two months, then I thought, No, look at Howard Donald, he's sex.

Tony: I loved Robbie. I liked the look of him and what he did in the video. But then Gary became my favourite. He said that the one person he'd most like to meet is George Michael. I've worshipped George Michael since I was twelve.

Julie: I was always into Jason.

Tony: You liked him because he was a vegetarian and he was into spiritual stuff.

Julie: And he was a twin, like Matt and Luke. That was important.

Tony: After Bros we said that we would never get into another boy band.

Julie: We tried not to be fans.

Brett: They resisted.

Julie: Then Luke wrote that book. It was about him being so sad and having such an awful life. 'I Owe You Nothing' was my favourite Bros song and he had to make it into this metaphor.

Tony: On the last page he says that he appreciated the support from the fans and the fact we were there, but at the end of the day what he realised was that he owed us nothing.

Julie: To me that was a slap in the face. I wanted to kill him. All the other fans thought the book was great. The only other person who understood how I felt was Tony.

Tony: I just felt gypped. My whole life was that band. Luke Goss owed me a lot.

Take Four—The wanting and the waiting

All the jumping in and out of cars, waiting at airports, following them, hanging outside hotels—a lot of people don't understand what that's all about.

Julie: It's the wanting that makes the waiting worthwhile. That's a quote from a Bros documentary. That's what it's like. You can sit out there until four o'clock in the morning and freeze your arse off but, if you really want it, it's worth it.

Sue Stafford

FANTALES

Tony: The thing is that there's a sense of camaraderie. You wouldn't do it by yourself. There's all these other people you can bond with. You've been with these people for hours and you play games and you've got little in-jokes and you talk about everything you've done.

Julie: And with Take That you knew you were going to get something eventually.

Tony: Something good happened every single day.

Brett: We camped out for four days for Take That tickets, outside the Entertainment Centre in the middle of June. We had beds made up on the grass. It was so cold. We were abused, kicked, spat on. People would call us freaks.

Why do you need to be there four days before tickets go on sale?
Tony: It's important! Imagine if we'd just said, 'It's OK, we'll just get up at seven in the morning and go down there because there'll be no-one else there.' There'd be twenty people there already.

Julie: We knew every single Take That fan …

Tony: And we knew what they were capable of.

Brett: We had to be …

Tony, Julie and Brett together: … anywhere within the first three rows!

Julie: That's my rule. I got it from the movie *Splash*. Tom Hanks says to someone, 'You can sit anywhere in the first three rows because you're in the bridal party.'

Take Five—It was like we were on tour

Julie (*showing me her photo album*): These are photos of the 1994 tour, with lots of pictures of Take That. And this is the 1995 tour, with pictures of friends. That was what 1995 was about—it was about people, about friendship. About us.

Tony: We spent more time hanging out with each other and going to dinner and going to concerts and staying in five-star hotels and catching flights. It was like we were on tour.

Take Six—It's not like we've grown up

Will anything surpass your love of Take That, or is this it for you?
Brett: With the three of us, I think we knew Take That was going to be it. OK, we like The Spice Girls, but it's not the same. It's not as intense or emotional.

Tony: It's not like we've grown up and we're saying we're over it. It's just that we experienced something really intense with a particular band we were very passionate about, and I don't think anything else will ever reach those dizzy heights.

Julie: Bros was like idol worship …

Tony: But by the time we got to Take That we were older and more cynical and more aware of the industry as a whole. We appreciated the hype and the way they worked things.

Julie: Plus it was more our age group. They could really be our friends. They weren't that far above us.

Brett: We never had to remind them who we were. They would talk to us and they knew about us. They made an impact on us, but we also made an impact on them. It was a two-way thing.

BANDS AS FANS

Tim Rogers from You Am I

I'm figuring myself as the worst kind of fan … the one who ain't too loyal, doesn't put out, and isn't big on merchandise, y'know? I'm not giving much back to the icon. Malcolm Blight gets evicted for Brian Jones, Townshend gets shafted for Horace Silver … it's a revolving door and no-one's walking out better off for the privilege. The lack of loyalty thing ain't borne out of malice, it's more a hungry dog thing— y'know, if I see a fella wearing a fine hat, or a trumpet player who sweats good, well, they're IT, until the next husky-throated singer replaces 'em on my wall. Speaking o' chain smoking, my pencil case was being rented by The Replacements for an above-average term. I been stuck in too many moot trials as to their worth since, but at the time—I was fifteen I guess when I first heard their *Tim* album—a lotta things took shape. Unfortunately, in this book's context, any obsessiveness was kept to other elements o' my time—I didn't want to root 'em, or read myself into the lyrics, or carve the monicker into my arm (circa 1979 … Kiss). Nah, the band felt familiar. They rocked, but it was part clumsy. It weren't cocaine and solos, it was beer and D chords. Cool. The only manifestation of my fan(ity) was that for the next seven years I wanted to be *that* guy in *that* band. Hey, clarity like that may be pathetic, but it sure helped. Nineteen woulda been total crap otherwise. By the time I got to speak to Westerberg (I was interviewing him for *Beat* magazine in 1996) I no longer wanted to be *that* guy. Maybe I could use a bit o' that nineteen-year-old acne'd clarity—it may've prevented some o' the crapper moments on You Am I records … hmm … Anyhoo, I froze up a bunch, asked nothing revelatory, he was charming and quotable. Job done then, but I couldn't help ponder on where I lost those 'fan' traits—wonder and unabashed acceptance. Just too wrapped up in my own thing (?!), or the guy's songs just didn't hit me like they did before, or perhaps I ran into too many other

spotty boys wanting to be *that* guy or *that* band. As vanity would seem to be the driving force behind this last option, I'll wear it. I guess compared to Sam Cooke or Selena(!), Westerberg got off lightly—he got a dull interviewer, and I just got a brief smoking habit and too many songs in D.

LET'S TALK ABOUT SEX, BABY'

'I always get it up for the touch of the younger kind'

—The Knack, 'My Sharona'

137

'**I**f there was something else that was just as exciting, then I guess I would do it,' Gene Simmons once told me, talking about possible career alternatives to being a rock star. 'Even being the Pope doesn't get you groupies. Well, I guess you'd get some, but not of the same calibre.'

According to the bass player of Kiss—the God Of Thunder, the bloke who spews blood and flies up into the air like a winged demon, the man who some Christian fundamentalists claim is a servant of Satan—he is a teetotaller who has never been drunk or high in his life. He told me that his mother—whom he described as a woman who sounds like Zsa Zsa Gabor—was very heavy about the evils of drugs and alcohol. And Gene was a good Jewish boy who listened to his mama. Subsequently, his weaknesses run to other areas.

'Well, I like cookies,' he admitted. 'Unfortunately there's an American chocolate chip and macadamia cookie that's about half a foot across, and I can eat one of those with a quart of milk easy. It's not really good for you but, once in a while, that's my weak point. Girls and cookies, not necessarily in that order. If a girl shows up with a cookie, I'm set. Cookies in between the thighs of your sister.'

Gene Simmons has met a lot of guys' sisters. And he has taken photos of them during these meetings. His collection is legendary.

'They're no different to the photos you see in certain magazines on newsstands, except I take personal photos instead of selling them,' he argued. 'I do nothing different than you do with your appendage. We all have a piece of the puzzle that's missing, and we try to fit a square peg in a round hole, or whatever.'

Yes, but Gene seems to play the game with a lot more fequency, and with many more different opponents than, say, me. Paula Yates says she saw some of his collection when she visited Simmons to ask him to pose for her book of stars photographed in their underwear. In her autobiography, she writes about the page after page of Polaroids featuring Gene's penis and a succession of girls 'all gazing with a mixture of awe and exhaustion at Gene's mighty member'.

Anne-Lise Larsen set herself a task on the Kiss reunion tour of Australia. Her aim was to get into Gene Simmons's hotel room. Possibly she would even get a look at that mighty member. She had talked to someone who knew Simmons, and this woman had given Anne-Lise a few pointers.

Well, one pointer really—OK, maybe two—have large breasts.

Anne-Lise was alright on that count. She has large breasts. She is also vivacious, intelligent, articulate and a classically trained cellist.

She had already met Simmons on the 1995 tour, and was encouraged by the fact that he had referred to her as a sex goddess. Of course, she wasn't deluding herself that he would remember, but her philosophy was that if he noticed her once, he'd notice her again. Sure enough, when the band arrived at Brisbane Airport, they made contact.

'I'm not a shy woman by any means, so I called out, "Gene!" and started shimmying. I was really

LET'S TALK ABOUT SEX, BABY

excited, so certain parts of my anatomy were rather goose pimply. He came over and said, "Oh my goodness!" and started poking my nipples. I was saying, "Go for it! Take me, baby!"'

Later that night, Anne-Lise hung around a nightclub where she'd heard that Kiss would be turning up.

'I was wearing this really low-cut top, and I knew they had to go up this certain flight of stairs to get to the exclusive part of the nightclub. Gene turned up and saw me and said, "I just have to hold you for a minute." He grabbed me around the waist and pulled me up against him and he was going, "Oh baby! Oh!" I could feel everything. There wasn't even a little pocket of air between us. We hung out, and basically he was just feeling me up all night.'

Gene was cupping her breasts and fondling her, and calling over to his entourage to marvel at Anne-Lise's attributes. She was thinking that things were going really well and that maybe this time she would get lucky. Then she started talking about music. She tried to discuss bass lines with him. She told him about her cello playing.

'It was the most bizarre thing. Up until that point he had been treating me like a piece of meat, and then after that he tilted his head and gave me a look like he'd totally summed me up incorrectly. He realised I wasn't a bimbo.'

Thinking about it, she laughs at herself a little self-mockingly. 'And I was trying really hard to be a bimbo! It just didn't work. After that he ignored me. He didn't touch me. Nothing. That was a bit disappointing.'

But what if she'd kept up the bimbo routine? Does she think things would have gone to their logical conclusion?

'I've never had a one-night stand, no matter who it was. Even Gene Simmons. I would have gone to his hotel room, fooled around, and I would have made him happy, but I wouldn't have done it.'

But doesn't she think that he might possibly have expected that she wanted to go all the way with him?

Mirror Australian Telegraph Publications

Kiss's Paul Stanley with his own Penthouse pet in Australia, 1980.

'Yeah. But the thing is that they want someone they can kick out of their hotel room straight after it's over. When it comes to real people they don't want to get involved.'

Surprisingly, the whole experience hasn't really tainted her opinion of the group, as she maintains a healthy cynicism about Kiss's 'just doing it for the fans' party line while still worshipping them.

'These are guys I've loved since I was ten years old. The thing with Kiss is that they're so famous and so rich and they have everyone saying 'yes, yes, yes' all the time, that I don't think they have much of a grip on reality.'

Reality, of course, is a bit of a rubbery commodity in the rock world. And when it comes to musicians, fans and sex, it's a volatile formula.

Here's Henry Rollins imagining his perfect meeting with a woman. The scene is a laundromat. Henry is washing his vast collection of black t-shirts and black shorts.

Woman: Can I borrow some soap?
Rollins: Sure.
Woman: I hate this place, the soap machine's always broken.
Rollins: Yeah, I know. That's why I always bring my own.
Woman: So what do you do?
Rollins: I'm in this group called The Rollins Band.
Woman: Huh? I've never heard of you guys.
Rollins: You want to go out and eat some dinner after the dryer cycle's over?

If for some reason you're reading this and you want to go out with Henry Rollins (hey, each to his or her own), here's a hint—don't be a fan. And, preferably, don't even be aware of who he is. Of course, this is a little difficult, as he's built like an outhouse made of bricks, and he has a huge angry sun with the words Search & Destroy tattooed across his back.

Of the women Rollins has been out with, only a couple didn't know about him from his work as a singer, author, actor, book publisher or spoken-word performer. One of them had seen him once at a spoken-word performance but admitted that she wasn't really impressed. Henry fell in love with her immediately. They ended up together for a few weeks and then she dumped him. There are songs about her on both *The End Of Silence* and *The Weight*.

'She wrote me a postcard last year and I was like, "Aaaargghh! It still lives!" She said that she saw a letter I had written to her a few years ago while she was going through a box and she was thinking about me. I was like *(adopts little bashful voice)*, "Get away!"

'Of course I wrote one of those things back to her that was like *(adopts casual, breezy voice)*, "Good luck with whatever you're doing!"'

The Rollins Band, he claims, is not much of a groupie magnet. He says that they're more like King Crimson or Frank Black than Mötley Crüe. 'Metal bands and strippers are buddies for life,' he nods sagely.

He's quick to point out that he is no monk. He has slept with women. Lots of women. In all kinds of countries. It's just that when someone comes up to him and breathlessly mouths platitudes like, 'I've always loved your work', it's an immediate turn-off. It's just not going to be an honest, 50/50 relationship.

'It's like I know every card in the deck and I'm going to deal you a hand now. I know how it's going to go. What image does this person have of me? She got it from a magazine and saw me in a photo. Is that going to be real, or has it sat in the sun for twenty minutes too long, and it's a little off?'

Does this sort of thought process go through the mind of the drummer from Whitesnake when a nubile babe rubs up against him in the backstage area? Possibly not. But Rollins isn't always so philosophical about things, either.

'If things are going to be on a surface level—you look good to me, I look good to you, fine, let's fuck madly for the next six weeks—I can do that, too. As long as everybody knows what the deal is. They ask, "Are you sleeping with someone else?" And I say, "Yes I am. And I'm conducting myself safely. And when I go on tour, I will write to you about once every nine years, and I'll see you when I see you. Can you hang with that?" If she says, "No, I don't think that's cool", I'm like, "Then let's just stop right now and just be buddies. I don't want to delude you."'

Loretta Tolnay thinks she may have had her first orgasm at the age of fourteen. She was surrounded by 8000 people at the time. It was at a Bon Jovi concert, and—another new experience—it was the first concert she had ever seen. Her love for Michael Jackson was even greater, however.

'I am attracted to Michael sexually. I think he's a very sexual person on stage. I would love to sleep with Michael, just cuddle up to him and kiss his face and be gentle. If I was the kind of person who had one-night stands then I'd go further, but that's not who I am. I don't get intimate with strangers. As much as I love him and know about him, Michael is a stranger. He doesn't know about me.'

Girls who follow teen pop bands talk a lot about respect, and many of them seem shocked that anyone would even consider the possibility of anything sexual going on between guys in groups and the females who follow them. This is despite the fact that they routinely say that they love these guys more than anything in the world. They can get hysterical. They can wait for days outside hotels. They can hang around airports at ungodly hours of the morning. They can spend thousands of dollars in a couple of weeks, flying to different cities around the country and paying big hotel bills. They can pledge undying love.

And they can even write poetry. Here's one that a fifteen-year-old girl breathlessly read to me at a Boyzone appearance at a suburban Sydney shopping mall:

POEM FOR STEPHEN
The first time I saw you I felt sure it was meant to be,
The way you made my heart pound I knew you were the one for me,
A million other girls assured me they all felt the same way,
But I knew in my heart there was something special which would make you mine one day.
When you came outside we all made a big race,
Because we wanted to be the first to see your smiling face
There were fans and cameras everywhere,
And all the public turned to stare
But when you left I wondered why
All I could seem to do was cry.

The Stephen in question is a member of Boyzone. This girl first saw him in a blink-and-you'll-miss-it cameo appearance in *The Commitments*, and knew he was the one for her. But what would happen if Stephen asked her up to his hotel room and put the heavy word on her?

'Can I say something? That is a really stupid question to ask any fan of Stephen Gately. If he invited me, I'd go up there and talk. That's happened to me before. I went up to Mark Owen's room. We were talking, but nothing ever happened, thank God. They're nice guys. They wouldn't do anything to hurt their fans.'

'We're not there for that sort of thing,' her friend pipes up. 'It just wouldn't happen. They're not like that. Any girls that walk around thinking they're going to get anything like that is just being disrespectful, as well.'

Julie Ledger, who I have seen fanatically following Savage Garden, Gary Barlow, Mark Owen and Boyzone over the space of six months, is equally adamant that sex just doesn't enter the equation. And, at the age of 25, she is surely more aware of the possible ramifications of getting close to these groups than some of the more immature girls.

'I have respect for myself, and I'm not here to sleep with them. I'm here because I love their music and they're really nice people, not because I want to get into their pants. If that's the way they thought about me, then I'd feel bad about myself and I'd feel bad about them.'

Brett Price isn't quite so circumspect. He says that he has seen fourteen- and fifteen-year-old girls trying to sleep with pop stars. Brett is now 25, but back in his day it was only the fans over the age of seventeen who would do that sort of thing. What happens to these girls after they sleep with someone in a group?

'The girls try to get more, but they're shunned. The band don't ever talk to them again. They look down on them. And they just don't understand why that happens. I don't want that. I'm happy where I am.'

Brett is a guy in a girl's world, but he understands their attraction to these guys, because he is gay. His ideal man is ex-Take That member Howard Donald.

Courtesy of Polydor Records

Boyzone—the girls don't want to have sex with them, apparently.

'To me he is every gay boy's fantasy. His body is from God. He's an Adonis. And the thing between his legs in a pair of white Speedos, oh my God. That was enough for me. Then he got the dreadlocks, the eyebrow ring and the nipple ring, and I love the rough look. It was too much.'

Brett has met Howard on many occasions. In 1993 he remembers being the only male in a crowd of 500 which bustled around Take That before their concert at Wembley Arena. He followed the band on their Australian promotional tour in 1994, and again on the live tour in 1995, and was actually in London when Take That announced that they were closing up shop. He claims to have a friendship of sorts with this guy, but what would happen if the opportunity arose to take things further?

'I wouldn't do it,' he says without hesitation. 'I think I've earned his respect, so even if he was gay, which I know he's not, he would lose all respect for me.'

There's that respect word again, the word fans use over and over when talking about their idols and sex. With that said, Brett has slept with a pop star. Although he won't reveal the guy's name, he was in a group which was big in England, but not very successful in Australia, and the affair continued for three weeks. He has also twice 'mucked around' with a member of a four-piece Australian group who are no longer together. The guy was flirting with Brett from the stage, then afterwards they got drunk together and things went on from there. Although he liked the group a lot, he wasn't really overwhelmed by the fact that this person was in a pop group.

'He wasn't a Take That member,' Brett explains simply.

Gary Barlow was a Take That member. He gets sent letters. He gets sent flowers. He gets sent nude pictures. Girls proposition him, and he doesn't mind at all. But does he take advantage of it?

'Well, obviously there are a lot of youngsters around, and I hope I've never taken advantage of my position, but at the end of the day, sometimes you're in the bar at night, and there's a couple of 25-year-old girls there. That's life. That's human nature. It's not just the situation I'm in. I don't mind a bit of that.'

The myth of the asexual, kind-hearted dreamboat permeates each new teen band that is pushed on the public. Sure, the story goes, they could get as many women as they wanted, but they're only in it for the music, you know. The big surprise is how everyone acts outraged when it turns out that someone is a drug-snorting, groupie-shagging beast.

In the early 1970s David Cassidy gazed from the bedroom walls of teenage girls everywhere, his shirt unbuttoned to reveal a hairless chest, his big, brown eyes staring kindly down on all he surveyed, and that shaggy hairdo shining healthily in the sun. Occasionally there were pictures of him with his shirt unbuttoned while he rode a horse, a marketing move of sheer genius, combining the stereotyped equine/pop obsessions of pubescent females in a single stroke.

As a member of the cast of 'The Partridge Family', he played a guy who was meant to be eternally seventeen, even though he was 24 by the time the show completed its four-year run. He was the cool big brother who occasionally went out on dates, but was really there for his single mum and his brothers and sisters.

'I lived a very different existence to that guy on TV,' Cassidy told me in an interview just before the release of his 1994 biography, *C'Mon Get Happy ... Fear and Loathing on the Partridge Family Bus*. 'I couldn't live up to this perfect, white knight, heroic-guy-next-door image. I wasn't at all like that.'

No kidding. For a start he was playing songs like 'I Think I Love You' and 'Doesn't Somebody Want To Be Wanted?' for the screaming kids, but in his dressing room he was cranking Hendrix, Jeff Beck and The Bluesbreakers. And secondly, he wouldn't have had the time or the inclination in real life to argue with Danny over his annoying habits, or give Laurie advice about guys, or help Shirley with the washing-up. Why? Because he was shagging anything that moved.

'I was twenty-one years old, my dick was always hard, and they were all so willing,' he wrote in the book.

Cassidy apparently considered sexual intercourse to be a little sacred, so he wouldn't always go all the way with the women who made themselves available to him many times during the course of each day he spent as a heart-throb. But as for oral sex, well, that was nothing. He'd get off on asking these girls how they fantasised about him and then get (ahem!) down to it. He details his

LET'S TALK ABOUT SEX, BABY

sexual exploits in *C'Mon Get Happy*, everything from a seven-minute encounter with a woman who was having an affair with a diplomat in the room down the hall in a Tokyo hotel, to a girl who just pressed his intercom buzzer at home, and ended up giving him a blowjob through his front gate. He says that even though a lot of his sexual experiences were empty, his life was such an unreal experience at the time, and he was dissociated from reality in so many ways, that meeting these women was the closest he got to dealing with the outside world.

Virgin sacrifice might sound like the stuff of bad voodoo B-movies, or maybe Ozzy Osbourne tours, but Cassidy claims that the most beautiful fourteen-year-old girl he had ever seen in his life seriously offered herself up to him. His conscience got the better of him and he turned her down.

According to Greg Macainsh from Skyhooks, the same thing happened to his band during the 1970s. Backstage after a concert, or via letters, thirteen-, fourteen- and fifteen-year-old girls would tell him that they were ready for sex with a member of Skyhooks.

'I mean, we were in our early twenties, so at the time we thought they were too young for us. Thinking about it now, it's horrifying that these kids offered themselves up to grown men.'

With that said, he acknowledges that the bulk of letters revolved around four words which could only have any sort of currency and meaning between the years 1974 and 1977—'We think you're spunky!'

As far as the sexually active fans of the time went, Macainsh uses the pat line that just about everyone involved in a big band during the 1970s and the first half of the 1980s uses— you have to remember, times were different back then. Most of the things you picked up from unprotected sex could be fixed up with a shot of penicillin.

'It was pretty wild in the early 1980s, because it was pre-AIDS,' says James Reyne, who at the time was the chisel-jawed lead singer with Australian Crawl. 'When it's thrown at you and you're in your early twenties in a band with

James Reyne occasionally found himself out on a limb (or two).

your mates and you're seeing the country, having fantastic experiences, and these things are laid in your lap, what are you going to do? You're away from home for months and months at a time. As long as people don't get hurt by it, that's fine.'

Some people, he is quick to add, did get hurt by it. Reyne admits that with the alcohol and other substances that were imbibed around this time, his judgement wasn't always 100 per cent. He recounts times when he had to feign a morning meeting, then disappear around the corner to a cafe until his overnight guest vacated his residence or hotel room, before creeping back.

'Sometimes you'd have to deal with these nightmares in the morning. Sometimes they just wouldn't leave. They'd think, "Fuck you! You had me, so I'm not leaving. Now you owe me." I always said, "Look, no-one had anybody here. It works both ways. You used me too." '

Reyne, like a number of other Australian band members from the 1970s and 1980s, says that when it comes to Sin City, Adelaide wins hands down.

'I don't know why,' says Boom Crash Opera's Peter Farnan. 'It's got lots of churches, lots of murders, and it's just loose. Adelaide was always the big city for relationships falling apart because of indiscretions which became public.'

The band christened one group of ardent young female followers from Adelaide 'The Creche'.

'Adelaide was maybe trying to prove that it could swing more than Melbourne. I must confess, I've swung in Adelaide. But with these younger girls in The Creche, you ended up just being like a big-brother figure. I didn't want to fuck them. You'd talk to them, and then you'd get involved in their lives, because they'd be hanging around looking lonesome and winsome. They were too young to even be thinking about trying to bed the band or the crew, but as they grew up some of them would move that way.'

Mark Seymour has had the odd lewd suggestion made to him in his time as the lead singer with Hunters & Collectors. In fact, he ended up marrying one woman who chatted him up. 'I let her do what she suggested,' he laughs. 'Now we have two kids.'

He says that the groupie scene was a lot more upfront in the early days of the band, but maintains that he was such a frightened little Catholic boy that he never took as much advantage of it as he might.

'It was much more prevalent when we used to come up to Darlinghurst in Sydney and play for the groovy inner-city scene, because we were a very groovy band back then. It subsided as we became more of a suburban band, which is something we actively embraced. I've just never really been that promiscuous. My behaviour in that area has been pretty disastrous really.'

Trying to get bands to open up about their sexual shenanigans is a little like extracting teeth. Unless they're under the influence of a numbing drug, those gums are not going to flap. Surely Dave Gleeson, a man who fronts the Screaming Jets, and was renowned a few years ago for his provocative stage banter and foul mouth, will have tales to tell. He maintains that the band's audience has gone through phases relating directly to his behaviour. When they started in 1990 they were followed

LET'S TALK ABOUT SEX, BABY

by rock chicks and metalheads. Then there were Dave's self-confessed 'dark years', between 1992 and 1994. During that period, you couldn't see a girl in the first couple of rows at a Screaming Jets show. Why?

'Because they didn't want vomit or spit or ridicule,' says Gleeson, before giving a sheepish, snaggle-toothed grin. 'There's no denying that in our gigs there's a lot of sex and lewdness involved, but for a couple of years there it was just pure rage and testosterone.'

Sometimes people ask Gleeson if he feels he got a hard time from the press back then. He says that he got what he asked for. He blames his behaviour on the simultaneous death of his mother and breakdown of his relationship with Baby Animals singer Suze De Marchi.

'There were always chicks backstage willing to indulge in coitus with the band,' he admits. 'But we've always been open with the punters about our situations. Now we have lives and stability, whereas before it was like, "Bring on the circus!" '

He still claims that the Screaming Jets weren't a very big groupie band. He maintains that they're more of a bloke band. Even in his 'Bukowski period', as he calls his two-year reign of terror, he was more interested in getting completely out of it than shagging groupies.

'We were definitely not leaders in the field. To this day, I'm still the guy in nightclubs who ends up in a corner with all these blokes going, "Ah, you wannanother beer, mate?" And we end up talking about the footy. Which I don't mind at all.'

For the definitive, no-holds-barred summing up of the complex band/fan sexual ethos, perhaps we have to go back to that great philosopher Shirley Strachan, when he was talking about the career of Skyhooks in the book *Ego Is Not A Dirty Word*.

'What do you reckon—we were in the business for money? No. We were getting paid in roots.'

Groupie Hall of Fame

Few may have been born great, many may have had greatness (ahem!) thrust upon them, but some have become great in their own right.

Cynthia Plaster Caster

WHO IS SHE?
Most famous member of the Chicago trio, The Plaster Casters, completed by Dianne and Marilyn.

WHAT'S HER STORY?
The Plaster Casters became infamous for taking plaster casts of band members' erect members. Their very first subject was Jimi Hendrix, whose trophy they named the Penis De Milo. Other notables included Roger Daltrey, Eric Burdon, Buffalo Springfield and The Monkees. Cynthia got the idea for the project while studying art at the University of Illinois.

SHE SAYS
'I had my new gimmick—this was the way I could capture bands, make them talk to me, and get their pants down.'

WHERE IS SHE NOW?
After a long legal battle, she retrieved her collection from someone who had been looking after it and then decided to hold on to the lot. She still plies her trade from time to time, but will only immortalise the penises of bands she admires. She does occasional spoken-word nights, and is considering writing an autobiography. Marilyn Plaster Caster became a born-again Christian.

POP CULTURAL ARTEFACT
Kiss wrote a song about Cynthia called 'Plaster Caster'.

FANBREAK

Bebe Buell

WHO IS SHE?
A fashion model from the 1970s who went on to become a fixture on the arms of many rock stars.

WHAT'S HER STORY?
The first concert she saw was The Rolling Stones when she was eleven, and she remembers the bulge in Mick Jagger's pants more than anything else. Modelling herself on rock girlfriends of the day—Marianne Faithfull, Jane Asher, Anita Pallenberg—singer/songwriter Todd Rundgren became her first paramour. Has also had relationships with Steven Tyler, Elvis Costello and Stiv Bators, and many flings, including Mick Jagger, Iggy Pop, Jimmy Page and Rod Stewart.

SHE SAYS
'I think people should look at it this way: instead of thinking that when a woman is with a man of professional stature she must have gotten out her butterfly net and snared him, why not think that the man chose her too? It's mutual.'

WHERE IS SHE NOW?
Married to singer Coyote Shivers, and managing Deborah Harry.

POP CULTURAL ARTEFACT
She blessed the world with her daughter, Liv Tyler, whose father is Aerosmith's Steven Tyler. Also played in two bands, the B-Sides and The Gargoyles.

Pamela Des Barres

WHO IS SHE?
An LA teenager who became a 'supergroupie' in the 1960s and early 1970s.

WHAT'S HER STORY?
She became obsessed with pop music via The Beatles, then hung around The Doors and The Byrds. Tiny Tim dubbed her Miss Pamela. She banded together with a bunch of friends to become the GTOs (Girls Together Outrageously). By this stage she was nanny for Frank Zappa's kids, and he produced a GTOs album. Rock stars on her hit-list included Mick Jagger and Jimmy Page. Then she started seeing Don Johnson, before fourteen-year-old Melanie Griffith came onto the scene.

SHE SAYS
About Mick Jagger: 'He gave new meaning to giving head. Those lips. Please! We made love for hours, but I kept flashing back to squatting in front of my hi-fi, touching myself for the first time while Mick groaned about being a king bee coming inside, and here he was right on top of me doing just that.'

WHERE IS SHE NOW?
Married (now separated) Michael Des Barres, from Silverhead and Power Station, and had a son, Nicky, now eighteen years old. Authored last year's *Rock Bottom*, about life, death and bad behaviour in the music business.

POP CULTURAL ARTEFACT
Wrote *I'm with the Band: Confessions of a Groupie* and *Take Another Piece of My Heart: A Groupie Grows Up.*

Jenny Fabian

WHO IS SHE?
British groupie from the late 1960s.

WHAT'S HER STORY?
Jenny had flings with Pink Floyd's Syd Barret and pre-Police man Andy Summers, when he was in Dantalion's Chariot. Hung out with English group Family, and had a relationship with their tour manager.

SHE SAYS
'If they weren't nice, you didn't suck their dicks, did you?'

WHERE IS SHE NOW?
After drug problems and marriage, she retired to the English country-side.

POP CULTURAL ARTEFACT
Groupie, a thinly disguised autobiography she co-wrote with Johnny Byrne in 1968 and 1969. Gave the general public terms like 'hung up' (in love) and 'plating' (fellatio). Re-released last year.

COME TOGETHER III
Waiting for Barlow

5.30 am
Why? Why? Oh why? And this seemed like such a good idea yesterday. As I stand under the shower I go over my plan—to get a fan's eye view of the airport greeting of a pop star, hopefully followed by a wild car chase and a bit of hotel-stalking. Gary Barlow, ex-Take That member, is arriving in Australia for a promo tour, after visiting Japan. He is not turning up at a civilised time, but 7 am. My taxi driver thinks I am an idiot when I explain what I'm doing. Sadly, I tend to agree with him.

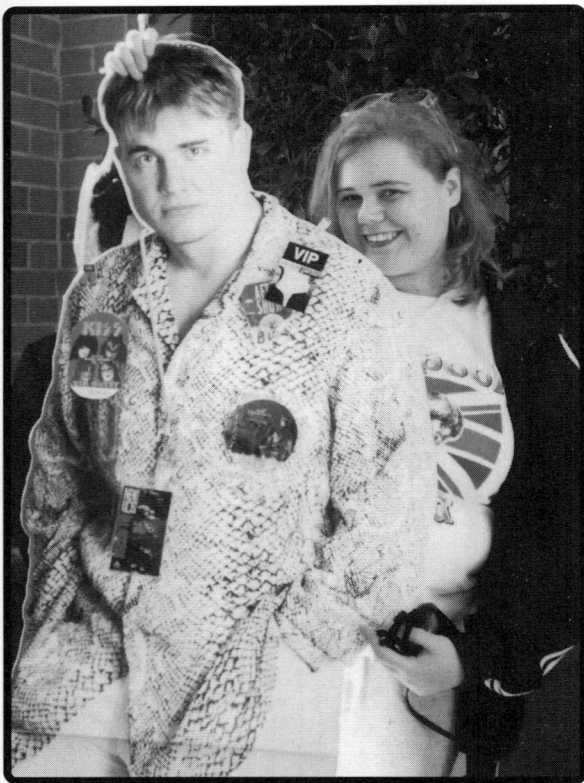

Barry Divola

6.20 am
Arrive at airport. But where are the kids? Gary will be touching down in a mere 40 minutes. I've done three circuits of the arrivals lounge and can't spot one fan. Have ex-Take That members lost all currency in the pop stock market?

6.25 am
Read arrivals board. Flight QF022 has been delayed until 8.02 am. Lesson one—before leaving home ring airport to confirm incoming flight is arriving on time.

6.30 am
Reading the paper and drinking a coffee, pondering what a stupid idea this was.

6.45 am
Do another circuit of arrivals lounge. I can see a few teenage girls here and there, but there are no cameras or flowers or cardboard Gary Barlow effigies in evidence, so I'd feel like a sleaze going up and saying, 'Psst! You a Barlow fan?'

COME TOGETHER

6.50 am

Finally see a couple of familiar faces. Julie and Tony, two Sydney fans, and Michelle from Melbourne have arrived. 'Where is everyone?' I ask. 'Over there,' says Julie, pointing out a small cluster of girls behind a pillar. 'And over there,' adds Tony, directing my gaze to a quartet in a doorway. I soon learn that fans are like those butterflies in wildlife documentaries that can blend into their surroundings without being detected.

7.00 am

The arrival of Tony, Julie and Michelle on the scene has brought everyone out of their little corners, and soon about 30 fans are milling around, swapping bits of information that they've gleaned. Everyone knows which hotel Gary is staying in. Tony, Julie and Michelle have already booked a $280-a-night room there. Julie estimates that over the next seven days, with accommodation, car hire, expenses and flights between Sydney and Melbourne, she will spend $1000 following Gary Barlow around. She hardly slept at all last night, and this morning she was so worked up that she locked the only key to her suitcase … inside the suitcase. All three of them are in new clothes they have bought for the tour. They like to co-ordinate their look for each different tour. This time out they're favouring dark blue.

7.20 am

There are a couple of older women in the crowd. It turns out that they're actually mothers of two of the fans. I ask one of these women what's inside the gold wrapping paper of the parcel she's holding. It's a small teddy bear. I assume that she's holding it for her daughter, but it turns out she has brought it herself. She's a huge Gary Barlow fan, and as the time ticks by she appears to get more and more nervous. 'Where's your camera? You've got to take photos!' her daughter berates her. 'I'm too nervous to do that now!' she shoots back.

7:30 am

Another look at the board reveals that the flight has been delayed further. It will now come in at 8.26 am.

7.50 am

'Are you a Gary fan?' I ask the fortysomething woman who is standing with her sixteen-year-old daughter.

'Oh, no, I'm more into Howard,' she replies, referring to dreadlocked ex-Take That member Howard Donald. 'I like his bum and his six-pack.'

Sharan (the daughter) has brought along a portrait of Gary she has painstakingly drawn with pencil over the last two days. Cheryl (the mother) saw The Beatles when she was fifteen, and has been hooked on pop music ever since. She still recalls coming to the airport in 1964 and being pressed up against the observation deck railing as the Fab Four walked off the plane. The crowd was so large and so hysterical that at one point she was afraid the whole railing would give way. She also talks about the shrill screaming that reverberated around The Stadium at the band's show.

8.10 am
The life of a fan involves a lot of standing around. Absolutely nothing is happening.

8.20 am
I spy a woman I know from Gary Barlow's record company and wander over to say hello. She doesn't know which gate Gary is meant to be coming through, but she does reveal that his parents have come in on an earlier flight, as they're holidaying while their son is doing his promo tour. She tells me this quietly, aware that fans are nearby. She could have used a loud hailer. They already know. They probably found out before she did. They even know what alias Gary uses on tour—Mr Popstar.

8.30 am
The fans have noticed I've been talking to the record company woman. They choose to call her 'The Driver'. They start casually pumping me for information. One fan tells me that during the Mark Owen tour, a record company person became irritable because she was hanging around Mark too much. 'I think you've had enough,' the woman told her. 'You can never have enough!' she replied.

8.45 am
The tension is rising. Now fans are clustered around the ramp that leads out of arrival gate B. They're sure this is where he will emerge. Cameras hang around necks. Presents are clutched nervously. Eyes scan the area for any sight of anything Barlowesque.

9.10 am
Panic. The more eagle-eyed fans have spotted a man with close-cropped hair sussing out the crowd. The ones in-the-know recognise him as Gary's tour manager. 'Don't look like a fan!' Julie whispers to me as we lean against a wall trying to look unfanlike. I'm a guy in my thirties. Do I look like I would come out to the airport at six o'clock on a Thursday morning to harass an ex-member of Take That?

9.15 am
More panic. The tour manager has gone to the back of the arrivals lounge and walked off with an older couple. It's Gary's parents! A bunch of fans start tailing them from a distance. Does this mean that Gary might be smuggled out through a different exit?

9.17 am
While the younger fans remain clustered around the off-ramp, the older ones have gathered halfway between arrival gate B and a lounge area where they suspect Gary may be hanging, waiting to move out. Should they stay at the arrival gate or stand around the exit of the lounge?

COME TOGETHER

9.19 am
This is it! 'The Driver' has emerged from the lounge with the tour manager and two women who the fans recognise as English record company and management staff. Julie is certain that they're heading off to get the Tarago, bring it around to the front door, and quickly transfer Gary into it. We race back to the arrival gate.

9.20 am
Still waiting at arrival gate.

9.22 am
Still waiting at arrival gate.

9.25 am
Still waiting at arrival gate. 'Did they actually go out to get the van?' someone asks Julie. 'Yes! Yes!' she replies, exasperated. 'I'm so stressed!'

9.30 am
'The Driver' walks up to the group.
    'There are too many planes and too many people,' she tells them. 'Gary said he'll see you at the hotel.'
    'Which hotel?' a young fan asks weakly.
    'Quay West Apartments,' she replies.
    I got up at 5.30 am on a Thursday, got a cab to the airport, hung around here for over three hours, and now we're not even going to see this guy?

9.31 am
All the fans race outside to look for the van. A decision is made. Julie, Tony and Michelle will drive into the city, check into the hotel and try to catch Gary there. I hitch a ride with them.

9.34 am
We're on the road.

9:36 am
We took a wrong turn and we're heading away from the city. We chuck a U-ee.

9.37 am
They confirm their hotel reservation on the mobile phone and ask for a room with harbour views.

9.44 am
Stuck in traffic. Tony rings his hairdresser to say he's going to be a little late for his appointment.

9.50 am

Julie: It's a bit disappointing. And a bit confusing. A record company person has never done this before.

Tony: Too many planes? What does that mean? It's an airport! Record company people are sly and everything they say you have to take with a grain of salt.

9.55 am

Still in traffic. Michelle's mother rings from Melbourne to see how she got on with meeting Gary. 'She understands all this,' Michelle says after she hangs up. 'She was really into The Beatles. And she still does it—she saw Tom Jones in a hotel and invited him over to have a drink.'

10.05 am

We're discussing record company people.

Michelle: When you're applying for the job, on your application you have to write that you're a bitch.

Tony: And you have to have no passion for music whatsoever.

Barry Divola

COME TOGETHER

10.09 am
We've finally made it into the city. The phone rings again. It's another fan, who is already at the hotel. Gary has still not arrived. 'Oh no!' exclaims Michelle. 'Do you think we've been sold the dummy?'

10.12 am
We drop Tony off at his hairdresser.

10.15 am
Julie has become noticeably quiet. She seems very stressed about not being there when Gary arrives. 'It's important that he knows we are here for him,' she explains.

10.20 am
We arrive at the hotel.

10:22 am
All of a sudden, the Tarago pulls up, Gary steps out, cameras are flashing, autographs are signed, nervous pleasantries are exchanged, gifts are proffered.

10.25 am
And he's gone. Five hours from the start of this journey, the result is about three minutes with Gary Barlow. Although they're still peeved about the airport scenario, the fans seem OK about that work/result ratio, as they're still basking in the glow of meeting him. Most of them hang around after he's disappeared. They'll stand vigil outside the hotel for the rest of the day, waiting for Gary to re-emerge. I go home for a late breakfast.

SEALED WITH A KISS

**'And then while I'm away, I'll write home every day
And I'll send all my loving to you'**

—The Beatles, 'All My Loving'

Afriend of mine once told a school buddy that she had a new boyfriend. She said that she couldn't reveal his name, but his initials were B.A. What she didn't tell her friend was that she had a crush on Berton Averre. You may have never heard of him. That's because he was the lead guitarist in The Knack. While the band was at the height of their success with their only hit, 'My Sharona', she penned a fan letter to them, making special mentions of the playing skills (love that solo) and brooding good looks (love that curly hair) of Berton. She never got a reply. And as a result she never wrote another fan letter to anyone. Like The Knack themselves, her missive was a one-hit wonder.

Why bother? What's the point of sending a letter to someone who will probably never read it, let alone reply? In 1964 Paul McCartney pointed out that many of the letters to The Beatles that he read—imagine how many he didn't quite get around to—started out with the line 'You probably won't get this letter'. American indie rockers Pavement make it obvious from the outset that their fans won't get a reply when, in one of their CD booklets, they refer to fans as 'our one-way corresponders'.

So what exactly are people after when they pen some carefully chosen words to their idols? Well, some are just after information—tour dates, reports on the progress of the new album, chords for a particular song. Some want to say how much they love them. Some actually send photos or videos to express how much they really, really love them. Some include marriage proposals. Most want to share with the artist how much his or her music has affected their lives.

But with the slim chances of a band of any magnitude actually reading every letter, don't people realise that it may be a futile exercise?

Probably. Without wanting to come over all mystical and Eastern, however, it's the writing that's the thing, and the destination of the letter isn't always the point. A fan letter is self-expression. It's about sitting and obsessing long enough over someone until you just have to let it out. It's about using a stranger as a sounding board for your own ideas and theories about life. It's about getting the words just right—not too fawning, not too idiotic. It's about letting an idol know that they've hit their mark, and that you're on their wavelength. It's about writing a ten-page drunken letter to Elvis Costello and not sending it.

Here's what a few artists had to say when I asked them about the fan mail they received.

GARY BARLOW

I get a lot of mail to my house. Record companies and agents think they're the ones who can read the market, but I'm the one who knows. I'm on the shop floor with everybody. I read these letters, and it's important to know the people who are right behind you. It's so good to read their reactions to TV shows or the album. That's the real reaction. I get a lot of flowers. I love flowers at home, so I get this endless supply. It's amazing. Sometimes I get nude pictures. That's always a good one. All sorts of strange things. They're just trying to attract your attention. It can get a bit dangerous now and then.

JOHN PAUL YOUNG
It was the usual stuff. Can I have an autograph? Can I have a photo? I love you, I love you, I love you. I want to marry you. I don't remember it all. There was so much crammed into my life back then. I really was a passenger. God love 'em, they really do some wonderful things and I love them all dearly, but the amount of money they would spend on presents and trinkets and things. I still get that every now and then. Not an awful lot, but occasionally. Easter eggs and gold charms on a necklace, and people used to to do embroidery and knick-knacks. And scarves. I happened to mention once that I was a Celtics fan and next thing I get this 48-foot-long green and white scarf. I ended up giving a lot of those fluffy toys away to charity. There were just so many. My daughter Amanda couldn't move in her room for fluffy toys. Far be it from turning away when Amanda was born, the fans got right into it and were sending me gifts for the baby.

DAVE GLEESON
Some chick from Melbourne who I'd met a few times was a bit of a casualty, and she'd send letters saying that we were soulmates and everything I said on stage she could relate to, and as soon as something like that happens you think of John Lennon. That's one person sending me a letter, but he must have had a million people sending letters that said 'John, you wrote that song for me!' It's selfish, but you have to say, 'Look, I wrote it for me, and what I do, I do for me.' I met this chick and I said, 'I know people suffer, and your story is a sad story, but all I can tell you is that what I write is about what I feel, and if you get off on that then I think, Well, I'm not alone, but I don't want you to say I wrote it for you and follow me around.'

RONAN KEATING (Boyzone)
We get some mad gifts. Calvin Klein underwear and aftershave. In Japan we get CD-Roms and picture discs. It's unbelievable. Then they make dolls and lovely cards and presents and chocolates.

MARK SEYMOUR
I very carefully screen all the letters I get, but this one girl keeps writing, and has done for the last five years, about two or three letters a year. She sends me lyrics. It's very sad. She thinks I'm on the same astral plane. There was this one person who I would see at gigs and they'd be very pleasant,

and then I'd get letters from them saying, 'I feel as though I've already written those words in that new song you do.' I would just sort of laugh nervously when I saw them and then try to extricate myself as politely as possible. I also get the odd bouquet of flowers. I've had one bra given to me in a sixteen-year career. We're a pretty blokey band.

BOY GEORGE
In the early days it was the usual stuff—I love you, you're beautiful, you've got a fabulous voice. It was mostly girls. Just before Culture Club got into the charts it was all androgynous boys with make-up and punky/goth girls. Then we hit the big time and it was a squillion girls. Literally overnight we lost all those hardcore avant garde fans, and they were replaced by teenyboppers.

CAROL VAN DIJK (Bettie Serveert)
It depends. Sometimes they're asking about t-shirts or lyrics. Nowadays I send the lyrics to the fan-club so they can send them. Sometimes we get very passionate letters from people who for different reasons felt that the music was a comfort to them, which is great. I've had people who want to marry me. That's really awkward. I've always been a very shy person and I've only had a couple of boyfriends in my entire life, so it's really weird.

JAMES REYNE
Brad [Robinson, ex-Australian Crawl guitarist] would get a lot of girls who just wanted to sleep with him or marry him. I'd get what I call the 'one trip too many' ones. They'd write me weird letters. My parents would be sent stuff. They insisted on keeping their name in the phone book. I told them that they should get a silent number but they had some weird principle about it. They'd pass these letters on to me. I said, 'Mum, just throw them away.' But she'd feel guilty and say, 'Some poor fan is trying to get through to you.' There were some who were very persistent. Some would write these cryptic messages with dates and codes and a picture of a death head on them. I always seemed to get them rather than the other guys. There was a woman in her sixties who I used to call the witch. She had long grey hair and wore purple and black robes. She'd stand right at the front of the crowd in the middle. She used to send me these envelopes with strange things written in them. Sometimes she'd just put them on the stage. I don't think she meant any harm. She found out where I lived at one stage and she'd drop garbage bags full of clothes outside. There would be weird tan flares and t-shirts and ties. Then she disappeared. Brad would get the teddy bears and I would get the rubbish bags full of clothes and weird coded messages.

DAVE DEDERER (ex-Presidents of the United States of America)
I've got to say that the greatest thing I got from a fan was from this guy in New Jersey who sent me a three-string slide guitar he made out of a cigar box. It's pretty goddamn cool.

SEALED WITH A KISS

STEVE MALKMUS (Pavement)
Most of them just want information. Ninety per cent of people have probably written to ten other bands at the same time. I wrote to this girl from Tacoma, and she got all offended by my response to her letter. All I was doing was saying I got your letter, thanks for writing, I don't want to bond with you, and I don't have time for a penpal. The bands I used to like as a kid seemed so huge that I didn't even think I'd get anything out of writing to them. At the time I would have wanted to write to Kiss or Devo, but I wouldn't have known what to write anyway. By the time I got around to Butthole Surfers and The Dead Kennedys, I could just go to the shows and say 'Hey'.

HENRY ROLLINS
During album and tour cycles the mail is heaviest because we're in magazines and on TV. Downtime, it's more like ten letters a day, one to ten e-mails a day. Usually the content of the letters is about the spoken-word shows or about the books. Very rarely is there a letter concerning the music. Maybe five in every 100 letters. 'When are you coming back? Saw you last night, blew my mind. Read your book, that was cool. Heard your band—ah, doesn't really do that much for me. I've seen you four times this year. I wanted to ask you about that guy you talked about—what was the name of the album he did? What was that book you talked about in that interview? I want to be a writer, I don't know what to do. No-one in my school likes me—what do I do? I'm gay, and I'm afraid of telling somebody—what do I do? I want to lift weights—can you put me on a workout? I'm twenty years old and I think I have one minute to live, I see no point in going on—can you help me? My friends think I'm weird because I wear black clothing and I like stuff like you and Bukowski and Nine Inch Nails.'

Henry Rollins spots a few penpals in the crowd.

Sophie Howarth

That's what I get. Rarely do I get a postcard that says, 'Hey man, love what you do. Cool.' I get nine-page bullet-proof letters that you can't stick a knife through and they desperately need a reply immediately. 'You've got to write back! This is really important! I've read all your books, now a little bit of me. I was born in 1978, wrote my first book in 1991, it's coming to you in a separate package.' And it's like 90 pages of teen angst. 'Think you wanna put this out?' And it's like this scrawl you can't even read.

Or you get poetry. 'I'm sitting in my lonely room, thinking my lonely thoughts of doom, here comes the night, it fills me with ...' Come on, help me out here ... 'fright!'

It sounds lame, but I like these people who write to me. They're throwing their guard down and they don't know if it's going to get read by me. But they're sincerely trying to make contact, and you've got to respect that. That's why I read the mail. I'm not going to ignore some person contacting me and say, 'Oh, you don't exist.' I could never do that to someone, especially a young person. That was done to me and it fucking killed me.

But on the other hand, I wish they wouldn't write. I'm so fucking busy. You come home from two weeks of being away, you open up your e-mail, it takes nine minutes to download all this mail. There is a paper box next to your desk full of letters. I now have 170 people in my living room going, 'Dude! Dude! You gotta help me!'

I'm like, 'What about me?'

'Dude! I really like what you do!'

'If you like what I do then get out of my way and let me do it.'

When I'm home in LA I'll get up at six in the morning and do mail from 6.30 to 8.30. On the weekend I'll do four hours a day just trying to get through it. If I never got another letter again, no problem. I reply by postcards, make it short and do the best I can. I prefer e-mail because I can type and it's gone. I don't dislike these people, nor do I dislike their enthusiasm and their friendliness, but it's time and it's personal space.

DEBORAH CONWAY

We used to get poetry. Some of it was good. I'd hear about people's lives. I find it remarkable that they can do that. It's admirable that they can express themselves. They don't feel there's anyone they can talk to, and then they find someone they can talk to in us, and they're using it as an outlet. It's not like they're getting anything back. It doesn't matter what I think—it's about them. It's like therapy that they're getting for the price of a postage stamp. It's about them working themselves out. Apart from that, people just send letters of appreciation, or asking for chords for certain songs, or asking about where the songs come from.

DARREN HAYES (Savage Garden)

Our families run the fanclub, so we do get to see a lot of the letters. We can't physically read them all anymore, but my family do, and sometimes they'll bring special ones to me to read. I hear about everything. Ninety-five per cent of the time it's fantastic—they're congratulating you and talking about how they love the music. But the other five per cent ranges from fanatical worship to insane hatred. And, yes, it does upset me, but I'm talking only five per cent here. They say things like, 'We are soulmates, we were connected in a past life and we were burnt at the stake together and our mission is to join up now and save humanity from doom—will you call me?' And at the other end we get ones that say, 'You suck so badly, let me count the ways.' Or they say things like, 'I'm a big fan, I love you so much, but here are a few tips—you're not the best-looking guy in the world, and you're not what most girls would even call cute, but there's something about you. And your voice—it's less than amazing, let's face it, but I guess the way you use it is interesting. I love you.'

Join the Club

You know those addresses they always print at the back of CD booklets? The ones that say, 'Hey kids, want to find out more about (*insert name of artiste here*)?' Have you ever actually bothered to write in? Me neither.

But one day, 26 August 1997, I decided to go through a bunch of recently released CDs in my collection and send off some letters. My only stipulation was that I wouldn't send money (Wu-Tang Clan wanted US$24.95 upfront plus US$12 for postage and handling for their fan pack—forget it). I sent them all the same letter—it went like this:

> Hi
> I'm an eighteen-year-old girl writing to you from Sydney, Australia, and I just wanted to drop a line to tell you that your

latest album is my reason for living at the moment. Thanks for creating such a godlike disc. I was wondering if you send out autographed photos, posters, fanzines or other information to fans. I've enclosed an IRC (International Reply Coupon) for this purpose. Keep up the great work!
Regards,
Brenda Divola

Hey, I figured eighteen-year-old Brenda would have a better chance of a reply than crusty old music journalist Barry. Anyway, here are the results.

5 September
A prompt response from Obvious Gossip, the kd lang fanclub. But what looked at first glance like a fanzine turned out to be a merchandise catalogue. So basically they're after my money. Who knew kd was so big in this field? Greeting cards, key chains, necklaces, badges, t-shirts, caps, mugs and even sets of *All You Can Eat* chopsticks are all waiting for you, should you wish to give your credit card details and pay postage and handling fees. According to the introductory letter, kd herself helps design the logos on these items. We're also told that kd's fans are of great importance to her, 'but due to the huge amount of mail she receives, it is impossible for her to correspond with you on an individual basis'. Damn! Now I'll never find out what the hell *Salmonberries* was all about.

8 September
And second across the line is ... oh goodie, Suede. A single sheet of folded paper. Half of it tells me the cost for joining the Suede Information Service. It will set me back seventeen English pounds. Apparently this will get me a 'stylish regular magazine', my very own signed band photo and special invitations to 'legendary' fanclub-only shows. Because we all know how packed out those normal Suede shows can get, don't we? Think I'll hang on to that cash for now.

18 September
Three responses in my letterbox!

FANBREAK

And Madonna wrote back! Well, the Official Madonna Fan Club did, anyway. And they didn't actually put pen to paper. But at least on the glossy form letter there's a quote from the icon herself—'I really appreciate all of your love and support, it means more to me than you can imagine,' she writes, which makes me feel very good about myself. To! Join! The! Official! Fanclub! You! Have! To! Get! Through! A! Lot! Of! Exclamation Marks! But the bottom line is that if I send 39 American dollars I'll get a welcome letter, an autographed photo, a membership card, a merchandise catalogue and the latest issue of *ICON*, the Official Madonna Fan Magazine. And then there's something called *Boy Toy*, but I got a bit bored by that stage.

Next up is Patti Smith. A sparse one-page sheet informs me of *PHTP*, a new fanzine. And it wants us, Patti's fans, to send in articles, photos, reviews and … uh-oh … poetry. It will also boast a trading section, where you can swap all your Patti collectibles with other fans. 'Please note the trading policy will be strictly enforced,' the letter warns. 'The only person who should be making money off Patti's music and writing is Patti.' Sounds like a hoot, doesn't it? I could barely hang on to my five dollars and resist sending off for a copy.

And the third letter? A tissuelike bit of paper. A few scrawled lines. 'Dear Brenda, Nice to hear from you and I'm glad you liked that album that much.' But what's that signature? Why, it's Jonathan Richman! *The* Jonathan Richman! He answers his own fan mail. What a novel concept! This is the only artist who replies directly to any of the letters I send out. Bless him.

22 September

Two Britpoppers in one day. Supergrass weigh in lightly with a small merchandise form, but at least they also provide an info sheet on what the band has been up to over the last nine months, and a promise to answer any questions and queries I may have. Should I ask why Gaz looks like an extra from *Planet of the Apes*? Nah.

Meanwhile, over in Pulpville, a comprehensive newsletter informs us that 1997 got off to the worst possible start. No, not a world war or famine in Africa, but Russell leaving the group. 'But you've got to look at it from Russell's point of view,' they urge us. Er, right then. The merchandise sheet has dicky little hand-drawn pictures (that Pulp irony at work?) and is called *Pulp Boutique*. And for 30 US dollars, all of this could one day be mine—six newsletters, a *Disco Very Magazine,* a badge, volume two of the *Pulp Scrapbook*, a full-colour picture post-card and, apparently, surprise gifts when I least expect them. How they'll know when I least expect surprise gifts, I'm not sure.

13 October
I'd just about given up on the rest, when Ben Folds Five came through. And what's this? A free gift? Well, a sticker that's folded in half. I wonder if Ben Folds folded it himself. They also kindly list the dates for their Australian tour, which finished over a week ago. A per-sonal note at the bottom lets me know that if I send a large envelope and an IRC, they'd be pleased to send an autographed photo of the band. Nice offer, but I think I'll go and buy a coffee instead.

27 October
The Cure have finally heard my call. Well, they are getting on a bit, aren't they? And the International Information Service ('the cure do not have a fan club,' sniffs someone called Janie in the letter) comes through with something called *curenews*. Janie must be an e e cum-mings fan, because there are no capital letters in the whole thing. There's a detailed update on every movement of the tousel-haired quintet, a lengthy Q&A interview and, most entertainingly, a 'cure-friends' penpal section. I don't think I shall be corresponding with the 'fifteen-year-old antichrist/anarchist who smokes the chronic'. He informs readers that he doesn't dance, 'but the voices in my head do'. It's a mystery why he's advertising for company. Seems like he would be a very popular chap.

And that's about it. To Coolio, Depeche Mode, Sonic Youth, The Lemonheads, Blur, Spearhead, Fun Lovin' Criminals, Ash, Pavement, Michael Jackson, Hanson and The Spice Girls—thanks for nothing. Brenda is still waiting.

John McKechnie
Abba

Auburn flowing locks. Pouting lips. Sharply defined eyeshadow. A silky pair of shorts that are cut high enough to reveal a pair of slim, stockinged legs, finishing up in a pair of high-heeled boots. Meet John McKechnie.

If you watch *ABBA: The Movie,* and check out the footage of the concert just before Agnetha, Björn, Benny and Frida race out on stage at the beginning of 'Tiger', there's about five seconds of film where the camera pans up and over a group of fans. In the middle of them is a lanky, bespectacled nineteen-year-old. That's John. He got to Sydney Showground at nine in the morning of 3 March 1977. The gates didn't open until 4.30 in the afternoon. It rained. And rained. And rained some more. But he didn't care.

'I was obsessive about that tour,' he recalls. 'When the gates finally opened, we had to run a couple of hundred metres to the gates, and then our line was held up for four minutes, so by the time I got into the Showground I got a spot about seven rows back from the stage, but it wasn't too bad. Then of course the long wait was on, because they weren't on until eight o'clock.'

John still gets goosebumps thinking about that night. The regular chants of, 'We want Abba!' that rippled through the crowd every ten minutes. The roar from the grandstand when those higher up in the bleachers could see Abba arriving in limousines. The unbelievable excitement when the group finally appeared on stage after all the waiting. His only regret was that he had listened to his mother when she told him not to take his tape recorder.

'The memory of that tour is so special. It's not really looking back at simpler times on a personal level. I much prefer myself now, at 39. I think I'm far more together than when I was nineteen. But it's the way Abba as a group made me feel that was special.'

FANTALES

Nine months later, John was invited to a fancy dress party. He decided to go as a member of Abba. Benny or Björn would have been simple but a little boring. He decided to go as Frida, and that started him on a path which continues to this day. John plays drag queen Mary Jane Mangler, and sings songs by Belinda Carlisle, Kylie Minogue and Gloria Estefan. But because of his Abba fandom, performing as Frida means so much more. His first show was in 1979, then he performed at an Adelaide fan convention in 1983. But the big one came in 1987, at the ten-year tour anniversary celebration.

What is it about the gay community? Why has it championed Abba for so long and kept the flame burning?

'That's a tricky one. My theory is that Abba were so flashy when they came out, and I think a lot of gay people gravitated towards them because of that. I'm totally open, whether it's about being gay or what ever, so when it came to being an Abba fan, I was out there.'

And it hasn't always been easy. Although he has never been punched for wearing an Abba t-shirt, he recounts tales of being ridiculed for his fandom, especially in the late 1970s and early 1980s, not easy years for the Abba follower.

'I joined the fanclub in 1979, and that was when I found other Abba fans. I was a big fan, but apart from a couple of people who thought they were alright, I was by myself. It was almost like me against the world. It's like the old cliché about being young and gay and you think you're the only one. That's what it was like for me as an Abba fan.

'Then when I joined the fanclub I was so happy. There were all these other idiots like me that worshipped them.'

He can dance, he can jive—it's John McKechnie live.

ON THE INSIDE

'Taking care of business, every day, taking care of business, every way'

—Bachman Turner Overdrive, 'Taking Care Of Business'

I f you can't get near the people onstage, then the next best thing is to get near someone who is near the people onstage. Roadies, security, hotel staff, drivers and record company publicists are the ones who often get to see more of the fans than the bands themselves.

A guy in a black t-shirt and earpiece stands with fans for hours waiting for a star to arrive on stage, distributing water, chatting to relieve the boredom, and occasionally dragging out those who have been overwhelmed by the crush and the lack of oxygen. The road crew are there in the early afternoon setting up the PA, and they're still there at three in the morning, breaking the whole thing down and lugging it out—they're the ones who see the stragglers, groupies and autograph hounds.

Amongst the fans, some of these characters become almost as well known as the bands themselves. Ask anyone about roadies from particular eras and certain names keep coming up, some of them for their notorious extracurricular activities. Melbourne pop fans from the 'Countdown' era recall with fondness a guy called Paddy who manned the door for the weekly taping of the show. Certain security staff, hotel workers, record company people and van drivers are recognised on sight, and if they've helped out with imparting information, meeting a band, obtaining autographs or delivering gifts, then they'll never be forgotten. And if they've been mean and surly, then they'll never be forgotten, either. Fans have long memories.

The artist only has controlled contact with the public at concerts, instore appearances or when they're confronted at airports and hotels. The people who work with them and around them are more in the frontline. They're seen as gates or stepladders, ways for the fans to get that little bit closer. As a result they get sweet-talked, propositioned and hounded. The following five people are on the inside, and here they talk about their jobs and how they've related to fans through them.

ANDREW TATRAI
Head of ACES (Australian Concert and Entertainment Security)

Don't even try to hit Andrew Tatrai with excuses. He's heard them all in his seventeen years in the security business. He started out as a bouncer, and he has the hands to prove it. He holds up his fists, and the knuckles look like a relief map of Iceland—the peaks and valleys occur completely at random. Forming ACES to provide a safe environment for concert goers, Tatrai has overseen security at countless gigs and outdoor festivals like The Big Day Out, looked out for the 78 000 people at Eastern Creek Raceway who came to see Guns N' Roses, as well as personally looking after everyone from Elle Macpherson and Gillian Anderson to Kylie Minogue and Fergie.

Luckily what we usually have are single-focus crowds. It's not like a soccer crowd where you've got team A versus team B, where there's not a hope in hell of negotiating. When people are focused on the stage, then we can control the crowd quite easily. If we don't act like arseholes, they just want to see the band.

ON THE INSIDE

The only problem is when you get gangs in there who have specific agendas. That's when problems start. The heavy metal and thrash bands aren't really a problem. It's a younger audience, but despite the way they look and dress, they're not usually vicious. They're loud and they make a ruckus, but they're pretty harmless. There were some problems with bands like ZZ Top because of the bikie element, or George Thorogood with the Jack Daniels crowd. And the rap bands sometimes attract the gang element.

You hear some very elaborate excuses from people wanting to see the bands. Some of them infiltrate the hotels and wear uniforms to blend in and get into the rooms. We had girls wearing overcoats at the Sebel, lying down in the middle of Elizabeth Bay Road, and exposing themselves to the band who were looking out from the balcony. They'll do anything to get closer to the band. The ones I find amusing are the really arrogant ones, who when you say, 'Excuse me, where's your backstage pass?' they look at you and go, 'Don't you know who I am? You'll never work in this industry again.' Total confidence. A lot of them try to pose as guys delivering pizza. I guess they think all bands eat pizza so they'll get away with it. I think it's a bit old now. Sometimes it works. On Bon Jovi's last tour, by coincidence they did actually order pizzas for the crew, so we let this guy through, but then he headed off to the dressing room.

I know security do get propositioned, but it hasn't personally happened to me. I think the fans who really want to get to the band won't waste themselves on someone who is working for the band. They'll use all sorts of excuses to get through us, but, I mean, if they slept with us and then get to the band, what do they say? 'I slept with security and a roadie to get to you?' I don't think it would turn on the band member very much … or I assume it wouldn't (*laughs*).

I don't think roadies get as much as they say. I think a lot of it is bravado, and some of it is offers that are never substantiated. Even if you start off doing roadie work or security work because you like to be associated with celebrities, after a while it wears off. So a roadie can say, 'Sure, I look like shit. Sure, I get paid like shit. Sure, I work shitty hours. But all these beautiful girls blow me because I'm close to the band.' I take that with a truckload of salt.

Does security get asked to go out into the audience to choose girls for the band? The answer is yes, but I don't really want to talk about it too much. Basically the band points them out or gives you a description, but normally it's one of their own security guys or crew who then goes out. After a while the roadies know what the band members like, so they don't even have to be pointed out. I've decided not to do that because I want to rise above that. It's a little tacky.

I find the whole fan thing fascinating from a psychological point of view. When we had Gillian Anderson over here I was her personal security guard, and to see those thousands of people at shopping centres was absolutely terrifying, especially because she's a very private person. Girls were fainting and screaming. The most amazing reaction I've seen to anyone is Elle Macpherson, between the time she went from calendar girl to launching her first line of lingerie. In Brisbane they opened the doors at Grace Brothers and 4000 red-blooded young men just went screaming in. It was incredible.

I've always enjoyed watching people, and I like to make sure they're safe. It's a fatherlike thing. I've got two children and tend to think of what I do at work as what I do at home on a larger scale—let them do what they want to do, but make sure they don't get hurt or do anything dangerous.

I was part of the old days in the 1980s when bouncers were rough guys. It was pretty ugly. You had to live with your hands in those days. I decided that this was just a liability. I'd look at people getting hurt, and I thought, This is not what I want to do. So I changed things. If someone walks in looking for a job with us, and he goes on about being a black belt and he's got the glare in his eyes, then forget it.

GEOFFREY ARIGHO
St John's Ambulance Officer

Geoffrey Arigho's wife is always telling him to turn down the TV. After fifteen years tending to the casualties of the mosh pit, his ears have been bashed by a succession of bands. 'I wear earplugs now, but we never thought about that in the old days,' he says.

What sort of things do you have to treat?
It usually depends on the type of concert and the crowd. If there are a lot of young girls, then the most common problem will be hyperventilation from all the excitement. It's actually overbreathing. They breathe at a faster rate, so their oxygen level increases but their carbon dioxide level decreases. The side-effects are tingling in your fingers and difficulty in breathing. They have to be taken aside to get their carbon dioxide levels back to normal, and you have to reassure them.

Do you ever think, Why?
You get used to it and expect it after a while. I suppose they're there for their idols and they get pretty worked up.

Mirror Australian Telegraph Publications

ON THE INSIDE

What other common problems do you come across?
Lots of headaches, sometimes burst eardrums.

Have you noticed any big changes in crowd behaviour over the last fifteen years?
I guess these days concerts are a lot more controlled. Now a lot of the bigger groups play at the Entertainment Centre when they come to Sydney. Years ago they'd be at the Capitol Theatre or the Showground, and the crowds tended to be wilder and the injuries were worse. I remember seeing AC/DC years ago and there were people running around with knives. It was a combination of the drugs and alcohol problems too. This guy came up to me and he was right out of it. He said, 'Oh, I think I've cut myself.' It turned out he'd been slashed with a knife on his buttocks. In the old Capitol Theatre we were always pulling girls out of the toilets because they'd collapsed. They'd mix the alcohol they bought there with whatever tablets they'd brought along with them, and they'd just collapse. You could usually find them by smelling the dope in the air.

Do you find some girls don't want help, they just want to get back to the concert?
Oh yeah, for sure. They want to carry on. But you have to talk to them and calm them down if they're hysterical. At the Police concert at the Showground years ago we had to take this girl behind the barrier because she was hyperventilating. We started treating her, but as soon as she saw the steps to the stage she took off, and we had to grab her pretty quickly or she would have got up there.

Do you ever get to see anyone that you're a big fan of?
I like AC/DC and bands like The Angels. And I got to see Joe Cocker, which was good.

Are there any groups that made you feel like you were really earning your money by being there?
Gary Numan at the Capitol Theatre. I just thought he was strange.

ELEANOR JACKSON
Band driver/production runner
Here's what you need to do Eleanor Jackson's job:
1. Be reliable
2. Have a good general knowledge of back streets and short cuts
3. Know all about shopping facilities, tourist attractions and restaurants
4. Know how to sort out tricky technical and mechanical problems
5. Be excellent behind the wheel

So, you're a crash-hot driver?
Well, I know people feel pretty comfortable with me in the car. I know what I'm doing and I know how to get out of sticky situations. You need to be paparazzi-aware, and be able to avoid situations.

What sorts of experiences have you had with fans?
It depends on the act. For some bands there are huge crowds at the airport and they're fine about it. They obviously have their own security and bodyguards. Bands like Kiss are good with that. Others aren't so good with that, and they get really nervous around a lot of fans. Then you have to organise back entries or loading-dock entries for just about everything you do.

Do fans get in the path of the car or jump on the car?
That's a problem, especially when you get caught up in traffic leaving a venue. If we don't do a runner and the band hang around for a drink, then that can be a problem because there are fans waiting outside. It can get scary when a lot of fans bash on the windows. A lot of artists hate that. I get frightened that someone is going to get hurt if the window smashes. And if we're stuck at a red light, then it's a worry for the safety of my passengers. When fans get in front of the car, you have to slowly try to nudge past them, but they'll do anything to get a photo or an autograph.

What about fans who jump into taxis and chase you?
That usually happens with the younger groups like Boyzone. I don't know where these fans get their money, but they'll follow them all over the countryside and book rooms in the same hotels, and be there waiting as soon as they come out. If I go through an orange light, it'll be red by the time they go through, but they don't seem to worry. They really make it unsafe for everybody involved. They're oblivious. All they want to do is keep following the van. That's pretty scary. They're risking their own lives, plus that of anyone else who is on the road.

Have you ever felt in danger, especially in light of what happened to Princess Diana in 1997?
Not really. It has been that bad, but you're not going to risk everybody's life. My theory on the Diana thing was that it was negligence on the driver's part. No matter who you've got in the car and no matter what anybody else is saying to you, you're the driver and you should be in control. You might have to bend the rules a little bit, but you have to decide what's safe and what you won't do, no matter who is yelling at you.

Do fans recognise you now and try to get to the band through you?
Yeah, they do. Basically I just ignore them. It depends. A lot of them are really horrible about the whole thing, but if it's someone who you can see is quite genuine or they've been to a couple of shows and they want something signed, then you might help them out. But most of them are really quite demanding, and once you do something for one person, they'll all want it.

ON THE INSIDE

Which bands' fans are the most over the top?
Mainly the younger teenybopper groups with four or five boys in them. Apart from that, the Chili Peppers and Kiss fans are pretty crazy. And with Alanis Morissette it was more a paparazzi thing. Because she's very private we had a lot of problems with paparazzi. She hasn't had many photos taken, so people wanted to hunt out a photo of her.

Do you ever find that you have someone who you're a huge fan of in the back of the van?
Nup. (*laughs*) I guess that's also why I'm pretty good at my job. I've driven for The Stones and Plant and Page, and I thought, Wow, but I'm a bit oblivious to the whole thing, I guess. Obviously I think some of these people are great, but I've never got anything signed by anybody.

You're kidding …
No. If someone specifically gives me something, then I go, 'That's great, thanks.' But I never go after anything. I suppose in hindsight I'm probably pretty stupid and I should do it because it's worth money, and it would be nice to show my kids later on, but I've never really thought about it because it doesn't mean that much to me.

You're not much of a music fan?
No, I'm a music nut. But I see them as normal people. I respect what they do and love seeing the shows, but I never go ga-ga over anybody.

Are there many women in this line of work?
No. It's mainly a male-oriented thing. This is fairly seasonal work. For me, I'm capable of standing on my own. I've got a pretty good head on my shoulders. A lot of women get into this business for the wrong reasons, if you know what I mean. There have been other girls we've got for bigger shows, but they shoot themselves in the foot by doing the wrong thing. You've got to be professional about it even though it seems like fun and games.

HOWARD FREEMAN
Tour manager
He was there with Sherbert and The Ted Mulry Gang in the 1970s. For a while he steered Dragon through Australian tours. These days he looks after The Cruel Sea and Nick Cave when they hit the road. He's been there, he's done that, and—without pointing too many fingers and naming too many names—he dishes the dirt on some 'special' fan/band encounters.

Fans will hide in any part of the building to get close to the band, whether that's stairwells or food trolleys or the room next door. There used to be a lot more mystique to it. It wasn't smutty. They

Philip Morris

were your idols and you wanted to get close to them and you could say, 'Yeah I touched him,' or, 'Yeah I saw him'. Now a lot of that glamour has gone. A lot of the chicks who were chasing bands back then are probably chasing footballers now. They've probably decided that musicians are too fucked up to mess with. Footballers are going to have a hard arse and be reasonably fit.

In America it's different. It's a user-friendly facility. Chicks are straight up and in your face there. I'm here, you're there, fuck me. That's the difference. There's no bullshit at all. You have to decide who you think has been there before and whether you're going to go there. Now it's a completely different game with sexually transmitted diseases. Now you could be dead. Kids treat it differently. Then it was 'let's have a go'. Now it's 'well, this could knock me off'.

ON THE INSIDE

I was sharing a room with Ted Mulry one night and there was bashing on the door the next morning. It was this guy after his daughter. I'm hungover in bed, and Ted, as he usually was, was pissed in the other bed. The doona's on the ground between the window and his bed. I said to this guy, 'Get fucked, look at this room, she's not here!' Five minutes after he's gone the doona moves and this young chick climbs out and says, 'I better go to school now.'

There was a chick in Melbourne who used to bake cakes for every band who came to town and then service the band. And back in the days of Buffalo they had a shaving fetish, and they'd have the razor man, the towel man and the powder man, and they'd get chicks in there and shave all the hair off their bodies.

The real teenybopper fans just had stars in their eyes, and they'd skip school to hang out near the hotel. The predatory ones were older chicks and they just knew what they wanted and how they were going to get it. I'd say Ted was a legend in that department.

In Sherbert all the guys were pretty well set up in relationships in their lives, so it wasn't the free and easy thing. They were probably more responsible with their fans. It was bizarre to see 200 chicks sitting outside Garth Porter's place in Rose Bay. They'd wait in the park for him to walk in or out of the door.

With Sherbert, we started off using hire cars, but then we'd find the hubcaps and aerials would go. Everything was souvenired, so the car companies would basically charge us to rebuild bits of the car. The safest and most obvious way to get in and out of venues was an armoured van. You can't get into it, but they'd still hang off the back and throw themselves in front. They just had to get close. It was hysteria. One day a chick got her fingers stuck in the back door and I seriously thought there were going to be four fingers hanging there and dropping to the ground when I opened it again.

LUIGI GALUPO
Bar manager

One night during his seven years as bar manager at the Sebel Townhouse, Luigi Galupo was serving Roxette at one table, Dire Straits at another, while through the doorway he could see Phil Collins chatting to Julian Lennon in the lobby. From 1989 to 1996, before he left to manage the bar at the Observatory Hotel, Luigi saw many groups pass through the Sebel. And he says that, yes, it's true— whether you're a fan desperate to meet your idol or a megastar just needing someone to talk to in the wee small hours of the morning, you'll unload your secrets to a bartender.

Have times changed in the rock star's world since the 1980s?
There's much more control now. There used to be a lot more partying in the bar, but now they're more likely to have a quiet dinner after the show. It used to be more crazy. Things have become more boring. In the 1980s it was unbelievable, the number of people who would hang around outside the hotel waiting for a band to come out.

What sort of lengths would fans go to?
They'd go up to regular customers in the hotel and say, 'Please, can you get me inside with you?' Or they'd get to the hotel phones and try to ring up to the rooms. They'll try to blend into a crowd of people who are coming into the foyer. They know that the main act arrives first, but after that there's the crew and people like that. So they know that security will be there for the band, but after that it will be easier to sneak in. I've seen kids out there for ten hours waiting for a band. You see the same people, too. You'll see them there for Roxette and then you'll see them for Billy Joel. Some of them follow everyone.

What are some of the stranger things you've seen?
At the back of the hotel there is a flag pole and there was a ladder there so we could pull it up and down. We've had people climbing up there, but it's very hard to actually get in the hotel that way. Some girls walk in and manage to get into the lifts, then they might hide in a linen closet on the floor where the band is staying, and they'll wait until they hear the band in the hallway. One guy got into the laundry through the carpark and put on a hotel uniform. He was trying to get to Coolio. You used to pick up a paper and it would say so-and-so is staying at the Sebel, so everyone would be waiting there from the day before. Now it's more low-key, and they have to find out the information, unless the record company wants people to know. Now there's more security and you need a key to get anywhere and there are cameras everywhere.

What happened when New Kids On The Block stayed there?
These girls knew they were staying there, so they organised a 21st birthday party in the function room. Automatically they could wander into the bar and walk around the hotel. They were sitting in the bar when the group came in, and suddenly there were 30 people rushing around them. It got absolutely crazy.

What about East 17?
They had a very young crowd. All these girls managed to get in and met them up in the pool. The hardest part is when the band says to security, 'It's OK, they can stay with us.' They might be under-age and they might be upsetting the normal clientele, but you can't do anything.

Did you see Prince when he was there?
Prince had incredibly tight security. He came into the bar, and wanted the bar cleared. He sat in the corner, and his manager went out to the crowd and brought in a couple of good-looking girls, and Prince would just talk to them. He drank French wine and Evian. He had his own chef. He had someone to taste the food before he ate it. And they had to redecorate his room.

ON THE INSIDE

Was there anyone you really admired who you got to know through your job?
Mark Knopfler, Elton John, Billy Joel. It was incredible for me getting to know these people, and they always say hello and thank you for looking after them in the bar.

Did you see a lot of drug-taking in your time?
With older bands, they loved to drink and use different drugs. It was very big. There was lots of smoking and lots of cocaine. They would be up at eight o'clock in the morning still partying and I would be thinking, Go to bed! The bar used to take in incredible amounts of money. Elton John used to foot the bill for everybody in the bar.

What about bands picking up women in the bar?
The crew are the ones who meet most of the girls. They say, 'I can give you a ticket to the show tomorrow.' It's sad in a way, because the girls think they're going to get to the band, but they just end up with the sound man. It's rare that they get to meet a star through the sound man. The most they can say is that they went to bed with someone from the crew. There were girls who came into the bar regularly and you'd get to know them. Most of the time it's the men that start everything, even though the women come in there to meet them. Only once or twice have I seen a girl approach the star. Usually it's a manager or someone like that who asks me, 'Who are these beautiful ladies?' or, 'Can you send a drink over there to that girl?' They use the barman as the middle man. It's like a game. The girls are usually in couples, sometimes there's three. But never more than that.

You never felt tempted, with these women being so friendly to you?
I knew the game. I knew they weren't after me. They were after the bands. I'd be naive to think otherwise. For me it was good to have good-looking girls in the bar because it was good for business. So they were using me, but I was using them too.

I'm with the Band

Staff at Australian Concert and Entertainment Security have heard so many excuses from fans trying to get backstage that they immortalised them on a t-shirt. Here's a sample of the lame, the inventive, the desperate, the aggressive and the just plain bizarre:

- I'm a friend of the promoter.
- I went to school with the singer.
- I was backstage at the last gig.
- I'm a journalist—do you want a bad review?
- My sister has got a baby to the drummer.
- They invited me to audition for them.
- I'm on the same label.
- They asked me to bring them some coke.
- I'm in a band, too.
- I'm from MTV.
- I used to see them when they played pubs.
- I'll get you sacked if you don't let me in.
- The band often stays over at my place.
- I want to interview the band.
- The guitarist and I had a flat in Melbourne.
- I'm helping with the catering.
- I won a contest on Triple M to go backstage.
- You let me through before.

FANBREAK

🎸 My band supported them last time they toured.

🎸 Do you know who I am?

🎸 I'm the promoter!

🎸 They ate at my restaurant last night.

🎸 Is that twenty dollars on the ground yours or mine?

🎸 Trust me—would I lie to you?

🎸 I threw my bra at the singer—now I want it back.

🎸 I'm the musican's union rep, checking equity cards.

🎸 I sold them the guitars.

🎸 You can have my two sisters if you let me backstage.

🎸 I'm with the tax department.

🎸 I just want an autograph for my friend.

🎸 I'm the band's assistant manager.

🎸 I'm working on the load-out.

🎸 But I'm with security.

🎸 I'm the support act.

🎸 I drive the limo.

🎸 You know me.

🎸 I printed the t-shirts.

🎸 Molly sent me.

🎸 I'm Richard Wilkins's hairdresser.

🎸 I'm the blond the guitar roadie picked for the lead singer.

🎸 You'll never work in this industry again.

Sophie Howarth

FANTALES

Loretta Tolnay

Michael Jackson

'Fuck!'

It was the greatest moment of Loretta Tolnay's life, and she couldn't stop saying that word over and over again, like a mantra.

'Fuck! Fuck!'

A spotlight was on her, a camera crew was zooming in, and there she was in close-up, beamed onto two huge video screens, watched by 50 000 people.

'Fuck! Fuck! Fuck!'

On 21 November 1987, Loretta made a vow. She had failed to meet Michael Jackson during his Australian tour, but after seeing a girl chosen out of the audience to dance on stage, she made it her personal goal to one day do the same. It was almost nine years to the day when she finally got her chance. It was Jackson's 1996 tour, and she had a plan. First she had to camp out for tickets. She got a seat in the second row, and on the aisle, in a perfect position to be spotted by Jackson's people. She broke down in tears of joy at the ticket office. Then she started to think about how to attract attention to herself on the tour.

'I thought, I'll wear white—that will show up in the dark. So I went out and bought white jeans, white tops, white dresses. I wore white the whole tour, so every time he saw me, he'd go, "There's that girl in white." '

It was a process of total preparation. She started a series of appointments at a tanning salon so her skin would contrast with her clothing. She even bought new underwear. When Jackson arrived in Sydney, she took up permanent residence on the footpath outside the Ritz-Carlton Hotel. On the very first day she managed to hand him a

cylindrical Postpak with a poster inside. She tried to scream over the noise for him to look inside and sign the poster. There was so much screaming from the assembled fans that he just looked a little confused and signed the postpak instead. The camera crew who were following him around on tour decided to film a few fans, and Loretta was one of those chosen.

'Hi Michael, my name's Loretta, and I'm going to be sitting in seat one, Row B, to your left, on Thursday night,' she said into the camera lens. 'I'm going to be wearing white jeans and a white top, and I want you to look for me. And I want to dance with you during "You Are Not Alone".'

She was so excited about the progress she had made on the first day that she stayed outside the hotel until three the following morning. After four hours sleep, she returned at 8 am, and hung around until three the next morning, too—he didn't appear at all in that time, but her spirits were still up.

The next day was the day of the show, so Loretta decided to rest. She and her cousin ate Indian butter chicken for dinner, and she still associates that taste with Michael Jackson today. The two then started getting ready for the night, and they took photos of each other.

'I look at those photos, and I'm already radiant,' she says. 'There's a look about me, like I know that it's going to happen. I'm like a bride. I'm beaming.'

When she got into the Showground that night, she started crying, and couldn't stop. She was so overcome with emotion that the security people were giving her water and trying to calm her down. She managed to vaguely keep things under control. But then the concert started.

'I lost it big time,' she admits. 'I was shaking, I was so hysterical. I was pulling out my hair. I just kept screaming out his name.'

When she finally heard the introduction to 'You Are Not Alone', her cousin grabbed her by the arm, and kept screaming, 'It's you! It's you! It's you!' Just as Loretta was thinking that this might jinx her chances, the light from the camera crew hit her face. She remembers it as being like a scene from 'The X-Files', when the alien mother ship lands.

That's when she started saying, 'Fuck!'

FANTALES

Loretta still can't recall being taken over the stage barrier and up onto the edge of the catwalk. She does recall a roadie with tattoos holding onto her before the big moment and encouraging her to go for it, as this was her one chance to be onstage with Michael Jackson. 'As if I needed any encouragement! I felt like a greyhound or a racehorse in the stalls, waiting for the gates to open.'

But then when the big moment came, she froze. A mere two metres away from her idol, she was rooted to the spot. The roadie finally shoved her in the general direction of Jackson. What happened over the next one and a half minutes is something that Loretta has obviously gone over and over again in her mind ever since. As she recounts the story, her voice occasionally breaks with emotion.

'I ran towards him and grabbed his hands. I stopped for a second and then I just grabbed him so hard that I bumped the microphone. He's so strong. He's incredibly muscular. I was afraid that he'd arch his back and give me a fake hug and try not to touch me. But it was amazing. It was full body contact. He was rubbing my back. I was just touching every part that I could, within reason. He was really being warm back. I wanted him so much to know how much love I had for him. And the smell was intoxicating, it was all over me.

'Michael, of course, is the consummate dancer, and I'm not. People spoke to me afterwards and they thought it was rehearsed, because I actually managed to do this little twirly dance thing. Michael leads but makes it look like you're leading. He can do that. Then he broke away from me and I was just standing there, and he kneeled at my feet. That was when I became aware of the audience. I looked over to my left and there were 50 000 people, and there's Michael Jackson kneeling at my feet. I couldn't take not touching him when I knew I could, so I leaned down and grabbed him and pulled him up.

'I was feeling such rapture and such love that I just went down on my knees and grabbed him around the legs and I remember thinking, Be careful, don't touch it. I'm attracted to him, but I don't think I'd like it if a stranger buried their head in my crotch. So I was careful. I wasn't aware at the time, but watching the tape, I realise I did touch his backside quite a bit. I couldn't help it.

'That was the point when my total fantasy and dream had come true. I was totally unaware of everything else but Michael. I just

189

Mission accomplished—Loretta and Michael share a quiet moment on stage.

closed my eyes and I was away in another galaxy. Then he leaned down and pulled me up. He held his hand under my jaw and looked over my shoulder. I knew that then the minders were coming, so I wrapped my arms around him and kissed him all over the face. I was talking in his ear going, "I love you. Thank you so much." And he said, "I love you."

'When they grabbed me, my legs just went like jelly. They had to drag me away. As I was taken off the stage I turned around one more time, and the last thing I saw was the most beautiful thing—Michael standing there smiling and singing and reaching out for me, like he didn't want me to go.

FANTALES

'I wasn't nervous or scared when I was up there, because in my mind I'd rehearsed it so many times. It wasn't until I got off that suddenly my chest went tight and I couldn't breathe.'

After the show it took Loretta over an hour to get back to her car, because other fans recognised her and kept stopping to talk. Some wanted to touch her. Some asked for a hug, and she obliged them if she thought they were genuine. Some of them wanted to smell the top she was wearing, because it still had strong traces of Jackson's scent on it. It was the only time Loretta ever wore that top. She keeps it sealed in a plastic bag to preserve the aroma.

Of all the albums, books, t-shirts, scrapbooks and memorabilia she owns, if her house was burning down, the one thing Loretta Tolnay would take with her is the 90 seconds of video footage from that night.

'Everyone said, "Get real, 50 000 people and he's going to pick you?" ' But I did it. Getting on stage was more about me and less about Michael. It was about achieving my goal and doing what I always swore I was going to do, and proving everybody wrong.'

BREAKING UP IS HARD TO DO

'This is the end, my only friend, the end'

—The Doors, 'The End'

As Neil Sedaka (and, later, David Cassidy) so succinctly put it, 'cumma cumma down doobie doo down down, cumma cumma down doobie doo down down, cumma cumma down doobie doo down down, breaking up is hard to-oo-oo do'.

Although Sedaka probably had a guy/girl thing in mind (while David possibly thought of some teenybopper he'd bedded the night before), the sentiment easily crosses over to the band/fan relationship. You invest love, devotion, obsession, adoration and not inconsequential sums of money into a band, and unless they're The Rolling Stones or Kiss, who are apparently going to be the last things left on Earth after a nuclear holocaust apart from cockroaches, one day you're going to hear the announcement. The group is splitting up. It's all over. And where does that leave you?

'I am sorry—but I suppose, inevitably it had to happen.' It sounds like the opening of a Dear John letter, preparing the recipient for some bad news, letting him know that it's been great, but all things must end, and there's the door, don't slam it on the way out.

In fact, it's the opening line from the last letter to members of The Beatles fanclub in March 1972, officially announcing that almost two years after the band split, they were closing up shop. Ringo couldn't have made the blow any less harsh by being quoted as saying, 'It seems pointless to keep alive a myth.'

The myth was that the four members of The Beatles were still the chirpy, chummy bunch of mop-tops they had been in the early 1960s, when they first appeared on the scene. In April 1970, fractured by jealousies, romantic liaisons, lawyers and failed business ventures, not to mention that old 'musical differences' chestnut, they did the unthinkable. They broke up the band. Freda Kelly, who ran The Beatles fanclub, wrote to fans: 'Well, there it is … eleven years in which we have become a very strong, happy and close circle of friends, the like of which has never been seen, and it is likely never to be seen again, in the pop music industry.'

But on that last point she was wrong.

The strong, happy, close circle of friends which had built up around a common love for The Beatles would not be a one-off experience. The hysteria which was so great that it warranted its own term—Beatlemania—would happen with other groups who weren't necessarily major musical forces or critics' favourites: The Osmonds, The Bay City Rollers, Kiss, Sherbert, Duran Duran, New Kids On The Block.

The thirteenth of February 1996. If you were outside the teen-pop demographic in the 1990s, then this date won't mean anything to you. For followers of Take That, however, that day is their own personal 'Where were you when you found out JFK was shot?' experience.

BREAKING UP IS HARD TO DO

The Manchester quintet mightn't have even made a blip on your consciousness if you were outside the loop. After all, they only ever made two studio albums in their five years together. But to Take That fans, they are the most important group in the history of music. And they'll tell you that without a trace of doubt or irony.

In July of the previous year they had suffered a loss when Robbie Williams left the group. The token bad boy of the bunch, the tabloids had a field day reporting on his drinking and drug-taking, and featured snaps of him hanging out with his new buddies, the Gallagher brothers from Oasis. There was also a dispute as to whether he left of his own free will or if he was sacked. Whatever the case, phone lines were set up in the UK to console grieving fans. The other four members had vowed to go on without him.

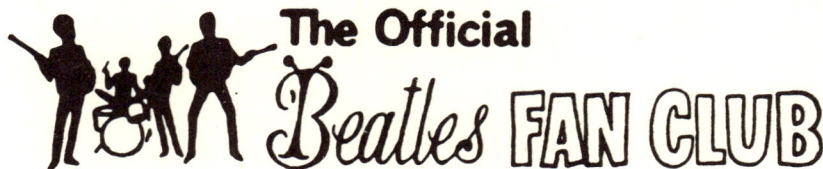

Sue Stafford

The Official
Beatles FAN CLUB

P.O. BOX No. 12, LIVERPOOL 1.
Telephone 051-709 2410.

Well . . . . this is, as you will doubtless have read in many sections of the Press, the last Newsletter. I am sorry — but I suppose, inevitably it had to happen. The Beatles are no longer together as a group, they are no more as a collective entity . . . . John, Paul, George and Ringo have each gone their separate ways, doing their own things and achieving great individual successes.

As I say, the Beatles no longer exist — and perhaps Ringo summed up the matter most concisely when he said "it seems pointless to keep alive a myth".

But this is no time for tears — it is one for happiness. For we all thank you very deeply for your support, your very great loyalty over the years and for me personally this friendship has helped to make the eleven years that the Club has been running a period of considerable happiness to which your letters, your thoughts, were a great and abiding contributiory factor.

Brett Price, who is now 25, travelled to England following his idols. He arrived on 12 February 1996, in the late afternoon, and collapsed into bed after the long flight. The next morning, at six o'clock, he switched on the television and couldn't believe what he heard.

'The first thing I saw was the announcement that Take That had split. My mouth hit the floor and I rang my friends, Tony and Julie, screaming. I was the only one over there from Australia for the break-up. Then I found out there was going to be a press conference on the Tuesday. I remember all of London standing still and listening to the radio. Girls were running out of schools crying.

'It didn't hit me until I saw the Brit Awards a week later and Chris Evans introduced them, and I thought, This is it. It's finished. Then I went to 'Top of the Pops' and stood outside for six freezing cold hours. They saw me and gave me a cuddle and told me to take care of myself, and they were off. I had a tear in my eye after that because a lot of fans realised that was the end, that was the last time they'd ever be on "Top of the Pops" as a group.'

I run into Brett's friend Tony Hamlyn at a Boyzone instore appearance in a shopping mall. He's had a history of dealing with break-ups and feels that he's learned from the experience.

'I'll be ready when Boyzone say it, but in the past I haven't been ready for it. There have been tears in the past, definitely. When I was fourteen I remember thinking, Is there life after Wham? When Matt and Luke Goss from Bros went their separate ways I thought I was going to die.

'But when Take That announced their split, that was a very sad day. People laugh at you and say, 'How could you be so pathetic?' but when you actually put that much heart and soul into something and you're that passionate about something and then all of a sudden it's over, you can't help but get upset.'

At least Brett and Tony actually got to see the group play. Others weren't so lucky. The most common word they use when describing their reaction to the break-up is 'devastated'.

'I missed out on the last Take That concert because I was in hospital,' said Theresa, 28. 'I consoled myself by saying they would come back, and then they broke up on me. I was devastated.'

'I came to school crying the next day,' said Stacey, thirteen. 'I was at home and my friends came over and said they'd heard on the radio that Take That had split up. And I went, "Oh yeah, sure." Then I heard it on the radio and I cried all night, and all the next morning. Shocking. I was devastated.'

'I was just so shocked because I knew they wouldn't come out again,' said Emma, sixteen. 'I'd missed the concert because of my stupid parents. They planned a holiday and I was so annoyed. I found out when a friend told me at assembly at school. I was devastated. I just started crying, it was so sad.'

At the press conference, while the remaining four members fended off probing questions with talk of finishing on top and looking forward to future projects, there was special emphasis placed on the role of the fans. This is a band which started out making four concert appearances a day—two in clubs at night, and two in schools during the day.

BREAKING UP IS HARD TO DO

'We hope the fans will understand that we feel we have done all we can do as Take That,' reasoned Mark Owen, the shortest member of Take That, and the most vocal during the final conference. 'We do very much care for the welfare of our fans, and if there are any problems I'm sure we can set up phone lines or whatever to sort that out, definitely.'

A year after he said those words, fans were still posting their feelings about the split on the Internet, and recalling where they were and how they reacted when they got the news. Page after page was filled with talk of crying for days, missing school, and retreating to bedrooms. One sixteen-year-old revealed that she stopped eating, and her family was so concerned that they took her to see a doctor, fearing for her health. A seventeen-year-old from Melbourne wrote, 'I ran into my room, grabbed the Mark doll and threw it, tore down some posters, sat on my bed, hit everything in sight, cried for ten million years, got depressed, rang people to cry with, and made my bedroom into a shrine.'

Most of those who logged onto the site talked about feeling numb, angry, sad and confused. These stages sound an awful lot like the periods one goes through when someone close has passed away. For these fans' someone close *had* passed away. Even though Gary Barlow, Mark Owen, Jason Orange, Robbie Williams and Howard Donald were still very much alive, the entity that they represented, Take That, was finished. Naturally, the diehards would follow the solo careers with interest, but the five- then, later, four-headed beast was the thing that had galvanised these kids. And now the beast was dead.

Peter Green has been through the death of a few beasts in his time. A public relations person who now organises fans' activities for a number of groups, he was involved in the final Crowded House concert, and was amazed at the outpouring of goodwill from fans who volunteered to work on stalls selling t-shirts, the proceeds of which were benefitting a children's hospital in Sydney. They would work all day for free, with only one stipulation. When Crowded House got onstage, the hospital would have to organise their own people to man the stalls.

After the concert, Green saw Neil Finn, who confided that he wasn't really able to cry. Green reminded him that he'd probably used up all his tears the first time around, when his first band, Split Enz, called it a day.

'I'm a tough old bastard, and that's one of the first times I cried,' Green recalls. 'I remember being at Festival Hall for the Enz With A Bang tour. When I saw Neil cry, I started crying too. Everywhere I looked people were crying, even some of the toughest people, like the road crew. No-one could help it.'

His first love had died years before that, however. As a teenager, Green had latched onto Skyhooks, and even after Red Symons and then Shirley Strachan left the fold, he remained loyal to them. The band's final album, *Hot For The Orient*, was released in 1980, and wasn't received favourably. Even Molly Meldrum, who gave just about everything a thumbs-up and a 'do yourself a favour' on 'Countdown', had slagged it off. Green organised fans to deluge the ABC with letters of outrage. 'I remember writing about 70 myself,' he recalls with a laugh.

Skyhooks were scheduled to appear on 'Countdown' soon afterwards, so Green turned up with a bunch of other fans, and was surprised to get a message from the band to meet him in the dressing-room.

'They said 'We've got something to tell you, you better have a drink.' I said "What? Are you going to break up?" And they said, 'Actually, we are. We're going to host "Countdown", but not tell Molly that it's over, so he can't get the scoop, so make sure no-one says a word.'

'At the time I was just really pissed off with Molly. He knew something weird was happening. He leaned over to Paddy (who looked after the door at 'Countdown') and said, "I'm really worried about the Skyhooks fans—I think they're going to get me." '

Subsequently, Meldrum called all the Skyhooks fans to sit around him. To this day, Green thinks Meldrum thought they would attack him en masse, and would refrain from doing so only if they were on camera. The next morning it was revealed in the paper that Skyhooks had broken up, so Molly didn't get the scoop.

'Skyhooks got me through a difficult period in my life,' Green says, when asked about the way he felt at the end. 'There are certain times in your life that are really not the best and that was one of them. The music helped me a lot. It was a great escape from a bitter reality. The band was really wonderful to us.'

New Year's Eve came early to Sydney in 1996. On Sunday, 24 November, to be exact.

Around the Sydney Opera House, they started gathering in their thousands from two in the afternoon. The previous two days had been unseasonably cold and blustery, but now the sky was blue and the sun was beating down. Vendors had set up makeshift barbecues to sell sausages. There was a festive feel in the air.

But the true giveaway that this was on a par with the last evening of the year was that people were selling large plastic bugles and those thin wormy necklaces filled with fluorescent liquid. Go figure.

The reason for this get-together? Crowded House, who had announced earlier in the year that they had decided to lock the door and throw away the key, were playing one final farewell concert. Who knew they would attract so many well-wishers? Why did this band, who played catchy yet strangely melancholy, low-key pop songs, whip up such an outpouring of goodwill from the public?

As they made their way through a performance that topped the two-hour mark, there were no stomping rhythms or screaming riffs. You don't punch the air to a Crowded House song, although

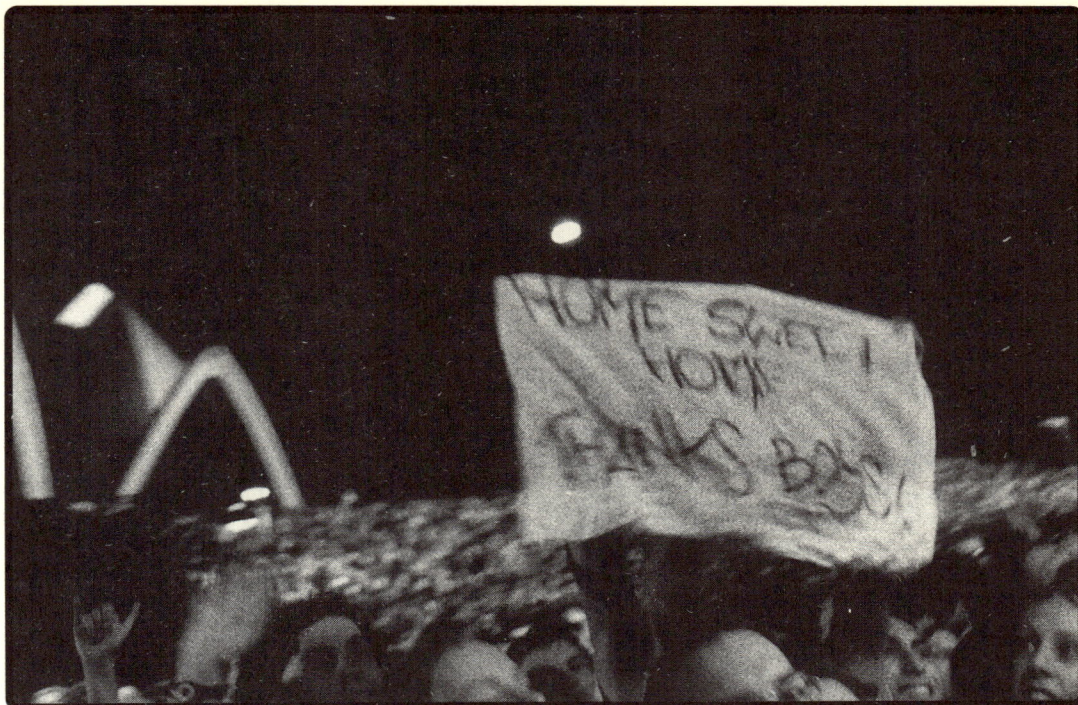

Sophie Howarth

Don't dream, it's over—fans at the Crowded House farewell concert.

many managed to crowd-surf, possibly one of the strangest imaginable soundtracks to that particular activity.

Somehow this group galvanised people. Tens of thousands waved their arms slowly from side to side during the lilting 'Four Seasons In One Day', and the effect was like a gigantic sea anemone stranded on the steps of the Opera House. I usually detest the old crowd singalong manoeuvre, but here it made sense, as Neil Finn allow the assembled to do their own chorus of 'Better Be Home Soon'. Even though there were at least 100 000 people crammed in (more enthusiastic estimates said up to 200 000) under very uncomfortable circumstances, there was a soothing feel to the massed chorus, almost as if they didn't want to break the spell.

Because, after all, this was a farewell. It had been ten years. There had been four albums in that time. And as Finn pointed out from the stage on that very Sydney kind of night, none of the band members even came from this city (although drummer Paul Hester cheekily points out that he had deposited some sperm there from time to time). There was a kind of reverie and a genuine feeling of community that was diametrically opposite to the corporate grandiosity of the Michael Jackson-meets-the-people stunt of the previous week.

'I suppose this is a funeral but it feels more like a celebration,' noted an obviously emotional Finn from the stage towards the end.

And he was right. The final two songs could easily become national anthems. In fact, anyone under the age of 50 can probably recall the lyrics more readily than those of 'Advance Australia Fair' or 'Waltzing Matilda', and their message of love and hope would do the job at Olympic ceremonies. A sparse and rousing cover of Hunters & Collectors' 'Throw Your Arms Around Me' had us all swaying patriotically in the breeze, and, finally, the last song Crowded House would ever perform, the gorgeous, swooning 'Don't Dream It's Over' drifted across the harbour, with every pair of lungs crooning the chorus with them.

'Goodbye, farewell, auf wiedersehn, goodnight,' boomed the Von Trapp family over the PA as fireworks explode across the night sky.

'I ran into two ex-girlfriends tonight, and they were with each other,' a guy marvelled to his friend. 'How weird is that?'

'Everyone was so happy and friendly—why doesn't that happen at other gigs?' a girl asked her companion.

Meanwhile, a conga line had developed as a sea of tired, blissful faces looked on, and we trudged our way back to Circular Quay. Crowded House waved goodbye, and for one night, they made us all feel like their flatmates.

There are good break-ups and bad break-ups. Some pull the plug at a peak or at least manage to leave with dignity. Many more go out with a whimper, a long time after their use-by date, smelling faintly of desperation. But whatever the manner of their exit, the strength of the bond between a fan and a band can't be underestimated. Like any relationship, it may have suffered setbacks along the way, but when you're waving goodbye and later flicking through the old record collection, as often happens after a bust-up, the feelings of loss are very real indeed.

I Hate the Music

As a great pop guru once wisely put it, for every action there is an equal and opposite reaction. The mass adulation and booming record sales of any big group will be counteracted by a bunch of naysayers who claim the band are a gaggle of no-talent idiots who are clogging up the airwaves and saturating the magazine market. Conveniently, most of these people live on the Internet, so it's easy to hear their gripes. They care enough to construct Web pages outlining in detail their hatred of particular groups, coming up with devious ways to demonstrate their feelings, then inevitably getting besieged with hate mail from fans, and causing an e-mail war in the process. Everybody hates somebody some time, and most of them are floating around cyberspace with their knives out, but here are the five big targets of the anti-fans.

Alanis Morissette

A surprisingly popular whipping girl among the anti-brigade. I was the 41 013th person to visit the People Against Alanis Morissette's Music page, but it was at the end of its cyber-tether. It seems that the page was receiving so much hate mail, racist comments, lewd sexual remarks, and even death threats, that they decided to call it a day. Apparently, like Alanis herself, her fans are not too familiar with the meaning of the word 'ironic'. Both this site and the I Hate Alanis Morissette's 'Music' Page (originally the I Hate Alanis Morissette Page—note the subtle difference) were at pains to point out that they wished the Canadian crooner no harm personally, nor did they want all her fans to suffer terrible deaths. It's just her music that bugs them. The main thrust of these pages appears to be that (a) Alanis is a sell-out because she basically used to be the Debbie Gibson of Canada, and (b) her music sucks. They point out that they don't support the 'Abuse Alanis' page. I immediately went there, and found a place where you could click on a picture of Morissette and progressively leave her more battered. Tasteful.

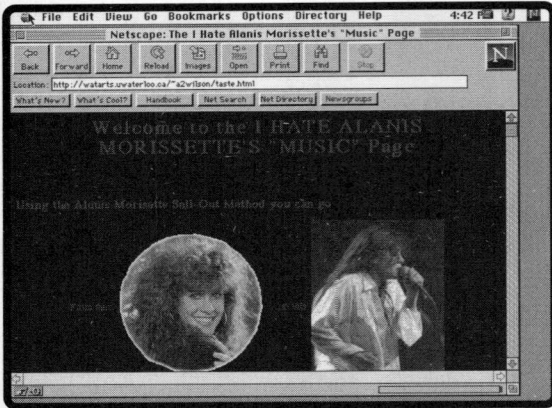

Oasis

The Official I Hate Oasis Page has two main arguments. One is that Liam is a monkey, and they have photographic evidence to back this up. The second is that he just has one continuous eyebrow rather than the standard-issue two. Very convincing and well argued.

Hanson

The three blond kids from Oklahoma not only became very popular very quickly, but they rapidly overtook most of the other regulars on the Web's most hated list, as anti-sites mushroomed soon after the release of their first single. Citizens For A Hanson Free America offers a glossary of common spelling and grammatical mistakes in hate letters to their site. With surveys such as 'What torture is most suitable for the Hanson brothers?' and the top-ten rejected Hanson movie titles, including *Two Girls and a Baby* and *Honey, I Exploited the Kids,* they can be assured of plenty of e-mail into the future. Hanson Is Evil uses mathematical formulae and Bible verses to prove that the pop trio is in fact the beast of the apocalypse. And just to prove that those fighting in the pop wars can occasionally join together, The Hanson Controversy is a site run by a Hanson lover and a Hanson hater, each giving their side of the story. One page is called Die Hanson! and the other is Hansonette. You figure out who's for and who's against.

silverchair

The Novocastrian trio don't escape the torch of anti-fans, either. At one point in 1997, silverchair's official Website was number two in the most visited music sites list, and I Hate silverchair was breathing down its neck at number five. One site is devoted to silverchair 'movies', which are basically roughly-drawn storyboard cartoons. In 'Nice To Meet You' the band gets shot. In 'Di-ing To Meet You', they get run over in 'la tunnel' after a gig in

Paris. And in 'Silver Fiction', the following exchange borrows dialogue from Quentin Tarantino.

You know what they call silverchair in France?

You mean they don't call them talentless little prats?

Nope, they call them 'le crap band'.

Man, that is seriously weird. What do they call Daniel over there?

They don't call him anything different over there. He is still known as 'dork'.

The Spice Girls

By far the five most popular backlash targets—and possibly the most criticised identities on the Net, full stop—are Scary, Sexy, Sporty, Posh and Baby. There are numerous hate sites, with self-explanatory names like Death To Spice Girls, Spice Girls Hate Organisation, Spice Girls! Kill! Kill! Kill! and Shite Girls. Here are just a few of the Spicy delights you'll find on these pages:

One of the most popular sites (and why not?) is Slap A Spice Girl, where you have to use your mouse to bash each girl on the head when they pop up from a series of holes on your screen. Extra points are given if you manage to hit the elusive original Spice Girl, Margaret Thatcher. Malky Alky, the chap who came up with this one, is himself one of the most hated people on the Net, and has incurred the wrath of Spice fans everywhere. Now he includes a disclaimer at the bottom of his page: 'This game does not in any way condone hitting women. It makes a joke out of delivering a cartoon slap to the manufactured, Tory loving, plastic, cartoon phenomenon that is The Spice Girls. The game delivers a cartoon slap to pretend people making pretend music in a pretend showbiz world.'

The Spice Girls Hate Organisation includes doctored pictures of the girls, featuring Victoria with facial hair and Emma dressed as Satan. Sporty Spice's picture is left alone. They consider her bad enough as she is.

Nick & Dave's Spice Girls Page includes their Ten Comandments, such as 'thy navel must forever be uncovered', 'thou must always dress according to thy Spicy nickname', and 'thou shalt not speak of Mel A'.

You'll find pages and pages of Spice Girls jokes. Sample?

Q: A blonde and The Spice Girls jumped off the Empire State Building. Who landed first?

A: The blonde. The Spice Girls had to stop and ask for directions.

'The Top 15 Questions On A Spice Tart Application' include 'Do you have any detectible vestige of talent, besides your hooters?', 'Choose an appropriate nickname: Sexy, Nasty, Sweetie, Chlamydia' and 'Explain the difficulties in identifying the source of individual free will in light of the deterministic theories of neurochemical medicine and modern behaviouralist psychology. Just kidding! Seriously, do you like leather mini-skirts?'

COME TOGETHER IV

Truly Madly Deeply

THE DATE: 25 MARCH 1997
THE PLACE: BLOCKBUSTER RECORD STORE, SYDNEY
THE OCCASION: SAVAGE GARDEN IN-STORE APPEARANCE
FANS: TINA, SEVENTEEN, AND KATRINA, NINETEEN

Why are you giving them flowers?
We have to give them flowers because they're great people and they deserve it. We've been into them since they came out.

What do you want to say to them when you meet them?
Can we have your babies?

Courtesy of Roadshow Music

205

What do Savage Garden songs say to you?
That they would treat a girl really good.

Can you see a time when you won't be into Savage Garden anymore?
No way. We'll always be into them.

Were you ever into New Kids On The Block?
No way. They're so gay.

Why are Savage Garden better than New Kids?
I don't know. These are hard questions. Don't ask us questions like that! We're too in awe.

FAN: DANIEL, EIGHTEEN
Is it hard being a Savage Garden fan who also happens to be a guy?
I don't know how many guys here actually like their music or if they're just here with girls, but I'm here because I bought the stuff. I heard their first single when it came out and it automatically clicked. Every song since then has been even better. I just like the music. The only singers I have everything of are John Farnham and Bon Jovi. This is going to be the next one.

Why Savage Garden?
They're different. A lot of the music coming out now is heavy metal, techno or rap with a lot of swearing and stuff. These guys know how to express themselves without that. They're musicians. Their songs have a lot more meaning than people notice.

What is 'I Want You' about?
It depends on who you're playing it for.

FAN: REBECCA, FOURTEEN
What do you like about Savage Garden?
Their music is different and they have good film clips and they sing good.

FANBREAK

Some people say they sound like Tears For Fears ...
Who's that?

A band from the 1980s. Have you heard of Duran Duran?
I've heard of them but I've never heard their music.

THE DATE: 6 MAY 1997
THE PLACE: ENMORE THEATRE, SYDNEY
THE OCCASION: SAVAGE GARDEN LIVE

FAN: JESSIE, SIXTEEN
How did you first hear them?
I'm blown out that I like them at all, because I'm a Pearl Jam, Stone Temple Pilots, Metallica person. My friend Sally played me 'Santa Monica' and I just fell in love. Then I bought the album and here we are. I had a dream that 'Santa Monica' was playing and I was in America. I don't want to tell you the rest because it was very risqué.

Are there any bands you used to like that now you're embarrassed about it?
New Kids, Bobby Brown, Girlfriend.

You were really into New Kids?
Oh yeah. Remember those mini tapes they used to have filled with bubblegum? Oh wow. Now I would not touch them with a ten-foot pole.

You don't think the same thing will happen with Savage Garden?
These songs will keep going because they're mellower. With New Kids, it was like, 'Hanging Tough'.

FANS: MELISSA, SEVENTEEN, AND ANDREA, SEVENTEEN
How do you feel?
Very, very nervous. I love Savage Garden. I can't wait.

What is it about them?
They're hot. Their lyrics are poetic and they have excellent music. They're appealing. I'm a huge fan. I have a scrapbook full of every single article I can find on them. I've got their CD and now I have a t-shirt and a poster. This is the first concert I've ever been to. They're going to be excellent. I'm freaking out.

I'm freaking out, too. *(they start to giggle, hyperventilating)*

They're just really cool. They write their own lyrics and their own music and they're cute. *(giggles)*

They have this appeal about them so that you can't stop listening and looking at them. *(giggles)*

They're just yum. *(giggles)*

THE DATE: 21 SEPTEMBER 1997
THE PLACE: MELBOURNE
THE OCCASION: It's the day before Melinda Ruffels, a sixteen-year-old schoolgirl, is due to have breakfast with Darren Hayes and Daniel Jones of Savage Garden. She won a radio station competition.

What is it about Savage Garden that makes you love them so much?
It's their music, and they're just the best guys ever. They're just so talented. After listening to interviews and seeing them on TV, I just thought they were excellent.

What did you think when you first heard them?
I'm ashamed to say this, but I didn't like them at the start. I thought they were girls. In their first film clip, 'I Want You', I really thought they were girls. Then I loved 'To The Moon And Back' and 'Truly Madly Deeply'.

Are you nervous about meeting them tomorrow?
I'm really nervous. I don't know what I'm going to say. I've been shopping all week for clothes—new pants, new top, new shoes, new make-up. I want to make a good impression. I've bought them presents, too. I got a big chocolate record and I'm buying them some roses.

FANBREAK

What's the most most fanatical thing you've done?
I sat by the phone for two weeks when they were running the competition. From the start I said, 'I'm going to win, I'm going to win.' I tried every night and couldn't get through. Then on this particular night the phone rang through and my heart started beating. I was just crazy.

Do all your friends like Savage Garden?
Some people at school hate them. I don't talk to them. They're usually big fans of someone else, so they should know how I feel.

Do you have a favourite member of the two?
Yep, Darren. He's gorgeous. Daniel's good-looking too, but Darren's my favourite.

What happened when you found out he was married?
I was crying. I was home from school that day, and after school my friend rang me and said, 'Are you sitting down? He's married.' We both started crying. He doesn't talk about it much. It's his own business, so I suppose it's private to him.

Are you over it now?
Well … yeah … I suppose. I want to know who she is. Some people have been saying it's one of the back-up singers. You don't know, do you?

Er, no.
I hope it's not one of them. I don't like them.

Why? Because they're too close to the band?
Yeah, kind of.

So you get jealous of them?
Yeah, I do.

Do you ever dream about them?
I had one dream that I missed an interview on television. That was really bad. It was something about a new single. I hate missing stuff

about them on telly. And I've got a file of stuff on them. I'm probably a bit obsessive. I buy all the magazines they're in and I can't miss any pictures of them.

Do you think your love for Savage Garden is something that will fade?
No way.

Who were you into two years ago?
I liked Take That, but not as much as this. I've never been into anyone as much as this.

THE DATE: 23 SEPTEMBER 1997
THE PLACE: MELBOURNE
THE OCCASION: The day after the big breakfast.

So, tell me about the whole day.
I got up at 3.30 in the morning and the flight was at six o'clock. Because I'd never flown before, I wasn't sure if I was really nervous because of the plane or if it was because I was meeting them. I think it was meeting them. I was feeling sick and my legs were like jelly. I was so nervous. The girl from 2DAY FM picked me up at the airport. We went straight to the Sebel Townhouse and I met Leonie (the group's promotions manager) from Roadshow. Then we went into this little room and there was a big fruit platter and food everywhere. I didn't eat anything. I felt really sick and nervous and I wasn't sure what I was going to say to them. Then some people from 2DAY and Roadshow turned up, and Leonie went to get them. The door was closed and I heard Daniel's voice outside. My heart was beating so bad. And then they walked in, and I had tears in my eyes. I hugged them, and then they sat me down between them.

What did you talk about?
I just looked at them for a while. Daniel was asking me about how I won and what year I was in. Darren was just on a high and happy to be home. They'd just arrived from Germany on Sunday night. He was talking and talking. They ordered their food. Do you want me to tell you what they ate?

FANBREAK

Can you remember?
Of course! Darren was eating some fruit at the start, then he had an omelette with mushrooms, because he's vegetarian, and he left his tomato. Daniel had some scrambled eggs and bacon and sausages.

What about you?
I didn't have a thing. I had an orange juice and that's all. I just couldn't eat. I was really nervous. Darren was talking about overseas and he was saying that in Tokyo everyone smoked, and he doesn't like that. Daniel smokes. That surprised me. I didn't know that. He went out to have a cigarette afterwards. We got on to Hanson and Daniel reckons that that little Zac guy doesn't play the drums. That was interesting.

Overall, did they live up to your expectations?
Darren was what I expected. Just a beautiful person and really nice and sweet, and he talked a lot. I don't know what I was expecting

from Daniel, but he was different. I can't explain it. They were really nice guys. There's no way I was disappointed.

What do your friends think about all this?
All last night and today my friends were ringing me, wanting to know what it was like. I got all my singles signed and my Savage Garden top and my favourite picture. And they also gave me this plaque with their CD cover and a thing thanking me for showing my support.

Now that you've met them and hugged them and had breakfast and got everything signed, is there anything else you could wish for?
No. It was like my dream come true. I don't think I can believe it yet. It doesn't feel real to me. There's nothing else I could ask for, unless they wanted to get married. *(laughs)*

THE DATE: 11 NOVEMBER 1997
THE PLACE: Brisbane
THE OCCASION: Darren Hayes shares some thoughts on his fans via mobile phone.

I love being someone that people want to meet. I enjoy inspiring people. It's a big compliment when someone comes up to you and says, 'Your song changed my life', or, 'I look up to you' or when little kids say, 'You're my hero'—that's the most humbling thing that anyone could ever say to you. It's just beautiful. If I'm feeling sick or whatever, I'd rather not do a meet-and-greet because I don't want to disappoint someone. What if for one hour out of your day you're feeling tired and grumpy, and in that hour you meet someone who's your biggest fan? That will be their impression of you forever. When someone meets you in the street, that's their one moment, and if you're just remotely cool, they'll see you as arrogant. I'm beginning to realise how many people I meet and how many hands I shake, and I don't remember them all. You smile and you pose for photographs, but it doesn't really leave a lasting impression.

As a fan, you delude yourself that you'll be the one and you'll have this special bond, but there's only so much room in a person's life for special relationships. My world of friendships and relationships is actually shrinking—I've got my wife, my best friends, Daniel and my immediate family. That's pretty much my whole world. There isn't room for people to get close outside of that. So you try to give the love you have in performance and the work that you do. You physically couldn't satisfy the need that's out there. Someone like Michael Jackson has it down pat—he's completely inaccessible because if he tried to satisfy that need he'd go insane.

BANDS AS FANS

Darren Hayes from Savage Garden

When I was a kid I worshipped Michael Jackson. I used to collect every single picture of Michael ever printed. I used to think I was Michael. I wrote him a fan letter once. I was about sixteen. I wrote this seventeen-page letter, and said things like, 'I love the sound of your buckles when you move, Michael—is this intentional?' My favourite albums of his are the older ones like *Off The Wall* and *Thriller*. He doesn't really exist in the same way for me anymore. I enjoy Michael from a distance now. I don't understand him anymore.

It's been Bono for ages. My brother had been into U2 for years, but they were a little bit too rock and roll for me. I remember listening to *Achtung Baby* in my car six months after it came out and I just thought, Oh my god! I get this! It completely made sense to me. I think the reason my hair is black is because of Bono. I wanted to be like him. Around the time of *ZOO TV* I decided that I had to own the vinyl pants and the wrap-around fly shades. As a performer, he gave me the confidence I didn't have. Before we got a record deal I was masquerading as Bono for a couple of years. I'm a mimic—I just transferred my ability to pretend to be Michael Jackson to my ability to pretend to be Bono. By the time we made our own music I realised I could sound like me and our music could sound like us. That day was quite liberating, but he definitely influenced me.

As far as collecting stuff, with Michael, it was like when you're a kid from a lower-middle-class home, you buy a cheap K-Mart red vinyl jacket that kind of looks like the one in *Thriller*, and you get your mum to take your pants up to the required length so you can see the white socks. With U2, I'd collect coloured vinyl, limited-edition discs, rare designs, bootlegs, anything I could get my hands on. I carry a lot of my U2 stuff around in a CD folder and its probably my most prized possession. I carry it on most aeroplanes with my Walkman.

BANDS AS FANS

We went to see the Pop Mart show in LA. I was front-row centre. I was surrounded by these kids who absolutely adored him. A few people recognised me, but I was just thinking, I don't care—I'm a fan and I'm in the front row! I stared at him the whole show and watched every tiny little thing he did. We got backstage passes and had the chance to go and meet them, but I chose not to. Seeing U2 in LA was like being backstage at the magic show and seeing a few tricks, and I was just enjoying having an idol, someone I can still keep on a pedestal. I realised I didn't want to be the one-millionth hand that Bono had shaken.

Courtesy of Roadshow Music

THE DAY THE MUSIC DIED

'The letter said that he was a hero, she should be proud he died that way—I heard she threw the letter away'

—Paper Lace, 'Billy Don't Be A Hero'

217

Every picture tells a story, and in this particular snapshot my eyes are going in independent directions and there's dried wax on my hands.

It's 16 August 1994, and I'm outside Gracelands with my friend Frank. We're wearing matching Elvis memorial t-shirts, and apart from looking like a couple of dorks, we're looking worse for wear. It's 2.30 in the morning, and we have just spent three hours in a long line with flickering candles in hand. It's towards the end of a pilgrimage which has taken us from Los Angeles, across Arizona, Texas and Arkansas. Our aim? To stop at every tacky roadside attraction we can possibly find in two weeks. Highlights have included The World's Biggest Roadrunner, Tiny Town in Hot Springs, and an amusement park outside Austin, Texas, which is built around the talents of Ralph, a swimming pig.

And we've finally made it to the biggest, tackiest, most famous roadside attraction of all.

There's only one day each year that you can actually walk up the driveway of the King's mansion and reverently pause at his graveside with candlewax dripping down your arm. For the rest of the year, you can only gain access by buying a ticket across the road then boarding a minibus for the 30-second drive to the front steps. But we're here on the anniversary of Elvis Presley's death. And we're in for the long haul.

Earlier in the day we found ourselves speaking to a skinny, balding impersonator from Wisconsin, who wiggled his hips almost exactly the way Elvis didn't. We also had an audience with a thirtyish guy at the very front of the line at the gates of Graceland. He told us that he'd been there for three days. 'At least he's not addicted to drugs or alcohol,' a woman beside us interjected as we tried to talk to him about his Elvis obsession. 'He's not weird, you know.'

It turned out that this was his mother.

Meanwhile, a bunch of men and women in matching red t-shirts line-danced to the Elvis tunes that's constantly piped over the loudspeaker system as if it's heavenly muzak. It was kind of like a David Lynch film.

As the line laboriously moves a metre at a time and we snake our way towards the gate, we pass impersonators, couples dressed in tuxedos and ballgowns, eight-year-olds with stick-on sideburns, families in co-ordinated home-made outfits, and one woman who silently mouths words while clutching a prayer shawl.

But a funny thing happens as we get near the end of our journey. As we look back into a darkness that is punctuated with hundreds and hundreds of flickering candles, we both get a little bit misty. Sure, we've been taking all of this with largish bags of salt. But we're also fans. We realise this whole operation is a kitsch merchandising exercise, but maybe all those Elvisly thoughts being sent up by the assembled throng are actually having an effect. We arrived with a strange mix of cynicism and true fandom, but by the time we get to the graveside then wander back past all those points of light, we understand that there is genuine feeling coming from these people.

Elvis mightn't have meant shit to Public Enemy, but he really was a hero to these folks.

THE DAY THE MUSIC DIED

Exactly three years later, and I'm trying to keep my footing in Melbourne. The wind is howling through a cemetery in Carlton. It threatens to blow away the small but faithful group of people clustered around a gravestone festooned with flowers.

Searching for the site, you pass stones marked with names such as Francavilla, Bongiorno, Venuto and Mascitti. In such company, a memorial with the name Elvis Presley on it looks strangely out of place. This is a focal point for Presley followers in this part of the world. It's the twentieth anniversary of his death, and it's an extra special day for them.

Sylvia, an Italian woman in her fifties, has arrived dressed smartly in a black dress and cream jacket. She has been coming here at least once a month for the last seven years, to clean the memorial, clear away any rubbish that has accumulated, and bring fresh flowers.

'Before that time I didn't want to know because I was still very much hurt inside,' she tells me. 'I'm still hurt. I was crying in the car today.'

Sylvia's family was in the movie business, and she says that she met Elvis on many occasions. She likes to remember him filling up a room with his presence but at the same time shying away from the spotlight. She claims to have seen him twelve months before he died, and was shocked at his condition. She heard the news of his death at work, where she was teased about her fandom.

'People at work told me he had died, and they were pleased about it. I felt like an arm or a leg was taken away from me. I felt all broken in. It's hard to describe. But at work I carried on because I didn't want to give them the satisfaction.'

Her voice starts to waver a little. She starts speaking about Elvis in the present tense, as if he's still with us.

'I'm in love with him. I've always been in love with him. He's warm and caring. He's good-looking too, but there are a lot of good-looking people around, so it's more than that.'

Sylvia touches my arm and lowers her voice, making sure the others around the memorial can't hear.

'The best person I ever met in my life was my father. He was very giving and very generous. And Elvis was as good as my father.'

Graffiti in the nearby rotunda:

Once in a lifetime—Elvis Aron Presley 8.1.35—16.8.77

Elvis—We love you tender

Elvis was no legend—he was a walking plate of jelly

Why Elvis? Let's write about Jimi Hendrix or Jim Morrison, the best ever

What about Kurt? Forget the baby boomer fuckers

In beloved memory of Tupac Shakur 1971–1996

On 16 August 1985, Poli Papapetrou was bored. She had been in bed with the flu that week and just wanted to get out of the house. She went for a walk and ended up wandering through the cemetery. As she strolled in between the gravestones she kept hearing snatches of Elvis songs. Tracing the origin of the music, she finally came across the Presley memorial. As a keen photographer, she carried her camera with her everywhere, so when she saw that Elvis fans had gathered to commemorate his death, she started photographing them at the site. Now she returns every year to document the day, and her pictures have been collated in two exhibitions, *Elvis Lives (In Melbourne)* and *Elvis Immortal*. Poli is not so much an Elvis fan as a fan of Elvis fans.

'I kind of got infected by it,' she says. 'I'm just really interested in the type of people who follow him. It's a fascination with me.'

Poli has seen people returning each year, telling their stories, updating their lives, and revealing how much Elvis means to them. There were Dulcie and Joanne Garvin, a mother and daughter team whose house was a virtual shrine to Presley. Dulcie's other child, Jimmy, would also show up, but five years ago he committed suicide by sitting in his car and setting it on fire. The mother and daughter attended the next anniversary but haven't turned up since.

THE DAY THE MUSIC DIED

There was Maryanne Ragos, who was there in 1997 for the first time in six years. She revealed that her mother had died in 1990, and she couldn't face the Elvis memorial for a while. She was so close to her mother, and her mother loved Elvis, so she couldn't do it without her. Turning up in 1997 was like her coming out, a forward step in her healing process.

Then there's Nancy Nunez, a young woman who arrived every year from 1985 to 1992, each time with a different man. The strange thing is that they all looked the same—greased-back hair, sharp cheekbones, rocker threads. Did she finally meet the right one in 1992? No-one is really sure.

And perhaps most touching of all is Alan Lang. His birthday is actually on 16 August, but after 1977 he stopped celebrating it because it was the day Elvis died. Alan used to say that he sometimes wished he was a woman, so that he could idolise and love Elvis more strongly.

As we stand there talking about all these characters, a succession of people arrive to pay their respects, bringing bouquets and candles. Some stay to chat with the assembled group, the breaks in conversation marked by solemn looks at the memorial. Others quietly lay bunches of flowers at the site, pause a few minutes for silent reflection, then leave without saying a word. One woman painstakingly arranges her wreath in a number of different positions before she's happy with it, then remains kneeling and intently mouths a silent prayer. It's hard to know if she's talking to God or Elvis. Maybe in her mind they're one and the same thing.

'It's not the early Elvis they're identifying with,' says Poli. 'They tend to worship Elvis in his jumpsuit days—it's the older Elvis, the fat Elvis, the bloated Elvis, the Elvis who was on a downward spiral. They can identify with his pain and suffering. It's pain and suffering that eventually led to his death, a bit like Jesus. That's the human Elvis. I suppose Jesus in his last days of suffering was a human who ended up dying. In their minds, I think they're drawing these parallels.'

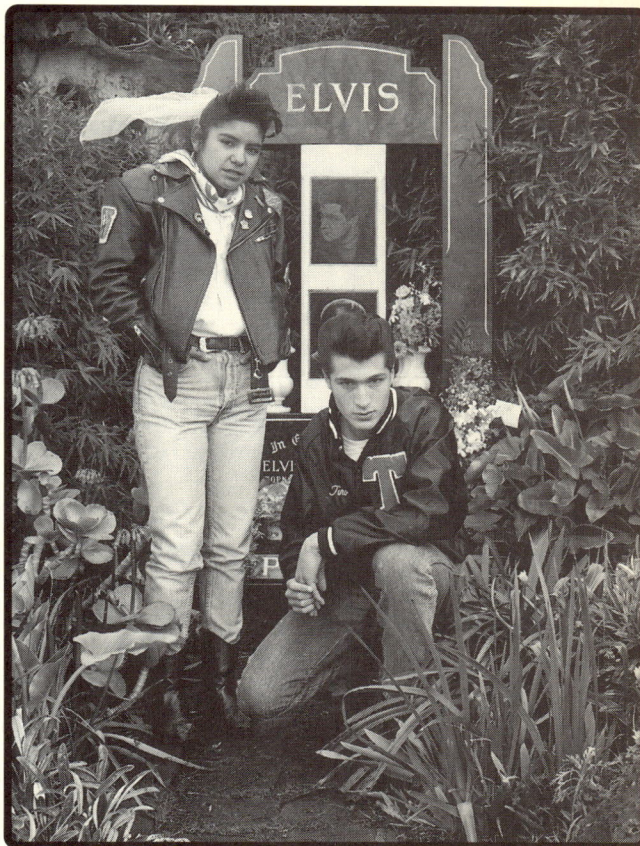

Polixeni Papapetrou

A strange thing happened to Elvis after his death. While the tabloids spewed out stories of his gargantuan size, his mammoth intake of prescription drugs and his bizarre eating habits, and the spooks said he didn't die at all but went to Mars for a little rest, his fans saw him as Jesus Christ with rhythm. He loved everybody and everything. He's the most generous man who ever walked the face of the Earth. The mere sound of his voice can incite them to hysteria or tears. Sometimes the mere sound of an impersonator's voice can do the same.

After visiting the Elvis memorial, I ventured out to the Melbourne Showground, where the Elvis Expo was nearing the peak of its two-week residency. Elvisphiles wandered through row after row of memorabilia, looking at rare movie posters and stills, bubblegum cards, sheet music and a wall of framed album covers. His films played constantly in a nearby theatrette and a woeful impersonator— all sneer, little rhythm and no voice—warbled his way through a medley of greatest hits.

Then Brendan Pearse, the organiser of the event, got onstage and addressed the crowd. He introduced Father Bob McGuire, who would perform a small memorial service.

Polixeni Papapetrou

'It doesn't matter whether you're Catholic, Jewish, Hindu, Buddhist, whatever,' Brendan told us. It was as if Elvis was there for everyone. He leaped religious boundaries. Our common love for him and his music meant that we were all one.

Father McGuire works with an organisation that helps street kids. 'We don't really have ghettos in Australia, but we have kids whose lives are in the ghetto,' he said, straining to make an analogy between an Elvis song and the lives of the people in this big shed.

'Do for others what you feel Elvis did for us,' he concluded.

Elvis may have left the building, but it sounds like he entered the church.

THE DAY THE MUSIC DIED

Like Elvis, Jim Morrison also expired in a bathroom, but across the Atlantic, in Paris. The focal point for his fans is his grave in Père Lachaise Cemetery. It's easy to find the site, as many of the other gravestones in the boneyard have the word 'JIM' scrawled on them, with an arrow pointing you in the right direction. On 3 July each year, the anniversary of the Lizard King's final trip, thousands of fans gather for a special vigil, where more tie-dyed t-shirts and out-of-tune acoustic guitars are gathered in one place than just about anywhere else on the planet.

Call them sacred sites. Call them the dead centre of town. Call them pop music's equivalent of shrines. They're the places where our heroes cashed in their chips, and for many fans it's a part of a pilgrimage when they visit these sites, and it gives them a sense that they're somehow getting closer to their idol by paying tribute in this way. Graceland is like a cathedral for middle America, albeit a cathedral incorporating lots of gift shops. Visiting such a site will bring fans in contact with other fans. What better place to communicate with people who are likely to share your mindset?

On 18 September 1973, Gram Parsons checked out of the Joshua Tree Inn in the Californian Desert in Yucca Valley. He'd been there and checked out many times before, as it was one of his favourite spots. But this time he checked out for good. A cult figure who pioneered country rock, and for a short time was a member of The Byrds, his point of departure attracts fervent followers who make the trip to stay in Room 8, where Parsons overdosed. There's a guest book in the room where they can write down their thoughts and musings. Evan Dando from The Lemonheads, who recorded a version of Parsons's 'Brass Buttons' on their *Lovey* album, made an entry in 1993—'I am addicted to Gram's singing but this room made me want to stay away from the hard stuff.' Some claim that the mirror in the room is haunted, although it must be pointed out that a proportion of those who make the Parsons pilgrimage take certain substances with them on their trip.

For followers of John Lennon, the Dakota building in New York City, where he lived throughout the 1970s and was shot on 8 December 1980, has special significance. In fact, his influence and fame is so great that many who aren't Lennonphiles visit out of sheer curiosity. Lennon's death was more significant than many other rock deaths because it came not by plane crash or car crash or accidental overdose or suicide or any other of the ways we prefer our celebrities to go. It was at the hands of a fan.

Across from the Dakota, in a clearing in Central Park, Yoko Ono had a simple memorial constructed, a circular mosaic with the word IMAGINE spelt out in the centre. In 1997 she spoke about being a famous widow in the weeks and months following the shooting, and described the process as being like sitting in a glasshouse for the world to see. She says that she gained strength and conquered negativity through her son, Sean, and realised that in turn she needed to be strong for him. But in addition she said something that suggested a kinship with those who followed her husband and admired his songs.

'The other strength was that I believed in the power of art and the power of pop music, and John's music was still there to protect us from becoming totally destructive. And when I say "us" I don't just mean me, Sean and the family—I also mean the fans. And that's why I feel such a responsibility to John's music.'

'It has become apparent to me that my son will not be walking out of the river. It is now time to make plans to celebrate a life that was golden.'

Five days after Jeff Buckley disappeared while swimming in a part of the Missisippi River known for its strong undertow, his mother made the above statement to the press. On the night of 29 May 1997, he had been hanging out with a friend in Memphis, where he was due to record the follow-up to his critically acclaimed debut album. The two went down to the river with a portable stereo to listen to music and hang out. Buckley decided to go for a swim fully clothed, and after a boat glided past and sent a heavy wake up to the shore, he disappeared into the depths. Apparently he was singing and laughing only minutes before as he splashed in the water.

When she heard the news, Gayle Kelemen, a 30-year-old New Yorker who runs a Jeff Buckley Web page, called up a few of her friends, and they all decided to head to the former site of the Sin-e cafe, where Buckley had played early in his career.

'We brought candles, flowers, Jeff's music and wine. Basically, we played his music and held the vigil from 10 pm to 5 am. We cried, we talked about his music and concerts, we told passers-by about him, we shared stories.'

For Gayle, the most emotional moment came when they all stood up, joined hands and sang along to Buckley's *Grace* album in its entirety. She admits that she was a little tipsy, but felt that it was good to express her sense of loss in that public way. Within a day or two there were 70 pages of postings on Gayle's site

Sophie Howarth

THE DAY THE MUSIC DIED

from fans expressing their feelings about Buckley's disappearance, and sharing their stories about the effect his music had on their lives. Gayle was stunned by the outpouring of emotion, especially when she read messages from people who had thought there weren't many other followers out there—many felt grateful for a community where they could mourn publicly.

Because of the six-day gap between Buckley's disappearance and the discovery of his body, there was an agonising delay for his family and fans—Gayle says that she just wanted to hear that he'd been found dead, so at least she could grieve and have peace. On 1 August, at St Ann and The Holy Trinity Church in Brooklyn Heights, New York, a memorial service was held.

'I met a lot of people I had previously known only through the Internet at Jeff's memorial,' says Gayle. 'A lot of bonding happened there, and in many ways that was more significant for me than the actual memorial. In a few instances those relationships—from the memorial, the vigil, and the last show we saw the week before he died—have expanded beyond the parameters of Jeff-related events and more into day-to-day life.

'Grief brings people together, I guess, and a lot of these people saw emotions of mine that don't frequently surface, and issues that I don't deal with often. And I found out about them and empathised with their grief. We experienced each other as a community, even though we were brought together by our relationship to Jeff.'

'He left a note for you.'

Those six words came from the mouth of Courtney Love on 10 April 1994. With that sentence, she initiated one of the most powerful, immediate interchanges between a group of fans and a dead star. Her husband, Kurt Cobain, had killed himself with a shotgun blast. He had left a suicide note, and Love chose to share it on a pre-recorded message which was broadcast to 6000 fans who had turned up for a vigil near the Space Needle in Seattle.

The reading worked on so many levels. For a start, it showed the world what was going through the mind of a major player in rock music just before he decided—in the words of the coroner who examined the dead body—'to obliterate himself, to literally become nothing'. And it gave the grieving fans something to hang onto. Portable cassette decks were blaring out Nirvana songs, and many of the kids were screaming along while dousing themselves in a nearby fountain. Others had set up shrines with handwritten notes to Cobain. Now their hero's widow was going to give them something even more personal. A parting gift. Kurt's last words.

But no-one, not even those who viewed Love as an attention-seeking harpie, could have predicted what happened as she read the note. Sure enough, there were sentences in there that referred directly to Nirvana's followers. 'The fact is I can't fool any of you: it simply isn't fair to you or to me,' he wrote. 'Thank you all from the pit of my burning, nauseous stomach for your letters and concern during the past years.'

To a fan, this was manna from … well, somewhere—wherever Kurt was floating around at the time. It was proof that he acknowledged them, even as he was loading the gun that would end his life.

But something else happened. While Love read the note, she started reacting to the words. 'So why didn't you fucking stay?' she said in response to her husband's line about loving people too much. 'God, you asshole,' she said, in answer to Cobain quoting Neil Young's line, 'it's better to burn out than to fade away'.

Finally, she addressed the crowd directly.

'I want you to yell, "asshole!" real loud. Say, "You're a fucker!" And then say that you love him.'

Here, in a couple of grief-stricken, confused, frustrated sentences, was everything that encapsulated being a fan—the transcendental highs and the crushing lows, the undying devotion and the bitter disappointments, the treasured memories and the shattered hopes, the way that everything is seen in black and white.

And, ultimately, how it's all a matter of life and death.

Many people see obsessive fans as pathetic individuals who are lacking something in their lives, emotionally stunted souls who can't quite cope with the real world. Why else would they get so emotional over a pop singer? Why else would they spend outrageous amounts of money on collectibles? Why else would they spend hours, days and weeks following their idols around?

Sure, if their fandom starts controlling them, and they find that they can't have a relationship or operate on a day-to-day basis as a result of it, then there's a problem. And, yes, if you can't quite share their enthusiasm or understand their taste in music, then their zeal can get wearing. But again and again in the writing of *Fanclub*, it was the unflagging enthusiasm and the fans' total empathy with their idols that impressed me. Whether it was the middle-aged women who worshipped at the Elvis memorial or the fourteen-year-old girls hyperventilating at the Savage Garden concert, there was a devotion evident that was impossible to ignore or dismiss out of hand. For them, this may have been filling a void, or providing a connection with other people. It may have given shy personalities a way to ease out of their shells, or just allowed hyperactive kids to get together and go absolutely crazy. In the end, why is actively following a pop star any different from collecting stamps

THE DAY THE MUSIC DIED

or supporting a football team or birdwatching or going surfing at six o'clock every morning? They're all absorbing pasttimes for those involved, and they all give people some release and order in their lives.

Finally, a funeral, two phone calls, a Bible verse, and the last word, which of course should come from a fan.

The twenty-seventh of November 1997, and it's like a sauna out here. A few hundred of us are standing outside St Andrew's Cathedral in Sydney. We're sweating, we're looking grim, and occasionally we gaze up at the black clouds that ominously move around the sky, gradually blocking out the sun. By the time Michael Hutchence's coffin makes the final trip back down the aisle to the waiting hearse, those clouds will spill buckets of rain down on us all. Over the loudspeakers that have been set up around the church, a priest is talking about the lead singer of INXS.

He says: 'We saw him, a distant figure on a stage, and somehow we felt we knew him.'

The two teenage kids across from me both look at the ground at the same time. One of them covers his eyes with a hand and stays that way for a while. We felt we knew him? He was a globetrotting glamour boy who went out with models and Kylie Minogue. We couldn't possibly know him. But through pop music, many of these people felt that they'd lost someone close to them. For some, INXS may have been part of the soundtrack to their youth. With the lead singer's passing, perhaps they were mourning something about themselves.

'Someone who was your rock is no more,' the priest continued, driving the point home a few more centimetres.

As I was adding the final touches to *Fanclub,* going back over what I'd written, checking facts, chasing up photos, and generally losing my remaining hair, I got a couple of calls from fans I'd met over the last year.

On Christmas Eve, around 10 pm, the phone rang. It was Annette Walsh, who had spoken to me about her Sherbert fandom. She was just about in tears. 'I'm really upset and I thought I should call you,' she said. Annette had read in a free weekly entertainment paper that a 1970s singer had been diagnosed with throat cancer. That night she had watched 'Carols By Candlelight' on television because she knew that John Paul Young was scheduled to appear. When he wasn't there in the line-up she put two and two together and started to panic. She was desperate for information. Did I know anything?

'I just need to know,' she said. 'Like I told you, Sherbert, TMG and JPY are a big part of me. I'm not going to sleep tonight.'

I felt bad that I couldn't enlighten her. The night before Christmas isn't exactly the best time for finding out that sort of information. In the cold light of day, the thought of a 38-year-old woman beside herself because of the possibility that a pop singer could be ill is a bit depressing. But I was touched by her concern. A little corner of her world was under threat.

Early in the new year, Julie Ledger and Tony Hamlyn left a message on my answering machine. I had to turn down the volume when I played it back because they were so excited. 'We just had to tell someone, and we thought you'd like to know—we just met Mel B from The Spice Girls!' Julie squealed. The passing of Wham!, Bros, New Kids On The Block and Take That didn't mean the passing of their fandom. These two would find new objects of affection. Bands come and bands go, but fans will always be there waiting for the next big thing—like those toy rabbits used for advertising batteries, their energy seems to be inexhaustible.

'Greater love has no-one than this, that one lay down his life for his friends.' John 15:13

Listen: Occasionally Loretta Tolnay has bad dreams about Michael Jackson's assassination. She says that it's probably one of her greatest fears.

'I'd love to think security could stop that happening, but it easily could happen. I would like to think security sized me up when I got up on stage with him, but I was never frisked—I could have killed him if I wanted to. But I'd like to think that they would have seen it in my eyes and killed me first.'

So, would you take an assassin's bullet for Michael Jackson?

'Of course I would. I would do that for anybody I loved. For Michael, of course.'

Why?

'Because it wouldn't be just for me, it would be for everybody. I wouldn't just be doing him a favour, I'd be doing the world a favour. It's not something that should happen to him.'

But it would be OK if it happened to you?

'In the bigger picture and the greater scheme of things, yes. I'm more dispensable than he is.'

Credits